AMERICAN PASTOR IN ROME

American Pastor in Rome

JAMES F. CUNNINGHAM, C.S.P.

1966

DOUBLEDAY & COMPANY, INC.

GARDEN CITY, NEW YORK

Nihil Obstat: Daniel V. Flynn, J.C.D.
Censor Librorum
Imprimatur: ☩ Terence J. Cooke, D.D., V.G.
Archdiocese of New York
June 8, 1966

The nihil obstat and imprimatur are official declarations
that a book or pamphlet is free of doctrinal or moral error. No implication is contained therein that those who
have granted the nihil obstat and imprimatur agree with
the contents, opinions, or statements expressed.

Contents

LIST OF ILLUSTRATIONS

following page 96

AMERICAN PASTOR IN ROME

Chapter 1

A HAPPY CHURCH

It was one of those soft, bright afternoons for which the Eternal City is famous. There was a fresh, alive feeling in the air. The Piazza San Bernardo was outlined with just the right proportion of lights and shadows, and the afternoon Roman sun did not seem in any hurry to shift the arrangement.

The scene at the doorstep of Santa Susanna's was a cheering combination of old and new. Many centuries earlier the Baths of Diocletian, the largest in all of pagan Rome, had spread like a giant mat from the square in front of Santa Susanna's to where the ultra-modern Main Railroad Station now stands. Parts of this bit of Roman antiquity were still on the scene as decorations, supports, and framework for other buildings, giving visitors a chance to piece together the story of Emperor Diocletian's crumbled monument.

Vehicles funneled into the piazza along a web of streets which appeared to reach out for them like fingers from a hand. The long finger of street which was pointed toward the Porta Pia, the arch-like gateway designed by Michelangelo, beckoned the largest number of vehicles into the piazza. The Porta Pia, a third of a mile to the left of Santa Susanna's, had been a pivotal battle point when troops fighting for the unification of Italy brought about the end of the Papal States by wresting temporal control of Rome from the Popes. That had been only a century ago, but on this mild Roman day it seemed like very ancient history.

In the center of the piazza, a white-gloved *vigile urbano*, directing the traffic, smoothly shepherded the vehicles on their way. There were several exits from Piazza San Bernardo, but most used the street which passed in front of the Grand Hotel. The vehicles were all sizes and shapes. There were automobiles almost as small as playtoys, chauffeur-driven limousines, elegant sports cars, tourist buses, horse-drawn carriages and wine carts, motor scooters ridden by young couples on the way to classes at the Rome university, and boys and old men on bicycles and tricycles which in the ingenious way of the Italians had been converted into serviceable delivery conveyances. The biggest of all the vehicles swirling through the piazza past Santa Susanna's were the City of Rome buses, modern in style but carrying a memory of times past with the large letters, S.P.Q.R., painted on their sides. Everything, from buses to bikes, mixed together in the piazza naturally. They had the look of belonging there.

The *vigile* communicated with the drivers silently, using neither word nor whistle. He relied solely on a system of gestures inspired by the actors of ancient Rome who had developed this means of communication when their theaters were immense and their voices could not travel to the thousands of spectators in the high, back rows. The hands of the *vigile*, moving quickly and easily, told more than the modern traffic lights on the corner. He himself was a holdover from the Rome of an earlier day. He was a direct descendant of the city policemen organized by Emperor Augustus, who reigned when Rome was 750 years old and Christ was born in the far-off Roman province of Palestine.

Cater-cornered from Santa Susanna's, the *Acqua Felice* fountain—built in the sixteenth century as an architectural experiment by Pope Sixtus V—splashed merrily around the feet of the heroic-sized figure of Moses in the central niche. Three large basins extended across the base of the fountain, and fresh water poured into them from the mouths of four lions. The lions reclined lazily along the edges of the basins. Visitors with guidebooks in their hands stood in front of the fountain, studying and seeking to identify the figures in the marbled alcoves alongside of Moses. One visitor was taking a picture. A workman in a hat made of newspaper waited patiently several yards away until the visitor had finished taking pictures. Then the workman matter-of-factly entered the fountain area through an opening in the marble railing and filled an empty straw-covered wine bottle with the clear water coming from the mouth of one of the lions.

Next door to Santa Susanna's a platoon of huge *corazziere* stepped from the Noble Guards' quarters to take their tour of duty down the street at the Quirinale, once the summer home of the Popes, later the royal palace for the Italian kingdom, and now the residence of the President of the Republic of Italy. Their silvered helmets, with fine plumes of horsehair streaming from them, caught the afternoon sun and, as if playfully, reflected it across the solemn fronts of the Ministry of Defense buildings which lined both sides of the street.

On the other side of the piazza from Santa Susanna's excursion buses squeezed through the Via Torino with new groups of visitors on their way from St. Mary Major's, one of the four patriarchal basilicas of Rome, to another holy site.

Churches of several denominations bordered Piazza San Bernardo. On the corner at the right of Santa Susanna's was the Evangelical Methodist Church of Italy, and just beyond it was a Presbyterian one, St. Andrew's Church of Scotland. Facing Santa Susanna's across the piazza was San Bernardo's Catholic Church. At the entrance to the piazza, opposite the *Moses* fountain, was the Carmelite church, Santa Maria della Vittoria, which has Bernini's famous statue of St. Teresa.

Day after day, for a dozen years, I watched that changing—yet never *really* changing—scene from the doorway of Santa Susanna's. During that period I was the pastor of Santa Susanna's. It was a period which reached from the hope and promise of the early postwar years to the Ecumenical Council. I have wonderful memories of those years at Santa Susanna's—memories I would share with you of the people who trooped through the portals of that lovely church and the experiences I had during those years in Rome.

Santa Susanna's has had a long history but it is a living, active parish of the twentieth century—a church with its roots in the ancient past but very much a part of today's world. What kind of a parish was this that I now was "running"? The query has always been a difficult one to answer, whether asked—in different ways and for different reasons—by high Vatican officials or boyhood friends from my hometown in Connecticut. In the early days after World War II, I could say simply that Santa Susanna's had been officially set aside by the Holy See as the national church for American Catholics in Rome. There was nothing complicated about that. It was their parish church away from home. But from then on, for the almost two decades I was associated with Santa Susanna's, its responsibilities kept growing. The church reached out, more and more, not only to American Catholics in Rome but to all Americans, regardless of their religion or even if they had no religion; whether they lived in Rome or whether they were tourists, pilgrims, international businessmen, diplomats, or military VIPs.

All Americans in Rome came to look upon Santa Susanna's as part of their homeland. Our non-Catholic friends never felt strange there. At the funeral of Mary McGurn, wife of Barrett McGurn, the noted correspondent, people of all religions in the American colony and in the foreign press corps turned out, and we had three Catholic ushers and three non-Catholic ones. It was the same for the funeral of Bill McHale, the Rome bureau chief of *Time-Life*. Bill had been accompanying the oil tycoon Enrico Mattei on an inspection trip when the Italian millionaire's private plane exploded in midair. While the Italian government was giving a state funeral for Mattei, Bill was buried from Santa Susanna's. Francis Cardinal Spellman, who happened to be in Rome at the time, also attended Bill's funeral, so it was really an American family affair.

We were not the only American church in Rome. (The American Episcopal church, St. Paul's, was only a few blocks away.) Yet there never seemed to be any rivalry or jealousy. Our parish bazaar was scheduled so as not to interfere with that of St. Paul's. For Santa Susanna's bazaar one year Mrs. Louis Skinitzero presented a large supply of dolls and toys. Her husband had gathered them from Italian manufacturers whom he had gotten to know during his long service as an Embassy official. There were so many toys and dolls, in fact, that fifty or sixty of them were left over at the end of the bazaar. St. Paul's bazaar, meanwhile, was only two weeks away so I called the pastor. Could he use them? He was delighted with this unexpected bonanza, and these surplus playthings were soon being carted from the American Catholic church in Rome to the American Episcopal church.

One Christmas Santa Susanna's helped make it merry in the home of two of St. Paul's leading parishioners, Colonel Gordon Dawson and his wife, Midge. The colonel, a wartime mountain-troop hero, was the Army attaché at the Embassy (later NATO security officer). He was the son of a Midwest Episcopal minister and he himself was a warden at St. Paul's. On this particular Christmas Eve he and his wife had just finished decorating the tree at home and had gone into the kitchen for a cup of coffee. A resounding crash echoed in their ears—the Christmas tree was a total loss. What to do? The stores were closed, and it was the weekend. One of them remembered the gay decorations they had seen at our pre-Christmas parish bazaar. They called the rectory to tell me of their Christmas Eve disaster. Within a few minutes the colonel and his wife arrived to pick up the decorations I had put away and stored for next year's bazaar. The two of them went back home as happy as a pair of youngsters who had received more from Santa Claus than they had counted on.

As for the question of the kind of church I was "running"—you could not even say that Santa Susanna's was only for Americans. English-speaking people of various nationalities adopted Santa Susanna's as their parish church. The parish bazaar, the greatest single source of revenue, was initiated by one of our English friends, Linda Graham Maingot, after getting the idea from her husband, Tony (now dead), a key British undercover agent in Portugal during the war. She was not even a Catholic at the time.

Many of our Italian friends dropped in to keep up their English. Minister of Interior Mario Scelba, who became famous for the imaginative methods he developed to handle Communist street mobs (spraying them with colored water, for example, so that they could be easily recognizable), attended Mass at Santa Susanna's several times to hear the English sermons, and refresh his knowledge of American English, before leaving on an official visit to the United States.

At dinner one night the Irish Ambassador to the Holy See, the late Joseph Walsh, was complaining about the lack of Italian men going to Mass and he said—perhaps rightly—that the churchgoers in Italy seem to be women. I remarked that I could show him a church in Rome where the men worshipers outnumber the women four and five to one every day during the week between seven-thirty and nine in the morning. The Ambassador found this hard to believe.

Then I told him of how high-ranking military officers, government officials, and civil servants from the near-by Ministries of Defense, Agriculture, and Finance drop in every weekday at Santa Susanna's to say a little prayer on their way to work. I told him, too, of one of the largest servers I have ever seen in my life: a six-foot-three, 250-pound member of the Noble Guards from next door. Morning after morning this *corazziere* would enter the church slowly, and with dignity, and would tiptoe up to the front, looking into the chapels along the way to see if there was a Mass he might serve.

Santa Susanna's often had pleasant surprises for the newly arrived American, offering religious experiences that could not be dreamed of in the parish church back home, or even in the cathedrals of our country. Leading figures of the American hierarchy were coming and going all the time. Cardinal Spellman often said Mass at Santa Susanna's over the years on his visits to Rome. Often he was accompanied by his good friend, Count Enrico Galeazzi, the highest-ranking layman in Vatican City and in effect its governor. Before leaving for the United States in 1959 to take up his duties as Apostolic Delegate, Archbishop Egidio Vagnozzi celebrated Mass for our guild. Bishop Fulton J. Sheen, on each visit to Rome, always preached at Santa Susanna's. I would ask him if he would speak and he would say: "Whenever you wish."

When Chicago's Loyola University opened its Rome center in 1962, the faculty and students, headed by Father John Felice, S.J., the rector, attended Mass in Santa Susanna's on the first day of classes. Monsignor Paul Marcinkus, a Chicagoan and an official in the Vatican Secretary of State's office, celebrated the Mass; I preached the sermon, and afterward the ladies of our guild served breakfast in the patio.

Sometimes I had to turn down the suggestions of friends who were trying to be helpful. My very old and cherished friend, Father J. Francis Tucker, accompanied the Prince and Princess of Monaco on one trip to Rome while he was their chaplain. He told me that Prince Rainier and Princess Grace planned to go to Mass at a convent where there was the same order of nuns who taught Grace Kelly as a young girl in the States. But Father Tucker said that if I wished he would try to persuade Their Serene Highnesses to come to Santa Susanna's for Mass. I was most grateful, but declined the offer. I have met the Prince and Princess several times in Rome at receptions given by the Legation of Monaco, and I have found them both charming (and the Princess beautiful!). But the following Sunday was the first Sunday of the month, when a larger number of parishioners than usual attend Mass because of our monthly Communion breakfast. For the Prince and Princess to come to Mass without publicity there would be no difficulty. But if the press and radio heard about it, then my own people would not be able to get into Santa Susanna's. It would be filled with strangers.

One morning in October 1959 I had a phone call from two journalist friends, Sam Steinman and Mike Stern, who are close to theatrical people. They told me that Mario Lanza had just died, and they thought it would be a wonderful idea to have his funeral from Santa Susanna's. (Both Sam and Mike we used to call our Jewish Catholics in Rome, and they never hesitated to help Santa Susanna's in any manner they could.) I asked Sam and Mike to hold us excused. The funeral for the Philadelphia-born singer would have many complications for Santa Susanna's. The church had just been repaired, for one thing. Furthermore, we did not have sufficient space for the large numbers expected, and the heart of the city (where we were) would be tied up for hours. The photographers would be climbing on the pews—even on the altar (I know these *paparazzi!*). Where Americans are concerned, we know how to handle the services and our people. But it is dangerous to try to regiment or control Italians who feel that a church, like Santa Susanna's, is theirs. They have their own way of doing things and will not be controllable. The dignity of Santa Susanna's had to be maintained, and I did not wish our church to be the center of a Roman circus.

Father Paul Maloney, my assistant, had baptized the four Lanza children at our church in Los Angeles, and I suggested to Sam and Mike that they talk over arrangements with him when he arrived at the dead singer's house. When the plans were drawn up, it was felt much easier to have the funeral from the church at Piazza Euclide in Parioli. Father Maloney celebrated the Mass. The church, and the piazza, were jammed. My two public relations men, Sam and Mike, both agreed that prudence had been the better part of valor. Some of the stories reported later were embarrassing—such as a photographer under the coffin taking a picture of Mrs. Lanza and the children.

Not all the experiences of visitors at Santa Susanna's were pleasant ones. Sometimes they were robbed right in church.

The first thing I would ask an empty-handed visitor coming into the church office was: "Do you have a purse or a bag of any kind?" When they said they had left them out in the church, I would tell them to get them right away. Constantly I would repeat the announcement that we must not place temptation before people. An American Dominican nun had just completed her doctor's thesis (the work of some three years), which was in her briefcase. A thief lifted it from her side as she was making her confession in one of our open-air Italian-style confessionals one afternoon. Fortunately for the poor nun the prayers of her fellow sisters were powerful. Two days later the briefcase, with the thesis intact, was thrown over the fence at the Embassy. On another occasion Mrs. George

Skouras of Hollywood, a long-time friend of Santa Susanna's, came to Mass at a very early hour one morning. She took a seat up in the front of the church while her driver remained in the rear. During the Mass a well-dressed man, full of piety but with larceny in his heart, knelt in the pew behind her. As she went to Communion, this man reached over, took the cash from her purse which she had left in the pew, and then walked casually to the door. Before anyone knew what had happened, the thief had disappeared.

Pilgrims robbed elsewhere often brought their troubles to us. One Saturday noon a California woman from Berkeley came into the office, distraught. She had been sitting in the Vatican Museum writing out postal cards. Her back was to her purse. When she finished her writing and turned to close her bag, she discovered her wallet, traveler's checks, tickets—everything of value—gone. She had reported this to the Embassy, but feeling that they did not take it seriously enough decided to come to us. I told her not to worry. The cash, I said, was gone for good. It was not too much anyway. But I assured her the other items, including her passport, would be returned in a couple of days.

The poor woman looked at me incredulously. She thought I was stretching the truth a bit. But I told her that several of my acquaintances were pickpockets, and I knew how they worked. I had met them while visiting some Americans incarcerated in Regina Coeli prison. I had often passed out a few cigarettes to these pickpockets in the jail. They had solemnly informed me they regretted the discomfort experienced by American tourists who suddenly discovered their passports were missing. But I was to assure their victims that the only thing a real pickpocket was interested in was cash. Everything else would be dropped into the nearest mailbox, and the police would see to it that it was returned to the Embassy. The pickpockets informed me, too, that only an amateur would let himself be caught with someone else's passport because it is a serious offense in Italy to be in possession of two passports.

Sure enough, on the following Tuesday morning the California lady came back and told me that everything had happened just as I had said it would.

The reputation of Regina Coeli as Italy's toughest prison—it has such a gentle name, "Queen of Heaven"— did not destroy the sense of humor of the prisoners. One time someone had given me a carton of king-size Chesterfields, which were still a novelty, and in arriving at the prison I handed them out. "Look at the size of these cigarettes," one of the pickpockets exclaimed. "The *Padre* must have made Monsignor!" And they all congratulated me.

Saturday afternoon was the usual time I went to Regina Coeli. It was not a convenient time for me, but it was for the regular chaplains who needed help with confessions. I would leave my passport with the chief warder, on entering, and would then be escorted to the sacristy. (The first time I was there the sacristan was a priest—and a prisoner! He had slapped a Communist sympathizer during an argument in his parish in Sicily and was sentenced to two years. Even in prison garb he was meticulously dressed.)

One of the people I visited at Regina Coeli was a likable American correspondent who, misunderstanding attention shown his wife by an Italian, waited for him as he got out of a taxicab and attacked him with a butcher knife. When anyone at the prison questioned why I visited the correspondent, even though he was not a Catholic, I explained that he was interested in learning the teachings of the Catholic Church and I was the only one from whom he wished to take instructions. For many months, apart from the staff of the Embassy, I was the only source of contact between this man and his wife. I brought mail to him, and took out notes to her and to his superior (the American magazine for whom he worked). I also brought in cigarettes, clothing, and other articles he needed. Until the day he left "Queen of Heaven" jail—and its 700-calorie a day subsistence diet—we met once a week. After being there ten and a half months he was sentenced to "time served" and given forty-eight hours to leave Italy, and never return. We still maintain contact with each other, although my instructions never reached the point of conversion and my mediation was unable to prevent the separation and divorce which followed.

The variety of requests I had to handle as pastor of this most unusual parish was extraordinary.

Typical of what I might expect took place one Sunday morning after the nine-o'clock Mass. About fifteen to eighteen people were waiting in the office when I came in. Some I recognized as golfers, such as Willie Goggins, a "pro," and Don Grant, a part-owner of the Mets baseball team. Others of the group were there to obtain invitations to visit the Holy Father. So to simplify problems I asked: "How many wish to see the Holy Father, and how many wish to play golf?"

Bishop James A. McNulty of Buffalo witnessed a somewhat similar confrontation on another day. He was attired in Mass vestments and was about to proceed to the altar with one of his diocesan priests when a heavy knock resounded on the sacristy door. I opened it and an athletic-looking man asked: "Are you the pastor?" I told him Yes, and he said: "I have just flown in from Libya with some other American Air Force officers. Our 'C.O.' told us you would arrange for us to play golf." The Bishop was listening to the conversation, and he heard me say: "Get back here—all of you—in fifteen minutes, and I'll have everything all set." In a reflective tone Bishop McNulty said: "You *do* get some rather unusual missions." Then, signaling wordlessly to the priest assisting him, His Excellency proceeded into the sanctuary to say Mass.

Not all the requests were easy ones. During the Ecumenical Council a New England Bishop who liked a cigar after dinner asked me for a box. Cigars are almost impossible to get at any time in Rome, and for some reason even the special Council office for American Bishops was unable to obtain any. In a similar situation I had borrowed a box previously from Colonel Peter Borre, a former law partner of Congressman John McCormack, but I did not want to approach him again. Two days later the Bishop again mentioned the cigars. I explained that my ordinary sources of supply seemed to have dried up— even the Navy Ship's Store at Naples had run out of cigars, and no one I knew was making a trip to the Army PX at Leghorn. The Bishop listened to my explanation with a slight smile. (It is always wrong to explain, or offer an alibi.) As the Bishop turned away, he said: "I thought you could do anything."

This was a challenge! So I paid the train fare of a sailor to go to Naples where Captain Larry Smith, the officer-in-charge of the Ship's Store gave him a note to a chaplain on one of the big carriers in the bay—and the Bishop had his box of cigars the next morning. As he tucked the cigars under his arm and walked away, he said: "Be sure and send me a bill." I didn't dare. How could I evaluate the time and money I spent to get the Bishop his box of cigars? So I wrote it off as an experience.

I frequently had to rely on friends for assistance. Vince McAloon, the director of the Notre Dame Hospitality Center of Rome, tells about being at St. Peter's one morning when he saw a clergyman working his way through the crowd. All Vince could see at first were a pair of waving arms and flashes of a white surplice. As the clergyman got closer, he saw that he was not an Italian. Then Vince recognized it was *I*, and I headed straight for him.

"Are you busy, Vince?" I asked. He told me No—he had just come for Mass. "Fine," I said, taking him by the arm and steering him through the throngs. "I'll give you a chance to attend three Masses." I had three weddings in St. Peter's for that morning—one right after the other—of personnel from the Arabian-American Oil Company in Saudi Arabia. They had one witness with them, but we needed a second one—and Vince filled the bill perfectly.

As pastor of Santa Susanna's I have presented at Papal audiences Superiors General of my Society of Missionary Priests of St. Paul the Apostle, the ladies of our guild, and men, women, and children of different religions and various points of origin. Among them was Brigham Young IV.

Pope Pius XII spent almost two thirds of a fifteen-minute special audience which included some thirty to forty people with three of my Jewish friends, Bernard Zucker, his late wife, Ruth, and his son Tony. Bernie, a C.P.A. in Waterbury, Connecticut, had been a friend of our family for years and I had grown up with him. Pope Pius liked young Tony and chatted with him about his European trip. Finally, turning to Mrs. Zucker, His Holiness said: "You have a fine boy here." Bernie had to speak for his wife, who was speechless at this special attention from His Holiness. As the Zuckers were leaving the audience chamber that day, an old Irish monsignor came up to Ruth and said: "Madame, you should cut off the boy's hair and keep it in a box because the Holy Father had his hand on the child's head." Then, somewhat ruefully, the old Irishman added: "You know, I have looked forward to this day for forty years. His Holiness spends most of the time talking to your little boy, and all he says to me is: 'God bless you, Monsignor'—and he hands me a medal!"

As tourism increased, more people unexpectedly ran out of funds in Rome, for one reason or another, and they would come by to see what I could do about it. I recall well one occasion during my years in Rome when a colored girl from New York City asked for help. She had run into perfectly understandable difficulty. Instead of her hotel bill costing five dollars a day, with meals, it turned out be 5000 lire (about $8.00) and only breakfast. So she was caught short. Within a month, she sent back the money I had loaned her, with a nice thank-you note.

A constant question asked of Santa Susanna's pastor was: "How do you adopt a baby?" Just as often there was the corollary question from an unwed mother-to-be of how she went about getting her child adopted. I have arranged the adoption of babies born in countries from Ireland to Germany, and some born right in Rome of American mothers. At the eight-o'clock Mass one Sunday a young American woman came in with her brother, a military official at the Embassy. She was eight months pregnant and had come to Rome to give birth to the child and put it up for adoption. I agreed to help her. At the ten-o'clock Mass, as it happened, there was a woman who had just flown in from Turkey. She and her husband were without children, and she was in Rome to see about the possibility of adopting one. Would she be interested in a newborn baby? Of course! Three hours after the baby was born at Salvator Mundi Hospital, she was with her new mother.

Father Francis X. Murphy, the noted Vatican II peritus whom many believe is the fabled Xavier Rynne, author of several controversial books on the Council, helped bring not a few unwanted babies to good homes and loving parents. When he stands before God in judgment, balancing what he is reported to have said about the Second Vatican Council will be some dozens of guardian angels he made happy through the care and attention he gave their charges at birth, as they came into the world, alone and friendless. He found homes and families for them and, one time, did not hesitate to carry a newborn infant on the long flight from Rome to San Francisco where the adopting parents were waiting at the airport to receive this little child who was literally coming down to them from the skies.

I was pastor of one of the most beautiful small churches in all of Rome—and a national monument! Architects and artists came from all over to study its beauty and design. Often on a Sunday afternoon I would turn the church over to a group of antiquarians who were studying Rome's great shrines. Not long after I became pastor I heard a wonderful old professor from the Fine Arts Commission giving a lecture about my church. "Look up at those angels in the arch over the sanctuary, and at the bronze ones on each side over the main altar," he told a group. "All of them are dancing. It's a happy church!"

Santa Susanna's had a happy pastor, too.

I first met Rome one midnight in January 1947. Not long before I had been elected Superior General of the Paulist Fathers and was flying into the Eternal City for a formal visit. Our plane landed at Ciampino airport, a few hundred yards from the umbrella pines and the catacombs of the old Appian Way. With me I was bringing some cigars and cigarettes for American priests and seminarians. Rome still had a long way to go to recover from the war. Necessities were being rationed. Luxuries, like tobacco, could not be found. Somehow, between the airplane and the customs shed, my two bags disappeared. This was not difficult to understand. Ciampino had been reopened only a short time and still was pockmarked by bomb hits.

We walked from the plane along a series of steel-mesh mats instead of the smooth level walks we are accustomed to at any good airfield today. Father Wilfrid Hurley and his brother, an American diplomat, met me, and I began crying "Diplomatic Immunity" on my missing bags. They were returned about twenty minutes later, but in the meantime they had been thoroughly searched, and the cigars and cigarettes had been carefully removed. Yet it was all done with such graciousness and cordiality that I found it hard to complain to anyone about it. From that moment on I felt completely at ease in Rome. For the next six years I was in and out of Rome constantly as Superior General of the Paulist Fathers. The following twelve years I was on permanent assignment there as pastor of Santa Susanna's and, simultaneously, as Procurator General for the Paulists (a kind of Ambassador to the Holy See). At all times during those eighteen years in Rome I was always right at home.

They were the Golden Days, and I savored them as they passed!

In Rome I met our last three American Presidents, and I had the unique privilege of serving under three Popes. On the steps of Santa Susanna's I welcomed thousands of American pilgrims to Rome in the Holy Year of 1950 and the Marian Year of 1954. I had an active part in the beatification ceremonies for two Americans, Mother Seton and Bishop Neumann, and Pope John appointed me to help in the preparations for the Ecumenical Council. "Good Pope John" was how he came to be called by everyone, but this title I heard for the first time from the lips of our own Richard Cardinal Cushing.

Pope John made me a member of the Christian Unity Secretariat for the Council, and I well remember his visit to a meeting of ours. His throne had been set up at the end of the room and as he entered he went immediately to it and spoke his appreciation for all the good work being done by the Secretariat. Then he came down from the throne and walked around the table—a very long table!—to greet some fifty members and consultors of the Secretariat. The Holy Father had a friendly word for each one at the table. When he came to me, I merely said: "Paulist Fathers—Santa Susanna's."

He gave me one of those warm thoughtful smiles of his and said: "Ah yes—the American church."

His Holiness spoke to me for fifteen or twenty seconds, but beyond those five words I don't recall what else he said.

In those Golden Days Rome was a great crossing point for many of my old friends.

On the occasion of the beatification of Pius X, the city was filled with visitors, and among them was Admiral Chester W. Nimitz, a man admired by all American Navy personnel. I had decided—with the help of our guild ladies—to put on a reception that evening to honor some of our distinguished visitors. Cardinal Spellman was among those invited, and he promised to attend. The reception was arranged for the big terrace of the McAdoo apartment in Parioli. Walter McAdoo, an old Navy man like myself, was delighted to learn that Admiral Nimitz was also coming. None of us ever forgot that party. The man who ran the entire Pacific Fleet operation in World War II found himself trapped in an Italian elevator, completely helpless, which stalled for twenty minutes between the second and third floors. When the admiral finally "came aboard" the McAdoo apartment, however, he did not seem unhappy about the experience. The next morning he visited me at Santa Susanna's. I obtained some religious articles he wanted for his daughter, a Dominican nun at San Rafael, California, and together we spent some pleasant moments talking about World War II, and the men who had fought it.

A special favorite among my Navy visitors in those years was Admiral Allan "Hoke" Smith, Jr., who had been my commanding officer on the battleship *South Dakota*. Neither one of us had ever forgotten that wartime day when he had called me to his cabin while he

was making out my fitness report as chaplain. He told
me he had the feeling that Catholics were more loyal to
the Catholic Church than they were to the ship. What
he wanted to know, he said, was what I would do if he
gave me an order in conflict with the teachings of my
church. And just as casual as his question had been was
my reply: "I would tell you, Captain, to go to hell." He
said: "I knew you would! And for that reason I am going
to give you a 'down' mark in loyalty." He did give me a
"gig," too, and had to write a letter to the Bureau of
Naval Personnel explaining the reason. From the view of
a career man whose life was the Navy, I certainly was not
a good loyalty risk!

At Santa Susanna's, too, I met again people on whom
I had looked from the pulpit of St. Paul the Apostle
Church in Westwood Village, Los Angeles, when I was
a newly ordained priest there in the Depression. Our
teen-agers at Santa Susanna's swooned one day when
Ricardo Montalban came to Mass with his wife. Georgi-
anna was one of the little children in my old-time Los
Angeles parish whom I used to drive to school in a rattle-
trap car.

When Bing Crosby and Bob Hope were making a
picture in London a few years ago, Dolores Hope and
Bing's wife, the former Kathy Grant, came over to Rome.
They stayed at the Grand Hotel, across the piazza from
Santa Susanna's, and we saw each other a number of
times. One morning about eight o'clock Dolores Hope
invited me over for breakfast. I had already had breakfast, but she said she had a special reason so I walked
over to the hotel. Going into the dining-room I went to
Mrs. Hope's table and, without any ado, she told me
that Kathy was going to have a baby in another six
weeks and had an insane desire for lemon ice cream for
breakfast. The problem was that Kathy was timid about
asking for such a thing. That is where I came in. Sitting

down at the table with them, I matter-of-factly told the waiter that the *signora*—and I nodded toward Mrs. Crosby—would like to have some lemon ice cream for breakfast, and nothing else.

The waiter bowed courteously, smiled at Mrs. Crosby, and said:

"Why, of course, *Signora*—why not?"

When I did not meet them in Rome, I often came across old friends elsewhere in Europe, or in North Africa, or in the Middle East. My pastoral work spread far beyond the ancient steps of Santa Susanna's. One time I might be giving a retreat for Americans in the oil fields of Saudi Arabia. Some other time, as Chaplain Delegate of the American Military Vicariate, I might be at a United States base in Spain or along the Bosporus in Turkey. I was the American Legion chaplain in Italy and attended all its conventions and on Memorial Day officiated at the services in the United States Military Cemetery at Nettuno.

One Memorial Day, accompanied by Legion Commander Reggie Perkins, I visited Haskell Rose's grave at Nettuno. Haskell had "caught it" in the Anzio landings. I had known the Rose family before the war when I ran a trailer mission in the Tennessee mountains. They were a big family—there must have been 400 of them at least—and I once went on a country picnic with them. Just before dying on the Anzio beach, Haskell—I found out later—told the Catholic chaplain that he had taken instructions under me back home in Tennessee. A brother and a sister of his had already entered the Church. He knew about the Catholic religion—Haskell said to the chaplain—and he, too, wanted to be baptized. He was, and received the last rites of the Catholic Church on the beachhead.

As Santa Susanna's pastor I regularly dealt with Vatican authorities on matters ranging from the most complex problems to audience tickets for visitors. There is always a tendency to be critical of official Rome. It is easy to forget that the prelates who work in the Vicariate and other Roman offices have to be most careful lest their sympathy for human weakness be used to challenge their orthodoxy. In all of my dealings with the Curia I have found a sympathy and understanding of human frailty far beyond that which I have encountered elsewhere. In the Navy we used to say, you could probably get away with anything except lying or stealing. In Rome you have a good opportunity to find rehabilitation from any failure.

On one occasion I was called to the Vicariate to explain what looked like scandalous conduct on the part of two American military chaplains. They had come through Rome, on their way from the Korean War zone, and were joined by some civilian friends at a local hotel. A rather querulous woman called me on the phone to say that these chaplains were with the people who were doing too much drinking. Knowing how quickly gossip travels in Rome—Rome has a reputation for being the most gossipy town in the world—I called one of the chaplains and told him of the complaint. He agreed that perhaps they had been indiscreet, and said there would be no further difficulty. The next morning Cardinal Clement Micara summoned me to his quarters and questioned me about a note he had just received complaining of the conduct of the chaplains. I assured the Cardinal-Vicar that there had been no scandal—that I had personally investigated.

"The two chaplains," I said, "were seen having a drink or two with their civilian friends in a cocktail lounge. However, Your Eminence, these are good men. They have been saying Mass each morning. They have had over a year and a half of extremely difficult combat duty, and have seen many of their friends die. This has been the first opportunity for them to relax in many months. And"—I added—"this morning after Mass they left Rome."

The old man took the note on his desk and, slowly tearing it up, said:

"My boy. We must always be tolerant. There is in all of us a little human weakness."

Rome was very good to me. I received high decorations and honors from my Church and from the Italian government. When well-meaning people asked me why I had been given this or that award, I am afraid that I frequently was as offhand and vague in my explanations as I once was with my friend Bill Fink, of *Our Sunday Visitor*, a long time ago. After the Battle of the Marianas the Navy released a story about my getting the Purple Heart and the Bronze Star. Bill Fink, for whom I had done some writing, wrote to ask me for more details.

My answer was a short one.

"I got the Bronze Star for ducking—and the Purple Heart for not ducking fast enough."

Lyndon Johnson was Vice-President when I met him in Rome in September 1962. He spoke at a luncheon meeting of the American Club of Rome, which I had helped found shortly after becoming pastor at Santa Susanna's. I met Vice-President Nixon at the home of Byron Snyder, the Embassy Counsellor for Consular Affairs.

During President Eisenhower's visit his personal interpreter, Colonel Vernon Walters (later Ambassador to Brazil), served the seven-o'clock Mass each morning at Santa Susanna's, and the head of the Secret Service detail, Paul Paterni (now Deputy Chief of the Secret Service), was a daily communicant.

At the Italian government reception for President Eisenhower there must have been 4000 people in the Quirinale Palace. Three clergymen were invited: Bishop

Ferdinando Baldelli, the late head of the Pontifical Relief Organization (POA); Monsignor Andrew Landi of Brooklyn, director of America's Catholic Relief Services in Italy; and myself, the pastor of Santa Susanna's.

We had been instructed that we were not to shake hands with the President when we greeted him. When the official party moved out of President Giovanni Gronchi's dining-room, Mr. Eisenhower said "good evening" to Bishop Baldelli, He also said "good evening" to Monsignor Landi. To me—dressed in a simple black cassock and without any ecclesiastical finery—our President said: "*Buona sera.*"

"I replied: "Welcome to Italy, Mr. Eisenhower. We are glad to have you with us."

—and he put out his hand.

Monsignor Landi said later that President Eisenhower either had to shake hands with me, or climb over me, because I had the way out of the dining-room blocked.

When President Kennedy visited Rome, Archbishop Martin J. O'Connor, rector of North American College, and I were the only two clergymen invited to the reception at the Quirinale. It was on a Monday evening in early July. Guests had been told to be present promptly at 9:15 P.M. in the palace gardens. The Italian President, Antonio Segni, was entertaining Mr. Kennedy and his party at dinner inside. Someone apparently talked too long for at 9:30 P.M., the time scheduled, there was no sign of the presidential party.

Bob Considine, the Connie Browns, Ed Hill and his wife, Gordon and Mrs. Dawson—together with a number of other journalists—gathered in one little group. Bob Considine, who in a column at the time referred to me as "the American Mayor of Rome," regaled us with stories of the inauguration. He told, for example, of Cardinal Cushing's long-drawn-out prayer. The press, cold and ankle-deep in snow underneath the inauguration stand, was shuffling and listening in silence as His Eminence talked on and on. Finally, Los Angeles *Times* man Bob Hartman, who is not a Catholic, said to all and sundry present: "Well, you can't say we didn't warn you Protestant so-and-so's."

Around 11 P.M. we were told that the President would be out shortly and were asked to form a line.

Colonel Dawson and myself were practically at the head of the line as President Kennedy came along. Up to this point no one had applauded, and the colonel whispered in my ear: "Don't you think we should give him a hand?"

We did. Mr. Kennedy glanced over at us and, smiling, said: "Thank you."

President Segni began introducing Mr. Kennedy to the many guests. The silver-haired Italian President, as classic-looking as if he had just stepped out of the Roman Forum, stood side by side with the strikingly alive young man who exuded the youth, the strength, and the hope of the New World. Pointing at me, the Italian President said to Mr. Kennedy:

"I go to his church to Mass. I say my prayers better there. His church is always orderly and quiet."

Being blessed by Popes and saluted by Presidents, as an American pastor in Rome, was something beyond the wildest expectations of a registered pharmacist from the state of Connecticut whose ambition in his early life was, some day, to own his own drugstore.

Chapter 2

DAYS OF YOUTH

I like hats.

In Rome, if you wear a cincture around the waist in the summertime, you do not have to wear a hat. I always wore a hat. If you took the Roman clergyman's hat and pushed up the sides and the back brim at the same time, you would find you were wearing the hat worn by the Minutemen at Lexington and Concord.

Since my earliest days I have had a preference for wearing hats. I am partial to hats because I was brought up in Danbury, the hat capital. It had a dozen factories with internationally known names, and the best hat-makers in the business. I grew up in the somber shadows of the huge illuminated derby at the railroad station. An electric sign blazed the noble thought:

DANBURY CROWNS THEM ALL

Times changed, like the people, and with the strikes families began to leave. The derby went out of style. The soft hat which took its place lost its appeal and men commenced to go without hats. Mallory now is only a memory for those of us who got their first real jobs there as boys, and the hat industry has little to offer the people of Danbury today.

My mother and father were Danbury hatters. They belonged to the United Hatters of North America trade union, and both of them worked in the John W. Green hat factory.

I was born in Nichols Street and I remember two

moves—first to Pleasant Street, and then to Town Hill Avenue. While we were on Town Hill Avenue, my father's mother died, and it was decided we should take over the old homestead where my grandfather lived on the outskirts of the city—the area now called Wooster Terrace. It was a two-family house, sitting on a hill lined by two rather high stone walls. My grandfather and his brother jointly owned the house and lived there.

The house was on a big farm—or at least it seemed big to me at the time. I guess there were ten or twelve acres. We had our own apple orchard, and there were some chickens and a horse. It was a workhorse, but on occasion three or four of us boys would get on its back and ride it to the water trough. Once in a while I would ride the horse while my father plowed.

We did lots of things for ourselves there. We raised our own potatoes, corn, and tomatoes, and butchered our own hogs. We put up our own sauerkraut, too. Everybody around agreed that our grapes and apples were wonderful. My mother canned the vegetables and made jellies which she stored for the winter. My grandfather was not idle either. He was a specialist in asparagus and had greenhouses in which to cultivate it. When the hat business was slow, my mother and father had the farm to keep things going. This combination life of farm and factory was not unusual. In many of the farm families you would find one of the men working in town.

Life in the farmhouse centered around a very large kitchen, and there was a parlor which we used frequently. The front room, on the other hand, was always closed and was used only when visitors came. Our next-door neighbors, the Brush family, lived almost exclusively in their basement. It was a beautiful homey room where they cooked and ate and did all the farmwork that normally goes on inside a house. In the ten years we lived alongside them, I remember only once being in the upper part of the house, and that was for the death of one of the family.

It was strictly a non-Catholic neighborhood. The families were mostly old New England Yankees. My cousins, the Claus family, lived near by, and so did Edgar White, a boy with whom I used to go fishing. But I don't recall more than one or two other Catholic familes in the whole area.

Summer was the time for picking berries. The hills around Lake Kenosha were filled with wild huckleberries and blackberries, and the lake was only a five-cent streetcar ride away. Kenneth Thompson, a non-Catholic friend, and I would take the first car in the morning and go berry-picking. Our mothers then would spend hours preserving the berries we had proudly brought home.

I liked to fish and was overjoyed when in time my friends all acquired bicycles. Then we were able to extend our fishing forays to Peach Lake, ten miles away.

A highlight of those boyhood days was the Danbury Fair—a means of creating interest in Danbury and its products. The fair grounds were only two miles from my home, and the week of the fair was a week of general hubbub. It was even more exciting than Christmas! Main Street was jammed, and visitors crowded in and out of the railroad station on White Street all day long. Every night there was a downtown parade.

Fairs are an old New England custom, and the Danbury Fair was one of the best. People showed off prize stock, women competed in cooking and in preparing special dishes, and prizes were awarded for the best jellies, jams, and pies. The Danbury Fair also had its carnival side, with magicians and fakirs, horseracing every day at the track, and a marvelous balloon ascension. As automobiles began coming into their own, auto racing was added. (One year at the fair I saw Ralph De Palma, a top auto racer of the time, go through the fence.)

The fair took place in the second week of October each year, and from the time we could walk all the youngsters of Danbury went to it with their parents. One day during the week was set aside as Danbury Day, and the family that did not attend the fair on that day was not a real Danbury family.

Many of us youngsters worked at the fair. One year my employer was a homeopathic medicine company from New York. All I had to do was stand behind the counter in the main tent and give out samples for a couple of hours. I was paid two dollars for my week's work. A Danbury family doctor who had seen me busily handing out the small bottles teased me later about my "wonder" medicine. "Take a pinch of salt and an ounce of distilled water, dump them into a barrel of rainwater, and stir vigorously," the doctor said gravely. "One teaspoonful after meals will have the same effect as your medicine."

His good-natured "kidding" did not bother me. The important thing was that, besides the pay, I received a free pass into the fair every day.

During the summer vacations in my first and second years at Danbury High School I worked at Mallory's hat factory. I was fourteen years old when I first went to work there. The pay was a dollar a day. I worked from seven in the morning until noon, and from twelve-thirty to five-thirty. Saturday was a half day.

In addition to men's hats, Mallory's, in the days when I worked there, marketed a woman's velour hat. It was very much like the Roman clerical hat I wore many years later as pastor of Santa Susanna's. The Roman hats are black while the Mallory hats for women—I think they were called "sailors"—came in many colors. My mother never quite got over the fact that out of my first week's pay I bought her an old rose velour hat. I did not realize that ladies' hats, like shoes, had special sizes. Fortunately the hat fit! Till the day she died she praised me for my thoughtfulness in spending a half day's pay on a hat for her.

I had finished eight years at St. Peter's parochial school in a routine way, but at Danbury High School, I am afraid, I was not too good a student. It was a period of uncertainty for me. Today, looking back, it is hard not to second-guess. But I know there was an uncertainty in my mind about what I wanted to make of my life. One thing I did know—making hats was not for me! I had seen too much of strikes and too much of the hat business to enter that field. I was an extrovert. I liked people, and liked being with them. I wanted to be in contact with people in some special way—just how, I had no idea. Then, an after-school job suddenly turned up in the Mahoney & Burns drugstore on White Street, near the railroad station, and I took it. I went to high school in the mornings, and from three in the afternoon until around ten at night I worked in the drugstore.

I found I liked the drug business. There was an opportunity for self-training. School seemed less and less important. So, midway in my third year, I left high school to take a full-time job in the Kinner & Benjamin store at Main and White. The six-dollars-a-week steady pay was a big help to the family, and that seemed more important to me than school.

Shortly after I took this job, my family became unhappy about the ever-recurring strikes at the hat factories. They decided to put the whole business behind them and start out anew. So we moved to Waterbury, the home of the brass industry, where there were opportunities for work. I myself stayed in the drug business and kept moving right along. By the time I was sixteen I had completed three years in pharmacy and was entitled to take the examination for assistant pharmacist. I took it, and I passed it.

My first job in Waterbury was with a wholesale drug

house, Apothecary Hall Company. They made me a clerk in the office, and during the summer I also worked in their retail store three or four nights a week. I kept up my study of pharmacy, but I was constantly restless without understanding why. It seemed to me that I was not doing what I wanted to do. I thought it was only because of the money involved that I was putting in overtime by working in the retail store. But it was not the attraction of extra money that made me do it apparently. The office job, I realized, was cutting me off from people and I saw that I was happiest when I was behind the counter of a drugstore instead of sitting at a desk. So after two years as a clerk in the wholesale end of things I returned to the retail side of the drug business. I went to work for the Wooten drugstore in my neighborhood on Washington Hill. That was to be the end of my job-changing in the drug business. Four years later I would be given the chance to have a store of my own in my newly adopted hometown of Waterbury.

Waterbury is something like Rome—a city built on at least seven hills. At that time it had a population of approximately 100,000 people and supported fifteen Catholic churches. More than sixty per cent of the people were Catholics. The population was mostly Irish, but there were French, Italians, and other nationalities as well. The Washington Hill section in which I lived housed a middle-class group. Our people worked in the brass factories, such as Scoville Manufacturing, American Brass, and the Button Company, and most of our parents were manual laborers. They worked ten hours a day in the factory and put in a five-and-a-half-day work week.

The houses of Washington Hill were wooden ones, two or three stories high. All of them were well kept, comfortable, and nicely appointed. But above all they were our homes—homes that no one of us through our lives ever needed to be ashamed of.

Our parish on Washington Hill was St. Francis Xavier's. Many police and firemen came from Washington Hill, and so did a number of teachers over the years. We had distinguished sons, too, such as John Gregory Murray, Archbishop of St. Paul, and Bishop Matthew Brady of Manchester, New Hampshire. Both of them are now dead. The Paulist Fathers have a church, St. Lawrence's, across the Mississippi from St. Paul in Minneapolis. When I became Superior General of the Paulist Fathers, I used to have to visit the Twin Cities in connection with my administrative duties, and I would call upon Archbishop Murray. He loved to discuss the old days in St. Francis Xavier's parish, and particularly the Washington Hill Grammar School out of which there were more vocations to the priesthood and religious life than any other public school in Connecticut. The Archbishop could call the old teachers by name, and he was almost reverential for a fine old Protestant lady named Miss Ella Bossity, who was school principal for many years. St. Francis Xavier's was a close-knit and vital parish—a parish proud of the name its sons and daughters had made for themselves. But no matter how far they went in the world, or how high they rose, they were always the boys and girls from Washington Hill.

Mayor Scully himself was one of our illustrious citizens from Washington Hill. The Waterbury mayor's son, Vincent—he became a lawyer like his father—was a tennis companion of mine. We usually played at Hamilton Park, and we defied tradition by wearing white flannel trousers. White flannels were not customary on Washington Hill. It was also an area where it was perilous to wear them. But we never had any trouble.

I played baseball, football, and basketball with the young men of my own age, and I joined the Waterbury Boys' Club where I satisfied a desire for athletic activity in an organized manner. On the Waterbury Boys' Club basketball team I played in competitions. One of my youthful goals was to go back to Danbury and play against the Congregational Church basketball team. All the boys on the Danbury team were old high school companions of mine—and Protestants. I thought we had a good chance to beat them because we had a forward named Hogan who was excellent. But, on arriving in Danbury two hours before the game, Hogan ordered hash in a restaurant. He maintained later that his hash "nailed" him to the floor of the Congregational Church "gym." We lost the game by a few points, but we gave a good account of ourselves.

Across the street from the Washington Hill drugstore where I worked was a firehouse, and out of it some of my friends and I developed a first-rate baseball team to play against other firehouses in the city. Once in a while I pitched for the Washington Hill firemen. In those days recreation activities were limited—maybe a movie every two weeks, or a dance now and then. Baseball, even the type we played, was a popular spectator sport. We had a great many pleasant and highly competitive games, with our friends there cheering along.

There was never a dull moment in Wooten's drugstore on Washington Hill!

An accident with a beer mug, for instance, might take place at the saloon, a half block away, and a man would have his skull cut open. The accident victim, either on his own steam or propelled by an innocent bystander, would head for the drugstore. "You'd better get to a doctor," I would say, meaning Dr. Quinn, who lived down the block. But the patient, wincing as he shook his injured head, would say:

"No, Jimmy. You fix it up!"

So, with the understanding approval of the doctor, I would take on neighborhood emergencies that went above and beyond the first-aid realm of scratches and bruises.

Thanks to a hard skull, my patients survived amateur repair work.

A constant flow of folks with minor ailments streamed into the drugstore for our attention. Someone with an annoying cough or with something in his eye. Would we take care of it, please?

At the drugstore we always knew when it was Graduation Day on Washington Hill. We would have a big run on ice cream. One Graduation Day was an unforgettable one in the Washington Hill drugstore. We had an emergency first-aid case on our very doorstep—and I was the cause of it!

It was a warm June day, and young people were coming by the dozens to get ice cream for graduation parties. Dr. Walter Keefe was working the front part of the store, while I was in the back filling prescriptions. Now and then he would call out for me to give him a hand. When he said he was running low on vanilla ice cream, I went out and got a fresh five-gallon can for the fountain, carrying it with a pair of sharp-pronged ice tongs. I was just about finished with this ice cream-shifting chore when a woman came into the store, saying she needed a prescription that I had been working on right away. I slipped the ice tongs on the back of a chair and took care of the prescription. The next thing I realized was that Walter was in the prescription room, laughing so hard he could scarcely talk. He did manage to say: "Mrs. Moran wants to see you."

Mrs. Moran was a sincere, heavy woman. She must have weighed 200 pounds. I went outside and leaned over the counter to see what she wanted. Piously, she said: "I just sat on those ice tongs." She pointed to the chair where I had left them.

Stunned, I watched her as she reached around and put her hand under one of her many petticoats.

"And I am bleeding, too," she told me.

"Go down to the doctor immediately," I said.

"I'll do no such thing. I'm going home."

"Those ice tongs were rusty and sharp," I told her worriedly.

"I know. I'm bleeding."

Not knowing what else to do, I gave her a two-ounce bottle of iodine, with a little paint brush, and instructed her to go home and apply it where it would do the most good. It must have been a painful experience for her. But I was the one who felt the full impact of the trauma resulting from the ice-tongs injury. (Mrs. Moran forgave me. When I said my first Mass, and gave my first blessing, at St. Francis Xavier's, she was right up in front. She looked completely recovered.)

While at the drugstore, too, I belatedly made up my high school education by going to night school. In my late teens I attended Collegiate Preparatory School in New Haven two afternoons a week. Four of us were studying pharmacy together and were good friends. My father would lend us his car for the one-hour trip to New Haven, and my three friends and I drove back and forth from school together. I was the only Christian in the group.

When the time came to take the "state boards" for registered pharmacist, the four of us went to Hartford together. The examination was spread over two days. The first morning, as we entered the corridors of the State Capitol, I noticed that my three Jewish friends were easing away from me and talking earnestly among themselves. Finally one of them—Bernie Litsky—came over to me and said:

"I hope you won't feel offended at what we are going to say, but we think you should take off that Knights of Columbus button. Four of the five pharmacy board examiners are Masons, and that button in your lapel is not going to do you any good."

I thanked Bernie, and my two other friends, and said I appreciated their good intentions.

"As for the button," I said, "I've worn it for years. A grand-uncle of mine, John McCarthy of the McCarthy Coal Company, was a charter member of Council No. 29 when it was founded in Emmet Hall on Main Street in Danbury in 1885. For better or worse, I'm going to continue wearing my Knights of Columbus button."

Whether the button helped or not—or whether the examiners even noticed it—I do not know. The examiners were all fine gentlemen of the old school. When the exam results were published a few weeks later, perhaps my Jewish friends felt they should have been wearing Knights of Columbus buttons, too. Of the four of us, I was the only one fortunate enough to pass!

During those four years of pharmacy work on Washington Hill, I met some wonderfully fine people. Most of them were Catholics, but a large number, such as my employer, were not. I came to know the priests better and one in particular, Father Jimmy Butler, the assistant pastor at St. Francis Xavier's. He and I would go fishing frequently. Another friend from the drugstore was Ed Stevens, a seminarian studying for the priesthood in the diocese of Richmond, Virginia. Ed was what is called a belated, or late, vocation. He was in his early thirties. He had been a lawyer and was already accredited to practice in the United States Supreme Court when he decided to become a priest. He had come back home from the seminary temporarily because his mother was dying. As it turned out, Ed spent almost a year taking care of her. The poor woman was in constant pain and had to be kept under sedation most of the time. Evenings, after Ed had given her the pills for the night and she had fallen asleep, he would come over to the drugstore and join me at the prescription counter. We would talk

about life at the seminary and about the priesthood—
and about the future in general.

St. Francis Xavier's parish was outstanding in the diocese for its many vocations to the priesthood, just as Waterbury itself was outstanding for its many college grad-
uates—particularly Holy Cross College. These young men
had come from poor families who made great sacrifices
so that their sons might have a college education. The
very nature of the parish of St. Francis Xavier's, and the
intense parochial life of the people, created the right sort
of climate for a budding vocation to the priesthood. If I
had any ideas along this particular line, the type of parish
in which I lived and worked gave it a little push. It was
not unusual, for instance, for young men of my age to go
to weekly confession and Communion. But today the Delaney girls, who were schoolteachers; and Rose Foley,
another teacher; and John Fitzmaurice; and the Byrons,
who owned the house in which we lived and who had four
daughters—and so many others—say they had me spotted
as a priest long before I made my first move. When I
would ask how they could tell, like everyone else on Washington Hill they would smile and shake their heads. They
just *knew,* they said.

I did not know it myself.

At least I certainly was not sure what I wanted to do
for the rest of my life. I had come to a crucial point. I was
twenty-one. Having obtained my senior pharmacy license,
I could now have my own drugstore. I had been dreaming
about that ever since the first day I stood behind the
counter, after school, at the drugstore near the Danbury
railroad station. Yet the unspoken desire to be a priest
persistently nagged at me from somewhere inside. One
thing I did know for sure. I had to make up my mind
once and for all.

A parish "must" on Washington Hill was the annual
novena to honor St. Francis Xavier, the great Jesuit

apostle of the Far East. The novena would be given by a Jesuit Father who was invited to the parish for just this purpose. In this year when I was trying to make up my mind I thought it would be a good idea to sound out our visiting Jesuit missionary. He struck me as being very intelligent and had a nice way about him in the pulpit. We would be able to talk confidentially and, what is more, he was a perfect stranger.

We had a fine chat. When I asked him some questions about his Society of Jesus, he suggested that I make a retreat. Taking a few days off for prayer and meditation under the spiritual direction of a regular retreat master would be helpful to me in reaching the right decision, he said. He proposed that I make the retreat at St. Andrew's on-the-Hudson, a Jesuit house in New York, near Poughkeepsie.

I made a visit to St. Andrew's—the farthest place from home that I had ever been—and spent a week trying to arrive at a decision. I had sort of hoped that the retreat master would tell me that, obviously, I was not qualified, and that I should forget the priesthood and concentrate on being a good pharmacist. On Washington Hill I was very much involved in the recreation and social life of the young men and women—the boys and girls of my own age—and I enjoyed it! Deep in my heart I knew that any decision I made at this point was going to be the one I would stand by.

The retreat master put the facts squarely before me. Without my realizing it, he forced me into a corner. At least it seemed so to me, whose uncertain but searching mind had to make a decision.

He told me that we are all here to work for God in one way or another. God gave each of us talents which could be used in diverse ways. It was up to each one to seek the best use of these talents to accomplish God's purpose.

"I know you want to save your soul, or you wouldn't be

here," the Jesuit told me. "We'll start out from that, and see in what manner you can best save your soul."

In our talks during that crucial week the Jesuit Father said it was clear I not only wanted to save my soul but that I wanted to help others in any way I could, and that I liked the chance to do things for other people. As I related to him my daily life in the drugstore on Washington Hill, the Jesuit nodded his head wisely. In the drugstore I was evidently helping others, he said. But he told me that I was helping people not only by putting iodine on their cuts and by bandaging them up but also by just listening to them and letting them talk about whatever they wanted to tell me about.

I listened, thoughtfully, as the retreat master spoke to me in that quiet, simply furnished room looking out on the Hudson.

"You have the talent and the ability to make a good priest," he said to me. "I think all of your background thus far points to this. Furthermore, from what you've been telling me, it seems to me that you have a special talent—the natural ability to get along with non-Catholics, whether they are Protestant or Jew, or whatever. You like them, and they like you."

I have never forgotten his final point. Looking me straight in the eye, he said:

"If you wish to help people, don't be an amateur. Be a professional. As a Catholic, to be the professional I think you should be, you need the graces and the help that come from the priesthood. God is calling you, I think, but only you know that for sure. You are the one who has to make the decision."

Before leaving the Jesuit house on the Hudson, I had made up my mind. My problem now was: how was I going to go about becoming a priest?

My seminarian friend Ed Stevens and I discussed the matter during the long winter evenings in the drugstore. I also began studying Latin on the side, under one of our high school professors, John Delaney. Because of my limited knowledge, I talked with Ed about the field of the apostolate I wanted to be in. My special desire was to be where I could do something for non-Catholics. Ed had two suggestions. First of all, he thought of the large non-Catholic population in his own diocese of Richmond. That sounded like a good idea, and I sent a letter to the Bishop of Richmond. I was told to complete four years of Latin before applying to the diocese to study to be a priest there.

Ed then talked to me about the Paulist Fathers and their non-Catholic mission apostolate. At that time I knew nothing about the Paulists except Father Finn's choir, which had sung in Waterbury on one of its annual tours. But I followed Ed's suggestion. I wrote to Washington where the Paulist seminary was located, asking for information. None was forthcoming—but the Paulists did send me an application blank.

Father Butler, my fishing companion from St. Francis Xavier's, and Ed and I talked over the whole matter after I received the Paulist application blank. From the two of them I got a fairly good idea of the Paulist Fathers—at least their ideals and aspirations, and their reason for being. The Paulists, they told me, were the first society of priests founded in the United States. Father Isaac Hecker, a native New Yorker, and four companions started the missionary society in 1858. Pope Pius IX had suggested that St. Paul might be an appropriate patron for the new American community. St. Paul had been outstanding in his zeal to obtain conversions for the Church, and Father Hecker (himself a convert) and his followers were making convert work the principal aim of the community they were establishing, so they took their name from St. Paul. As their mission field, the Paulist Fathers chose the

United States, and in a variety of ever up-to-date ways began working to convert Americans.

Since I wished to help people, and especially non-Catholics, the Paulist Fathers seemed to be the proper religious society for me. I filled out the application form and sent it in. Within two weeks I had a letter from Father Michael Carey, the rector of the Paulist seminary, asking me to report to Washington. I had been accepted!

The first Paulist I ever met was Father Tom Tierney of Ottawa, who greeted me at the seminary door when I arrived in Washington. From 1922, when I entered the seminary, until the present moment the Paulist Fathers have given me every opportunity to help people, and in a unique and most extraordinary way have led me into contact with non-Catholics throughout the world. The ecumenical movement, set in motion by Pope John, put the stamp of approval on the apostolate to our separated brethren, which is now recognized and authorized as an official work of the Church. Starting back in the drugstore, working with non-Catholics has always been my personal apostolate.

My decision to become a priest was happily received by my mother, whose sister was a Provincial of the Sisters of St. Joseph in Englewood, New Jersey, and my young brother, Will, seemed to be proud of my vocation. My father, on the other hand, was not very happy about it. He thought I was showing signs of mental deterioration. His main thesis was that there is no money in the priesthood. When I convinced him that I was not especially interested in money, he realized for sure he had brought up a crackpot son—and said so! But, shaking his head a few times and shrugging his shoulders, he said resignedly that if that was what I wanted, he would not interfere. Nor did he. From that time on, he was most cooperative and tried in every way to make my path easier.

It was not an easy path in those first months.

For the last couple of years prior to my departure for the seminary I had been managing a drugstore. The owner had taken on another place and had given me pretty much of a free hand in managing the original one. I was, therefore, used to taking responsibility and doing things on my own. Suddenly I was taken out of this environment and went into a seminary where I had to ask permission for everything and where I had to free myself of all responsibilities. Did I need a new pair of shoes, another tube of toothpaste, underwear? Did I have to write an extra letter home (one a week was allowed)? Did I want carfare into town to see a dentist? No matter what it was. I had to ask permission. A religious seminarian has nothing of his own except an abundance of energy, piety, and good will!

It took me a year or so to get adjusted and to refrain from making decisions without proper permission. Years later in the Navy, addressing brand-new sailors fresh out of "boot" camp, I recalled those seminary days. I told the young sailors as they reported for duty that they were no longer free men. "You are now slaves," I said. Once they took the oath of allegiance to the United States and put on a sailor's uniform, they would have to do what their superiors told them to do—with no if's, and's, or but's about it. The one thing the Navy demanded of everyone was Prompt Unquestioning Obedience. At the same time I promised them that if they ever got into trouble I would be right there to help them. But I said that a good ninety-five per cent of their trouble was going to come from not doing what they were told. "If you do what you are told," I said to the sailors, "you'll have an excellent tour of duty in the Navy. But if you cut corners, make your own rules, or do other than obey, you are in for real trouble."

I learned Prompt Unquestioning Obedience in my first

year in the seminary and recognized its importance. I found out at once that the young man entering a religious society owes his obedience from that moment on to his immediate superiors. Like anyone else, as a child and as a youth growing up, I had been obliged to obey my parents. Now I was transferring this obligation completely. Until the day I died I would never be free of the obligation to obey those above me. There would never be a time when what I taught, wrote, or said—or even my life itself—would not be subject to authority. There would be times, I was told at the seminary, when I would think my superiors were mistaken, misinformed, or unjust—or that they did not have a proper estimate of a particular situation. But I would never be permitted to question the sincerity of my superiors or their right to exact obedience from me and their other subjects. I think elderly men coming into the seminary—the late vocations—find the burden of obedience their heaviest cross.

(Today a new theology is being written on the subject of religious obedience. One may not obey blindly regarding the regulations of superiors as the will of God; one may question the right of a superior's actions, challenging his right in this or that area to give commands. One must obey his own conscience in respecting orders given. Between the theologians who write this emerging point of view and the superiors who must maintain order in church life and in the religious communities there is an abyss filled with uncertain souls. Until this gap is bridged and there is a meeting of minds, there will be broken spiritual lives and lost vocations.)

We learned at the seminary, too, that even the Ordinary of a diocese can be dethroned if he violates the rules laid down for the conduct of a Bishop. (Many years later, as pastor of Santa Susanna's, I had a firsthand example of this seminary teaching being put into practice. It took place, as a matter of fact, during the Ecumenical Council. There was a Scots Bishop who had gotten into the habit of visiting our library at Santa Susanna's, and he frequently borrowed books. After a while he began sending his housekeeper, who had come to Rome with him, to procure books for him at our library; our people thought they were wonderful, and the librarian was very fond of the housekeeper. Some of the priests from the Bishop's home diocese in Scotland did not approve of the housekeeper, and they presented their case to Rome. The Holy Father ordered the Bishop to get rid of the housekeeper. He refused, and within a year the Holy Father had him removed as the head of the diocese.)

My general seminary training followed the pattern that is more or less standard in religious societies. After the first year in Washington, I was allowed to go home on a visit. Then I entered the novitiate for a year of spiritual training, without any formal studies. The Paulist novitiate is now at Mount Paul, in Oak Ridge, New Jersey, but at that time it was close to home and brought back a memory or two. It was the former residence of the Knox Hat Company owners, at Ridgefield, Connecticut.

After the novitiate, I returned to Washington for the two years of philosophy and the four years of theology that led to ordination. The first year we seminarians lived at the Apostolic Mission House on the Catholic University campus, and we did our studies at the university. The Paulists had never had a "canonical" novitiate; ours was the first novitiate class in accordance with new rules. As we finished the year at Ridgefield, Connecticut, there was some question in the minds of superiors as to whether we should be in Saint Paul's College, the major seminary, with men who had followed the old tradition of a novitiate through the whole course of study. I was never quite sure of their thinking. Would we contaminate them, or they us? Would the major seminarians find us a problem? We were integrated starting our second year in Washington.

I do not think the "non-canonical" Paulists were too greatly inconvenienced in their religious life by us "Johnnies come lately."

Washington, in those busy twenties, was getting crowded and a great many families had moved into Brookland, where St. Paul's College is located. We had our own athletic teams at the seminary, and a very large and inviting sports field. I noticed that the neighborhood youngsters longingly eyed our field and would silently stand on the sidelines as we played. With the approval of the Father Superior of the seminary, I invited them to use the field and soon had them organized into baseball, football, track, and basketball teams of their own, according to age groups, and they competed with other teams. The boys were twelve to fifteen years old, and at one time there were seventy of them using our field. At least a third of them were non-Catholic, but we worked as a unit and turned out some fine teams. Everybody helped in outfitting the youngsters. Catholic University furnished the uniforms, for instance, and Clark Griffith of the Senators baseball team would provide baseballs. People like Joe Cronin and the late Harold "Muddy" Ruel, Walter Johnson's catcher, came out to talk to the boys on occasion. They played all year round, after school, baseball in the spring and football in the fall, and a bit of everything in between. Bill McAndrew, now president of news for NBC, learned his elementary football with one of these teams on the Paulist athletic field.

I was just as busy in the classroom. While studying for my master's degree at Catholic University, I took a special course in labor relations under Monsignor John Ryan. Because I was working so much with young people, my professors recommended I also take a course in adolescent psychology. When it came time to write a thesis for my master's degree, Father Paul Hanley Furfey, of Catholic University, suggested that I use "The Organization of Boys Clubs" as my theme.

After ordination on June 10, 1930, I was assigned to assist in the building of a new parish in West Los Angeles. The area, called Westwood Village, had been undeveloped, but now it was building up fast. Hollywood's fame as the world's motion-picture capital and the warm magnet that California has always been were attracting people who, in the 1929 crash, had lost everything but hope. Many Catholics were moving into the Westwood Village area, but there was no church for them. The Paulist Fathers were invited by the Archbishop of Los Angeles to come and build one.

I "flew" to Los Angeles—but in between New York and Burbank I had to spend two nights on a train, and my coast-to-coast trip took almost forty-eight hours. I left New York one night at six o'clock on the train and arrived the next morning in Port Columbus, Ohio. There we transferred to a tri-motored, corrugated-steel transcontinental plane that was noisy beyond description. We flew all day at about 3000 feet and 125 miles per hour to arrive that night, beaten, bedraggled, and with a mind completely unhinged in a little Oklahoma town called Waynoka. The airstrip was several miles outside of town, and we were driven into the Santa Fe railway depot. I was glad to see the depot. It had a beautiful grass lawn in front of it. I stretched out on the lawn and lay there in the grass waiting for the coming of the Santa Fe train, the Missionary. Food had no charm. I had been eating lemons all the way out on the plane to settle my stomach. The plane had been loaded with lemons! In those days the cure for airsickness was not pills, but lemons. You were told to suck on a lemon, and everything would be all right.

The next morning the train landed me and another hardy soul in Clovis, New Mexico. Once again we filed onto a plane, and after another day in the air I arrived late in the afternoon at the Burbank airport. I had sent a notification of my expected time and manner of arrival, but it apparently had gone astray. No one was there to meet me. The cab driver who took me to Westwood Village gave me the impression we were going around the world—we drove so far. Later I learned this was the normal California taxi ride.

It all seemed the perfectly natural way for a newly ordained twentieth-century missionary to arrive in an old mission land on his first mission.

Chapter 3

EARLY PRIESTHOOD

My first church, as a newly ordained Paulist Father, was a small store on Ashton Avenue in Westwood Village, ten miles from the heart of Los Angeles. We had movie-house style chairs, linked in threes, and could seat about a hundred people. Until a real church was built, by Christmas of the year after my arrival, the Ashton Avenue store was the center of parochial life for the recently established parish of St. Paul the Apostle.

I had my first experience with an earthquake in that store.

On Saturday afternoon I was hearing confessions when the building began to tremble. The confessional seemed unsteady, and I asked the penitent if he detected anything.

"Sure, Father," he said. "We're having an earthquake."

He reported later that the shepherd, saying, "Let's get out of here," beat the sheep to the door.

I met the parishioners quickly. I was not in Los Angeles more than two days when I found out that the pastor, Father Henry Stark, had arranged a reception for me at Theta Phi Alpha, the Catholic sorority at U.C.L.A., and the Altar Society was in charge. He told me I should be there at six o'clock. I arrived on schedule with Father Ben Bowling, who was down from St. Mary's College (where "Slip" Madigan coached), to help out for the summer. Father Bowling went off to say his breviary someplace, while the ladies had me act as jack-of-all-trades—moving furniture, rolling up carpets so people could dance, and lending a strong arm where necessary. When the reception line started, I was ready to go home!

Father Stark, my first pastor, was a pious, devout man. I never heard him say a harsh word about anybody—and he could have said plenty! He rarely forgot a birthday; he never forgot a favor. He was a dyed-in-the-wool Californian who believed his hometown of San Francisco was the greatest city in the world. "Go slowly, be kind always," he told me. "You never know the secret sorrows of another." (Father Stark later became Superior General of the Paulist Fathers and when I in turn succeeded him in that post I arranged for his reassignment to the church he and I had built in Los Angeles. On his beloved California soil, he died four months later.)

Our parish was surrounded on one side by Sawtelle and on the other by Good Shepherd Church in Beverly Hills. Sawtelle was a small parish—mostly Mexican—but Good Shepherd's was a large one, and Edmund Lowe and Skeets Gallagher (later one of *our* parishioners) used to take up the Sunday collection there. Wilshire Boulevard passed right through the heart of St. Paul the Apostle's parish, yet at that time you could shoot a cannon practically in any direction and hit no one. Month after month I continued a house-to-house visitation of our parish to find out who were Catholics and to let those who were know that there was a church in the vicinity and they were members of it.

The shining sun and the mild climate, the varied terrain, and the labor market made the Los Angeles region ideal movie-making country. In the parish was the great Twentieth-Century-Fox studio. A few blocks to the south, in Culver City, was Metro-Goldwyn-Mayer. The Warner Brothers studio was over the hill from us, in Burbank. Paramount was fifteen minutes away, in Hollywood. In our midst, as kings among their subjects, walked the new aristocrats, the Hollywood stars.

The store which housed our temporary church was on the edge of the parish, and Father Stark wanted the site of the future church to be much closer to the center. Within a short time he and I found just the right place. The tract belonged to the Harold Lloyd studio, but they were not interested in selling. Father Stark had a great devotion to St. Joseph. One night he took me for a walk to the lot he had his heart set on, dug a hole in the ground, and placed a small statue of St. Joseph in it. Then he began a novena, asking the saint to get the property for us.

His novena was a success—at least the studio decided to "sell." Not long afterward, Father Stark and I broke ground together, with a team of four horses pulling a plow, and in the second furrow we uncovered the small metal statue of our benefactor, St. Joseph. Ralph Huesman, one of our friends and the owner of the Desmond Stores, made the down payment on the land for us.

After our new church was ready, parish activity really began developing. We had no school, but many of our children attended Good Shepherd's in Beverly Hills. To encourage other families to send their children to Good Shepherd's also, I offered to take the youngsters in my Ford coupe. After seeing about sixteen children climbing out of my Ford one afternoon, as if it was a circus car, the mothers decided to take this transportation job out of my hands and find a better way to get their children back and forth to school.

The people who formed this fast-growing *Hollywood-USA*, and who made the studios tick, were our friends and, in many cases, our parishioners, too. Bankers, such as the head of the Bank of America, A. P. Giannini, attended St. Paul the Apostle's. So did many of the movie stars—Spencer Tracy and Tyrone Power, for example. During these days days I instructed the Whiting sisters so they could make their confession and First Communion. Loretta Young, Irene Dunne, Peggy Ann Garner, Andy Devine, Jimmy Cagney, Allen Jenkins, and Pat O'Brien were people I saw not only on Sunday but often during the week. Joe E. Brown and his two sons frequently joined me in evening softball games on the U.C.L.A. campus. Pat Costello, one of the new breed of Hollywood sound technicians who could make the people on the movie screen talk, found the time to become the heart of the parish Holy Name Society, while his wife, with Agatha Holtby, Kathleen O'Rourke, Julianna O'Reilly, and others, organized a Paulist Businesswoman's Club and worked with the Altar Society.

There was plenty of talent in our parish. With no difficulty I put together outstanding minstrel shows and started a fife, drum, and bugle corps. It started out for the boys of the parish, but we added girls when Mary Ellen Bodie and her sister Judie said they would like to join the band, and Tom and Jack Ingersoll, two of their young neighbors who were drummer boys, wanted to know why they could not. It ended up in a band of seventy-two boys and girls who called themselves the Paulist Cadets of Westwood Village.

Dr. Arnold Janss bought the band their uniforms. There were two Janss brothers, both real estate developers, and Protestants, who had just given property for the growing U.C.L.A. complex. Dr. Janss told me I should order the uniforms from his friend, Ralph Huesman, but he made me faithfully promise that the store owner was not to know of his part in the matter. These two wealthy men were practical jokers and seemed to get a keen delight in taking a few cents from each other. As owner of the property where Desmond's was located in Westwood Village, Dr. Janss received a ten to twenty per cent discount on all his purchases in the store. When the uniform bill came, I gave it to Dr. Janss, and he walked into Ralph Huesman's office with his checkbook and demanded his discount, knowing full well that as one of our substantial supporters Ralph had already cut the cost to rock bottom. The two had a great laugh over this.

Often, as our cadets practiced on Saturdays in front of the church, I noticed two little boys watching. One day I asked them if they wished to join us. That night their father, a Goethe scholar at U.C.L.A. named Dr. Diamond, came over to the rectory with them. "We are not Catholics," he said. "We are Jews." I told him a dozen children in our band were not Catholics, and that we made no religious demands on them. Music is international and universal, I said. I had issued the invitation to his sons because they looked lonesome—as if they had been left out—and I thought they would feel at home in our band.

They became cadets and would go to summer camp with the rest of the band. Nothing pleased the father more than to join us when we were at Hermosa Beach or in the High Sierras so that he could spend a day or two with his boys. He and I would eat together at the head table. Often, before the meal was finished, I would signal to the two boys that it was all right if they wanted to break away and go for a walk with their father. And how this distinguished professor would chuckle when they got up from the table, blessed themselves, and said Grace before running over to him!

In no time I began acquiring extra duties. The first was right in my back yard. Some of Hollywood's films were raising eyebrows across the country, and bishops throughout the United States were asking the Archbishop of Los Angeles what could be done about it. Archbishop John Joseph Cantwell set up a three-member committee to keep "this monster" under control and put me on it. The two other members were the editor of *Tidings*, the diocesan newspaper, and a Jesuit from the Blessed Sacrament Church on Sunset Boulevard, the biggest church in Hollywood. We found out quickly it was a problem too big for the three of us to handle—and too big for Archbishop Cantwell as well. But from this first committee of ours evolved the nation-wide Legion of Decency, which was established in 1933.

That did not end my contact with the Archbishop of Los Angeles by any means. It was only the beginning. Anyone who knew Archbishop Cantwell realized he could be as kindly and gracious a man as one would hope to find. They knew, too, that he could also be severe and vigorous. My subsequent dealings with him more than confirmed this observation.

More than once he let me know why I was being picked for special assignments rather than one of the regular priests of his diocese. With a bit of a twinkle in his eye—but you knew he was not fooling either—the Archbishop would say: "If one of my own men makes a mistake, I am stuck with him. But if you make a mistake, back to New York you go."

Out of the blue one day, the Archbishop put me in charge of the Newman Club at U.C.L.A. We at St. Paul's had been helping at the Catholic sorority house on the campus, but a member of the diocesan clergy had been handling the Newman Club. The Archbishop's instructions were brief and gruff. I was to look after all the Catholic students on the campus and work out a program of Catholic activity for them. The Archbishop did not say why my predecessor had been summarily taken from the work. He made it clear it was none of my business—and I did not dare ask (nor, for that matter, did I ever find out).

When I walked into the University Religious Conference building on the campus that afternoon, the Catholic students did not look particularly happy to see me. The Religious Conference was a truly ecumenical activity. Thirteen denominations, including the Catholic Newman Club, belonged to it, and all of them were housed together under one roof. I had hardly introduced myself as the new chaplain to Adeline Gunther, the conference secretary, when the Reverend Gale Seaman, the Baptist minister in the conference, came in to say hello. I told him I was a complete neophyte in the field and knew nothing about the work. He spoke about some of the problems I would face and in a paternal way said: "Your boys and girls are not going to like you because you are replacing someone they liked very much. At your first meeting I suggest you say you know nothing of what transpired before, that you have been appointed by the Archbishop, and that the program established by your predecessor will be continued. There will be new elections for officers in a few months, and then you'll have a chance to introduce your own program. But don't make any changes now."

It was safe advice I have never forgotten, and the Reverend Seaman and the other clergymen in the Religious Conference were always very helpful to me.

During Lent one year Archbishop Cantwell had me preaching every Sunday night in one of six Protestant churches between Long Beach and San Bernardino. His Excellency had found himself committed to an interfaith program in which the Protestant churches agreed on having rabbis, priests, and others explain their form of belief in a series of talks. The Archbishop assigned me to preach on one tropic: "Why I Am a Catholic."

It was most interesting work for a priest who likes to talk to non-Catholics and who had a captive audience. Some of the congregations were hostile, some friendly. Usually I asked the priest of the nearest Catholic church to accompany me. I remember the Irish priest of San Bernardino who appeared reluctant to go along with me. He told me that he had never before been in such a place —a Protestant church!—and seemed to be afraid that the roof would fall in on us. I assured him that the strong right arm of Archbishop Cantwell would hold up the roof.

I thought the roof might fall in at that, when I later sounded off publicly in front of the Archbishop about a big garment strike.

Los Angeles was the last frontier of the open shop, and the clothing industry had established a California beach-head there. In the silk and wool dress group alone, there were 118 manufacturers, and the work pool consisted largely of about 40,000 Mexicans. When a bitter organizing strike developed, I was asked about Catholic interest in it by some of my minister friends at the Religious Conference. They suggested I go and see the picket line for myself. Although those picketing were Catholics, the clergy did not seem to be interested, the ministers said.

I visited the picket line.

That afternoon it so happened that the regular clerical conference for the junior clergy of the diocese was taking place. After hearing two talks on Catholic principles in labor relations, Archbishop Cantwell looked around the room for comments. He spotted me. "We have here with us today a great man from the university," he said. "Would Father Cunningham like to comment on the papers that have just been read?"

It was all done in a humorous way, that is true. But, irked a little, and caught off guard—and with my mind filled with what I had seen that morning—I said more than I should have. I said we apparently were interested in theory, but not in practice. The 40,000 people on strike, I said, were Catholics, but the only assistance they were getting was from the Protestant ministers.

After the meeting the Archbishop motioned to me to come up front. "I want to see you in my office at the Chancery tomorrow morning at ten," he said.

I went home to Father Stark and said: "I guess you

are going to get a new assistant." I told him about my date with the Archbishop for the morning.

"Archbishop Cantwell is a just man," Father Stark said, "and I think you will have nothing to fear." But Father Stark said that only after he had first raised his eyes to heaven and murmured: "My, My, My." That was his way of indicating things were not so good.

The next morning the Archbishop said: "You young fellows think you are smart, don't you? Well, I am as interested in this strike as you are—and I am appointing you as my representative."

When I sat down a few hours later at the Mediation Board hearing, I was asked by the chairman, Campbell McCullough, what my business was in the conference room. I created a considerable amount of interest when I said I represented the Catholic Archbishop of Los Angeles. In an effort to settle the strike, McCullough, the head of Hollywood's Central Casting Corporation, had stepped in and formed a mediation board. Besides McCullough, the other members were a Hollywood rabbi, a U.S.C. professor, and a Los Angeles clubwoman. Within no time, I, too, was on the board.

The strike was settled by the board. Then Arthur Booth, of the manufacturers, and Israel Feinberg, the International Ladies Garment Workers' Union international vice-president on the Coast, asked me to be impartial chairman for the garment industry and handle its future union-management problems.

I accepted. When a strike threatened in the future, both sides would meet with me in the rectory. The first two hours of the meeting would be chaotic—everybody charging everyone else with larceny, felony, and all kinds of crimes. These men were old "pros." We would finally have a coffee "break," and in talking to Feinberg I would learn which of the twenty-two demands on his list were window-dressing and which ones the union would insist on before calling off the strike. Just as confidentally, Booth would tell me the maximum the manufacturers would agree to. After one or two more coffee "breaks," I would have them pretty close together, and I would make the decision. At once both sides would cry they had been robbed—that I was unfair. But this was for the record. There would be no strike. A day or two later they would laughingly tell me the ugly things they had said about me in reporting to their individual memberships. Out of these negotiations contracts were drawn up which lasted for years—and some of the close friendships are still in effect.

During these years I had an office in downtown Los Angeles where I worked till 1 P.M. daily and then went to the Newman Club at U.C.L.A. Two or three times a week I would have a call from the Butler Club—or, as later, from the Beverly Hills Athletic Club—that Pat O'Brien, Andy Devine, Jimmy Cagney, Allen Jenkins, Bud Collyer, or someone else was going to play handball. Would I make a fourth? I was always happy to! One day during a four-wall handball game at the Butler Club a knock came on the door. A friend reported he was having a discussion about the seminary training of priests. "Does a priest know Hebrew?" was the question. An interested observer was Al Jolson. My Hebrew was long gone, but I knew the alphabet because a Paulist priest in Washington, Father James McVann, had put it to music many years before to make it easier to commit to memory. So with a handball in my hand, and standing on the roof of the Equitable Building at Hollywood and Vine, I chanted the Hebrew alphabet—from *aleph* all the way through!

One of the many things neglected in seminary training, however, was how to put on a style show.

I proposed the style show to my colleagues at the Religious Conference. Each denomination at the conference had been staging its own card party or spaghetti dinner to raise funds, and no one was getting anywhere. Let's pool our efforts this time and put on a first-rate event, I said one day. Working together we can really do something nice, and all will profit from it.

Everyone pitched in. I was made chairman because of my contacts, but the other ministers all helped. We set the style show for the Los Angeles Biltmore, which has a dining-room like an arena, and arranged for Jimmy Greer to provide the music. The clothing was promised us by the manufacturers with whom I was working at the time, and a Twentieth-Century-Fox starlet was lined up to model a wedding ensemble. I figured the university girls, if they were in the show, would sell three to five tickets apiece. With the help of the ministers I assembled 150 girls from the sororities at U.C.L.A. and U.S.C. and told them they would be the models. Two professional models showed the coeds how it was done, but were not happy about the assignment. One professional model, who was especially hardboiled, exclaimed: "Father—where in God's name did you get this crowd? Look at 'em! Flat heels, stomachs sticking out, flat-chested. They don't know how to walk, stand, or turn around." But it all worked out beautifully, and our style show turned out to be as profitable as it was ecumenical!

When the new NRA moved into the labor field, I sighed with relief. The National Industrial Recovery Act established by the late President Roosevelt was a government-sponsored national assistance program. Later declared unconstitutional, it endeavored to assist labor and industry to get on their feet after a long and harrowing depression. With General Hugh Johnson at its head, it sparked and quickly developed the national economy. In each industry a secretary was appointed, called an "Authority," to establish fair prices and wages. A government representative came out from Washington to set up the

local office of the Dress Code Authority, which was to enforce fair practices in the industry. He felt there would
be no further need for me as impartial chairman because
the Dress Code Authority official could handle everything.
But after six weeks of negotiations, the man from Washington asked me to come back to work. "You are the only
one they will agree on," he said. And I found myself right
back in the middle of labor relations.

The New Deal was busy putting a mass of new labor
laws into effect, and it was a complex field—particularly
for someone unskilled like myself. However, both the
union officials and the manufacturers helped me to
avoid mistakes. They had plenty of practical advice, too.
I was listening to a case in the office one day when the
secretary came in with a question. Before I could answer,
a manufacturer said: "Father—say No. You can always
change your mind later. But once you say Yes, you are
committed—besides, I know that guy."

This was the beginning of large-scale involvement of
priests in labor-relations work. There were a dozen of
them across the country doing this type of thing, but I
was the only one in California. This, however, did not
impress my superiors back East: the Superior General and
Council. They regarded the field of labor relations as a
fad taken up by priests who were not quite mature or
who were a little left of center. They also took a dim view
of California and considered any statements made by
those who worked near the Hollywood picture people as
hardly worthy of credence.

They made no secret of their attitude either. The
archdiocese of Los Angeles, for instance, was financing
the construction of our church and rectory in Westwood
Village, but Father Stark and I thought it would be a
good idea for the Paulist Fathers themselves to pay for
the addition of a wing that could be used by the Paulist
Mission Band. It would give them facilities for more

extensive missionary work in the area, we felt. So, when I was going on a visit to my home in the East, Father Stark insisted I bring along the plans for our suggested wing and show them to Father John Harney. "Oh—you Californians are all alike," the Superior General said when he saw the plans. "You have big ideas, but nothing to back them up. You and your plans get out of here."

Father Harney was Superior General for eleven years, altogether, starting the first of his two terms in office the year before I was ordained. Many of the older Fathers knew him to be a dedicated missionary and a prolific and excellent writer. They also knew better than to cross his path because he could fly into a rage without a moment's hesitation. Yet if he felt that a man was being unjustly treated, no man had a greater champion. It just so happened that long before I was ordained we took different points of view, and this personality conflict was never resolved—not even on his deathbed. We respected each other's work and activity, but never in the farthest stretch of the imagination could we be called friends. One might say that our friendship was purely spiritual.

Four years in California were enough for me—Father Harney and the Council decided. Feeling that I would have a better opportunity to save my soul away from the fleshpots of Hollywood and the machinations of the manufacturers and the unions, they transferred me to Rome as an assistant in 1934. But when I arrived in New York that fall, someone was needed to run a bazaar at our church there, and the Rome assignment was canceled. I remained in New York for two years. Then I was appointed to the southern Mission Band.

Every Paulist Father in those days felt that the finest appointment was to work on the Mission Band, and I was no different. After returning to the East, I received my introductory training in mission work through my old drugstore friend, Ed Stevens. Monsignor Stevens, a pastor in Richmond, Virginia, invited me to give four weeks of missions in his diocese of Richmond—and they grew to twenty-eight weeks altogether.

But a special kind of mission apostolate was in store for me, farther south, in Tennessee. Tennessee had great possibilities for those of us Paulists who wished to do mission work in our own specific field, the non-Catholic apostolate. Since 1900 the Paulist Fathers had had a Mission Center for the rural South in Winchester, in the diocese of Nashville. There was a parochial school, in which half the 120 children enrolled were non-Catholics, and there was an active, predominantly non-Catholic Mothers Club. The priests at the Mission Center preached in the local schoolhouses and courthouses, and got out into the rural areas when and if they could. But this was not enough. In the previous ten years, despite the work of zealous priests, there had been only a few dozen converts. The school itself, in two decades, had produced no more than a handful. Father Harney was not at all satisfied with these results. In discussing the matter with him—he had called me off a mission in Norfolk to talk it over—I said that more could be done in our rural apostolate. However, we would need new methods and must move into the field and stay there. We could not be returning to headquarters in Winchester each night. We would have to devise means of keeping in contact with people interested. We later called this the "follow-up" work. Father Harney and I had disagreed on practically everything, but we were in accord on the need of this missionary apostolate. A new approach to the mission field was his idea, too, but how it was to be worked out he left to me, giving me complete support—and almost a free hand—in developing this activity.

I decided to put a chapel on wheels and cover the Tennessee mountain country by trailer. I had inquired

if there was anything like this already being done anywhere. "Oh yes!" someone would say—and I would be
given an example. Each time I ran down the lead I
found it was something else, and not a trailer mission.
One of my clerical friends—after I had spent ten days
on false leads—remarked that probably no one in the
world has more misinformation than the clergy.

So my trailer became a trailblazer.

With a young engineer in New York I designed and
built the trailer-chapel from the ground up. In my rural
apostolate I would be going into areas where the roads
were bad, and where it would be some time before TVA
and its electric lines reached. The engineer helping me
was a capable young man who knew exactly what the
newborn trailer industry could do. There were many
things, on the other hand, that people said we could
not do—such as finding room for an electricity-generat-
ing unit that was as big as an office desk. But a friend
got hold of a Ford coupe which had a special gear ratio
and heavy-duty springs in the rear. This coupe could,
therefore, carry the trailer load and (in place of the
rumble seat) the Kohler unit we needed to power the
public address system, the sound movies, and the cooking equipment. I drove the coupe into New York from
Waterbury—without the trailer or the generating unit—
and it was so high in the rear I felt like I was riding
downhill all the way.

I spent one whole summer getting the trailer made
just the way I wanted it. The chapel part opened at
the rear, making a speaking platform that became a fine
pulpit, and two loudspeakers could be attached. The
trailer had primitive living quarters for two priests. For
the first year Father Harney assigned me Father Thomas
Halloran because he was a Tennessean and knew the
area.

When people in the South later commented on the

trailer's colors, I would say: "The gray is for the Confederacy, and the blue in the piping and letters is for us Yankees operating it." But we painted it those colors for a practical reason. They would show the dust from the dirt roads least of all.

I called the trailer-chapel *Saint Lucy*. Lucy was the name of the daughter of Raymond Reiss of New York City, who made us a gift of the trailer. St. Lucy herself was the patron of the blind, and I hoped she would help open the eyes of those to whom we were going to preach, leading them out of the spiritual darkness.

By the end of the summer we were ready to move, and everything was in order—or so I thought. I had had a special waterproof canvas cover made for the bulky Kohler unit in the rumble seat, but this would not do for Father Harney and two of his inexpert advisers. It had to be a *metal* cover! It did not seem to bother them that I would be the one who would have to take this metal cover off and on each time the generating unit was used.

So I had a metal cover made. It was really an eyesore. But it satisfied the gentlemen who seemed to think this was all-important. Finally we pulled out of New York and started south. About fifty miles away I no longer could stand the rattling of the cover on the Kohler unit. I pulled up at the side of the road, took the metal cover off, and put my canvas one back on. Assisted by Father Halloran, I threw the metal cover over the fence and went merrily into the mission field.

It was a big mission field, covering seventeen counties and 7000 square miles. It extended down the state from Shelbyville (famous for its annual walking-horse show), and over the hills of Sewanee and Mount Eagle to South Pittsburg. On the east it went from the Alabama border almost as far north as Crossville. A quarter million people were living there, but when we moved in with the trailer there were only 250 Catholics in the whole area. All of Lincoln County had only one Catholic, and that was a woman living in Taft, near the Alabama line.

The chief occupation of the area was farming, although some manufacturing had begun to find its way in because of the abundance of inexpensive labor. The crops were corn, cotton, and tobacco. Tennessee was a "dry" state but over at Lynchburg special permission had been given to distill the famous sour-mash Jack Daniel. Around Winchester the potato crop was important and a standard source of revenue.

Many of the people had Irish backgrounds as well as Irish names. Their ancestors had "come over" in the early days of emigration from Ireland, had worked on the railroads, and going through the lush country of Tennessee had picked out beautiful valleys and good ground—and remained there. One priest who had gone with many of them died in a typhus epidemic and was buried near Cowan. From that point on, the people had little if any contact with the Catholic Church. We started the trailer mission at Cowan, which was only a few miles from Winchester, and gradually extended our operating circle.

It was not difficult to meet the people. I followed the practice of calling on leading farmers around noontime. Many times—particularly in the rural areas—we would come across people who had heard only evil about us, and were very suspicious. Some disliked the Church so much, and hated what we stood for, that they would go across the street to avoid speaking with us. But at noontime if you were the Devil himself—and that was our category so often!—you were invited to dinner and sat at the table with the family. We learned to talk about crops, and horses, and dogs, and fishing, and bird-shooting. Only when we were leaving did we say: "If you are free some evening, I'd like you to come down and hear our preaching."

We developed our own techniques. Each evening's program included a Question Box, an Evangelical-style sermon, and, of course, movies. Many of these rural people had never seen a motion picture before. As an opener we would use a ten-minute "short." This was intended for the children who came in great numbers, and who were well behaved once they found out the picture was for them. We told them each night they would have a moving picture like that if they remained quiet during the adults' part of the program. From the opening film—it might be an *Amos & Andy* animated cartoon—I would pick a particular subject to talk about which had reference to the ten-minute film—such as telling the truth. To keep the grownups interested after a question-and-answer period and a sermon, I used a real "spectacular," Cecil B. De Mille's *King of Kings* (I knew De Mille from the Religious Conference in Los Angeles—in fact, I instructed and received his son into the Church). Since it was only a film with sound effects, and not a "talkie," I sat beside the motion-picture machine with a microphone and gave a running commentary. After doing this for several weeks, I was asked by some of the people to read the *writing* on the film. They said it went too fast for them. The difficulty, actually, was that some did not read well, and some did not read at all.

These mountain people and I spoke the same language, but some words had a different meaning. I would talk about Christ, for example, and youngsters in the front row would look puzzled till one of them realized that I meant *Jesus*—and whispered this to the others. Catholics distinguish between "mortal" and "venial" sin. To my rural audience, sin was "doing anything wrong," and was punishable by Hell. One aged man with faded suspenders quoted a country preacher as having told them: "Sin is sin, and there ain't no two ways about it."

We had to get used to each other in other ways, too. For example, I had to become accustomed to being addressed as "Mister," or "Brother," without any offense being intended. In the same way, seeing me preaching in cassock and mission cross was a surprise for them. They could always identify me as a Catholic priest because I wore a Roman collar all the time—no matter how hot it was. As a matter of fact, it was in Tennessee that I acquired my lifelong habit of wearing black shirts. When it got too hot for a cassock or coat, I began wearing the Roman collar with a black shirt and rolling up my sleeves.

The title of our service was completely ecumenical. To Catholics the service would be a Mission, while Protestants would have called it a Revival. So I compromised, and in our handbills I always announced we were going to have a Mission-Revival.

Sunday was always a busy day. Many times I would say Mass at three different widely scattered places, finally breakfasting in South Pittsburg around 12:30 or 12:45 P.M. (These were still the days of the midnight fast.) By afternoon I would be in the hills at the foot of Sewanee Mountain for an open-air afternoon service with some 300 non-Catholics in attendance. Music would be furnished by the Long Family, led by "Uncle Good" Long who, though in his sixties and blind in one eye, played a real mountain fiddle. The Long girls played their guitars and sang. It was more like a country picnic than a Mission-Revival, and our non-Catholic friends enjoyed participating in it. (There were very few other distractions in the area.) I would return home around five-thirty in the evening, satisfied that I had put in a good day at what we called Muscular Christianity. Father Halloran left at the end of the first year. He was followed by Fathers Arthur Spear, John Mitchell, Frank Broome, and Henry Flautt. When I went into the Navy, the work was carried on by Father Broome.

Recreation was chiefly hunting and fishing. If some-one were to ask a parishioner in Winchester where the trailer was this week, the reply might be: "I hear there's good fishing up at Sparta—the bass are biting good." And if Sparta was on our mission itinerary, that is where the trailer would be.

A number of very fine people in Winchester were trying to build up the city and county and, through my interest in hunting and fishing, I became involved in civic affairs. The local sports club invited me to join, and in subsequent discussions there we talked about the problems of the high school football team which did not even have money for uniforms. I suggested football games on Friday nights as a way of raising money. The field had no lights, it is true, but Reuben Pritchard, the head of the local light company, offered to install them on a trial basis. I said we could use our trailer to broadcast the games over its public address system. Tom Gregory, the city clerk, volunteered to take on the other arrangements with the help of brothers of his from the Masonic lodge.

This was the first time anything like this had been done, and the people took to it. The first game made more money for the team than the whole previous season. For the six weeks of the football season we would close our trailer mission in the outlying areas on Thursday and move the trailer-chapel onto the playing field to broadcast the Friday-evening football game. The high school boys and girls were in and out of the trailer all the time and got to know us. After the first football game, we had no difficulty with anyone.

It was the same for the annual Crimson Clover Festival, which would draw 9000 people to the fair grounds. All activity centered around our trailer because all the arrangements were being made from there. One year the city fathers decided to commemorate the founding of Winchester with a day-long pageant. The historical happenings portrayed included the departure of the Winchester delegation in the Civil War to join Confederate General Edmund Kirby-Smith (who died in near-by Sewanee). It was a big family reunion, and everyone had some part in the festival. My part was to direct the activities: the singing, the recitations, and the other events on the day-long program.

With my trailer-chapel, *Saint Lucy,* I even broadcast several horse shows.

By the end of the first year all the people knew about us, and the trailer-chapel was a familiar sight on the highways. When we started our second year's work in Tullahoma, we were not in town twenty minutes before a dozen teen-agers—all non-Catholics—were in to see us. They said they had seen us at the football games in Winchester. We never had to search out a place to preach. The people searched us out and invited us to their community.

At Possum Trot one evening I was not so sure we were welcome. How the little village got that name I don't know. But I do know that the possum did not live who could trot up that hill. It was a steep, dusty mountain road, and we had trouble getting our trailer up it. With me on the opening night was Father Arthur Spear, an indefatigable worker. As we were getting ready, a very gruff character told me that before anything started some of the people wanted us to stand on the platform— facing them. "Make your act of contrition," I said to Father Spear. "I don't know what's going to happen." As we stood there waiting, twenty boys and girls walked past the platform, each putting on it a little bouquet of flowers they had picked that afternoon to show us we were welcome visitors.

The Muscular Christianity of those years was tiring, physically and mentally. It was much like a road-show routine—heavy equipment had to be set up, chairs placed, motion pictures arranged, and Mission-Revival announcements had to be stuffed into rural mailboxes. Our trailer accommodations were no Hilton suite. We had no showers, for instance, and very little room. Where two people live in such quarters, it is not difficult for them to get on each other's nerves. We lived like birds in a dusty ungilded cage. My own cross, I guess, was the lack of privacy.

But our strenuous efforts brought results. We made many friends and there were 300 converts, including one little girl who later became a Sister of Mercy. We built a small chapel at Possum Trot, and churches at Tullahoma, Shelbyville, and Alto.

The first funeral from our new church at Alto was Uncle Bud Kennedy's. Through the years of the trailer work there were many characters who crossed my path, as well as many fine religious people. Outstanding among them all was Uncle Bud Kennedy of Alto, Tennessee.

Uncle Bud ran a general store, and at the time I met him he was about seventy-two. He was a fairly big man, close to five-ten, with a shock of white hair and bright blue eyes that were set in an Irish face. His bronzed hands and face showed long exposure to the Tennessee sun. He had three sons and one daughter. All were married except the daughter, Miss Ida, a schoolteacher. Miss Ida lived with Uncle Bud and took care of him. Uncle Bud's store was at the junction of the Alto-Roark Cove road. The Alto road had been recently hard-topped, but the Roark road was still a dirt one. Uncle Bud's house was alongside of the store and back a little from the road. It was a roomy house, and it showed Miss Ida's influence.

After services one night, Uncle Bud came up to me with a broken rosary. He told me he had been baptized a Catholic but never remembered having practiced the religion. His father, on his deathbed, had passed the rosary to him. "Someday a man will come preaching, and will have one of these," Uncle Bud quoted his dying father as having told him.

Uncle Bud looked right at me. "Son," he said, "I've been waiting for you for almost sixty-five years."

According to Uncle Bud's Bible, he had been baptized at the age of six by Father Abram Ryan, the poet priest of the South and a Confederate Army captain, who now lies buried in Mobile, Alabama. Records put together in recent years by Father Christopher Murray of Sacred Heart Church in Lawrenceburg, Tennessee, confirm this. Uncle Bud is truly an historical figure.

I knew that Uncle Bud had seen some of the priests from Winchester during the year prior to our arrival. He knew Father Donald Barry and was known by Father Michael Frassrand but apparently he had not gotten around to talking religion with them. He was proud of the new rosary I gave him when I received him back into the Church and he made his first confession and Holy Communion. Later, with a group of young children, Uncle Bud was confirmed by Bishop William L. Adrian of Nashville, and in the last two years of his life was a pillar of the Church.

Uncle Bud was not one to move fast. At the start of our work in Alto, we used to have Mass in his front room. When I first asked permission for this, he told me he had to "think on it." I made two trips to Alto to ask about it, and each time Uncle Bud said he had not made up his mind yet. On my third time back—as he sat in the rocking chair on the front porch of the general store—I evidently

showed my impatience. I said I had to know now because
I wanted to tell the people about plans for Sunday Mass,
and the time was getting close. As he kept rocking, he
said: "The trouble with you, young man, is you have too
much of that damyankee uneasiness." Uncle Bud never
separated "damyankee" into two words.

His son Roy, a local farmer and fairly well-to-do, came
to Winchester one day to tell me his father was dying and
wanted to see me. Sitting beside Uncle Bud's deathbed
for the next two days I watched him fingering the rosary
I had given him. He always wore it around his neck. I
recalled how, sometimes driving past the farm, I would
see him in the field plowing, and I would stop for a chat.
Invariably he would ask me to explain the rosary. His
excuse was always the same: "I never can remember what
to say on these different buttons."

When Uncle Bud died, City Clerk Tom Gregory called
to ask how he could help with the funeral. Some of the
men in the Masonic lodge were wondering if they might
sing at the services, Tom said. I asked him if they knew
such hymns as *Faith of Our Fathers* and *Lead Kindly
Light*, which could be sung just as well in a Catholic
as in a Protestant church. Since we were working in the
field among non-Catholics, the Bishop of Nashville had
given us certain liberties—like using the King James Ver-
sion of the Bible for our preaching. So I took advantage
of these permissions. I would venture to say Uncle Bud
Kennedy's funeral service was probably the first "ecumenical songfest" which would have been recognized and
blessed by Pope John. The pews of our new church were
filled with lifelong friends of Uncle Bud. The rector of
the local Presbyterian church was there, and a double
quartet sang under the direction of Tom Gregory. There
were probably no more than ten Catholics among the
400 or 500 people in the church.

The impression given—and the one I retain all these

years—was that Uncle Bud Kennedy was a member of a great family of Christians, belonging to different churches but unified in their respect and affection for him. His funeral exemplified an ecumenical thesis that these were the people of God, taking part in a service as a family. From their various points of view they were asking a merciful judgment for a family member from the one God they all worshiped.

Miss Ida entered the Catholic Church and became one of our best catechism teachers. It was Uncle Bud's lead, I am quite sure, that brought others in his footsteps to the Church, which, rather than being neglected by them, had actually forgotten about *their* existence.

Chapter 4

ANCHORS AWEIGH

Hunting and fishing had introduced me into civic circles in my mission area with surprising results. This same outdoors interest suddenly brought me into a circle as big as the world because my hunting dogs led me into the Navy in a very real sense. The "brass" in Washington were beside themselves, and I don't blame them. I was being recommended to them as "Navy material," not because of my record as a priest or a missionary, but because of my years in the drugstore!

A pastime hobby of mine during my trailer mission days in Tennessee was to raise Llewelyn setters. They are short, shaggy-haired dogs that make excellent retrievers. They would scramble through the roughest brush to find a bird and point out its position. The mother of my dogs, Kaby, was a champion. Across the Alabama line, in Huntsville, a doctor was raising American pointers and on occasion we would get together, each bringing his own dog. For the dog-lover, or quail-shooter, it is a beautiful sight to see two dogs of a different breed quartering the field together—then, when one has found a covey of quail, to see the other respect the point and back it up.

When my hunting friend, the doctor, found out I was a registered pharmacist, he asked me to join the local Naval Reserve unit as a pharmacist's mate. My knowledge of naval procedure was practically nil. But since this would give me an opportunity to be with a large number of my non-Catholic friends at their meetings, I agreed to join.

Several weeks later I received a letter from Rear Admiral Robert DuBois Workman, the director of the Chaplains Division in the Bureau of Naval Personnel at the Navy Department in Washington. Chaplain Workman, a Presbyterian minister, implied that though my qualifications for the Navy, as exhibited by the unusual application I had sent him, were peculiar, he felt this lack might be overcome if I filled out the proper papers and applied to his office to be commissioned as a chaplain. Father Stark, my old pastor in Los Angeles, had recently been elected Superior General and, after getting permission from him, I made out all the papers and forwarded them.

Nothing happened until several months later when I received another letter from the office of the director of the Chaplains Division. This letter said my papers had indeed arrived, but had been misplaced. Would I please apply again?

I did. Still nothing happened. Since I had been trying to get into the Navy for almost two years, one way or the other, I decided I would just forget about it. The hunting season was upon us, and things looked glorious in the autumn colors of the Tennessee hills.

Late in that fall of 1940 I went to Chattanooga to give a retreat for the Alexian Brothers in their hospital on Signal Mountain. It was to be eight full days of talks, with six talks a day. During the third day of the retreat I received notice from the late Cardinal John F. O'Hara (at the time a Bishop and the head of the Military Ordinariate in New York) that I had been accepted as a chaplain in the Navy and that I was being assigned to Panama. I was the first Paulist—and the third of the Order priests in the country—to don military garb after President Roosevelt had declared a state of national emergency existed. A day later came another telegram—this time from Chaplain Workman. My orders were to report to Birmingham for a physical examination on December 11. I had only a matter of days!

Fortunately I was able to get Father Henry Flautt, from our Mission Center at Winchester, to take the eighth (and last) day of the retreat. I didn't have a minute to spare. I had to see the Superior General in New York, be fitted for uniforms, and get back to Birmingham in time for the Navy "physical." I was in such a hurry I did not even wait for Father Flautt to arrive, and after finishing the seventh day's talks I took the night train for New York.

When I sailed out of New Orleans on December 13, I thought I looked very glamorous in my "whites." On arriving in Panama, I was told by the Methodist chaplain —a fine man named Miller—that I had my shoulderboards on backward. That was a simple matter. The main difficulty about my naval wardrobe was that I had bought only blue and white uniforms in New York. When I got to Panama I found the working uniform was khaki.

Chaplain Miller had to take me under his wing, because in those days there was no such thing as a Chaplains School. Patiently he gave me daily briefings on naval procedure and the duties of a chaplain. We were doing very well, too, until I learned about something which was not on my indoctrination program: Navy feuds. In one small area at Panama there were three different Navy commands. Besides the Fleet Air Wing, and its PBY patrol squadrons, there was the Naval Air Station, at Upton, where I was stationed, and the submarine base at Coco Solo, to which Chaplain Miller was attached. Chaplain Miller and I agreed to conduct our respective services at each other's installation.

After about three or four sessions with Chaplain Miller, I was ordered one day to report immediately to the executive officer's office at the air station. "Why are you visiting Chaplain Miller each morning?" I was asked by the "exec," Lieutenant Commander Del Connolly. His tone was not at all cordial, and I was suddenly aware that he and my volunteer "teacher" were not getting along well at all. Naturally I did not know the rights or wrongs of the matter. But the executive officer's order was simple and explicit—I was to take no further instructions from Chaplain Miller. Furthermore, Commander Connolly informed me, Chaplain Miller would no longer be allowed to conduct Protestant services at the air station. In the future, I would be expected to conduct General Services (a non-denominational service which a Catholic chaplain may direct when no Protestant chaplain is available).

I obeyed orders. Chaplain Miller—an excellent person and one who did his chaplain's work well—was unhappy about my embarrassment. But, as he said, I had to do what the "exec" ordered. This was the first time I had come in contact with the internal difficulties of the Navy. I was getting indoctrinated.

In addition to the usual chaplain's duties, I took part in civil affairs, too. One night, for instance, there was a dinner for Arnulfo Arias, the President of Panama. This politician and doctor, who was educated in Panama and the United States, was very anti-American. The dinner was a stag affair. There were 400 men present—military, consulate, civilian—and each one had his own bottle of liquor on the table beside him. Like everyone else at the party, I was dressed in evening clothes (white jacket, black trousers, and black bow tie), and I was expected to lead the singing. I did, leading all hands in "Let Me Call You Sweetheart," "Girl of My Dreams," "Moonlight Bay," and one or two other nostalgic numbers of the twenties.

While on duty in Panama, I had to make a difficult personal decision. Pearl Harbor—as we were to learn shortly—was just around the corner. G-2 discovered that the Japs had infiltrated the hills near Rio Hato, on the Pacific side of the Canal, and were winning over the natives, who were Catholics. A high-ranking G-2 officer, searching for ways to combat this, asked if the chaplains had any ideas which might help.

A chaplains' retreat in the area was proposed, and I was chosen to give it. Eight chaplains participated. An architect working for the U. S. Army Engineers Corps loaned us his summer *hacienda* at El Valle, a town about sixty miles from Panama City. Army trucks carried us to the area and brought food and supplies. We set up a tent in the yard for a chapel and, stripping down a bar that had been in the patio, used it as an altar for Mass. Several of the Panamanian people working at the *hacienda* passed the word about our being priests and told their neighbors and friends that we were saying Mass there. Each afternoon, too, the other priests and myself would drift into the village, giving the people a chance to see us up close. Our military superiors were happy at the good will and understanding our presence in the hills created. That made me feel better because, just as we had gotten everything set up and were about to begin the retreat, I had received word—there in the hills—that my mother had died. My first reaction was to rush right home. But even if I was lucky enough to get transportation, one thing was certain: the whole plan that had been so minutely worked out would collapse. So I went on with the retreat.

On Sunday, December 7, 1941, I had just returned to the Bachelor Officers' Quarters where I lived, after having said Mass at three different Navy installations around Panama. The commanding officer, Commander "Buddy" Weber, was on the phone. He told me that Pearl Harbor had been attacked by the Japanese and asked me to help round up the young flying officers and have them report immediately to their squadron ready rooms. We had a large outdoor swimming pool at the submarine base. I am sure the officers, and the wives and girl friends, swimming there that day thought I had gone a little crazy when I walked out onto the diving board in my khaki uniform. But it did attract their attention and, from this improvised pulpit, I announced: "The Japs have just attacked Pearl Harbor." They were a sober and somber crowd as they climbed out of the water.

A couple of days after Pearl Harbor I myself was on the way by ship to Puerto Rico, having received orders to a new assignment. Puerto Rico, I found out, was to be used as a staging area. Within the first week of my arrival, the commanding officer, Captain "Squash" Griffin, took me on a tour of the base (which seemed bigger than it does today). He showed me a large structure, on a hillside, which had once been a Spanish munitions depot. The walls were three feet thick, and a wonderful promenade ran around the outside. Since it originally lay several hundred yards off the beach, on its own little island, it had been turned into an isolation hospital. The Navy had subsequently filled in the area between the mainland and the island, and the old Spanish landmark was now our property. Did I have any ideas about it? Captain Griffin asked.

"Well—it would make a fine chapel," I said. "But it would need a lot of fixing up."

He asked me how much I thought it would cost, and I said, "About $50,000." One thing the Navy had already taught me was never underestimate the cost of anything.

"Go ahead," Captain Griffin said. "You'll get the $50,-000."

Within a year I dedicated my new Santa Barbara chapel. I named it after Santa Barbara because it had been an old ammunition depot, and she is the patron saint of ordnance.

My chaplain's quarters on the base included a library and reading room. Pilots flying early that evening could not go to the Officers' Club and do any drinking so they would come over to my place and read the latest books

I had received. Or they would sit around and listen to the music—and, possibly, have a rum-and-Coca Cola. The young flyers, however, were abstemious and adhered very strictly to Navy regs on this matter. To supplement the regular Navy library, I would have Baker and Taylor, the book jobber in New York, ship me, from time to time, some new books. They would be sent to the Naval Air Station at Jacksonville, and the U. S. Navy Dispatcher there would put them on a plane for San Juan. I would give the pilot a gallon of Bacardi rum to take back to the States with him for his trouble. From each shipment I would send a half dozen books over to Admiral John Hoover with a marine orderly—slipping something of a religious nature among them. The admiral, invariably, would spot the religious book right away and send it back to me with the same orderly.

After twenty-two months in Puerto Rico I received orders to sea duty in the South Pacific. The battleship to which I was being transferred was the *South Dakota* and had been in the thick of the Pacific war from the Solomons on. The captain of the port in San Francisco was an old friend from San Juan days, and he set me up in style for the long sea voyage to join my ship "somewhere in the Southwest Pacific." He made me recreation director on a fast Dutch transport ship that was carrying combat personnel to the New Hebrides Islands (between Australia and the Fijis). Being a member of the ship's company assured me a cabin of my own. But when a Navy dental officer arrived and needed a berth, I made room for him in my cabin. Then, just as we were about to sail, Lieutenant Commander Ralph Emerson Duncan, a Navy medical officer from Kansas City, came aboard. His ship was to have sailed with us, but was being held back for emergency repairs. The Dutch captain of the troop transport asked me to see what I could do for the doctor. I solved that problem by inviting him to use the last spare bunk in my cabin.

It was a fine voyage. The captain allowed the radio operator to give me inning-by-inning reports of the World Series which I broadcast to the troops on the ship's public address system. I also arranged boxing matches. Since I was the only chaplain on board, I had to say Mass three times on Sunday in the mess hall (there were so many troops)—and three times conduct General Services.

Most of us disembarked at Espiritu Santo, going our separate ways. My doctor friend, Commander Duncan, for example, headed for his carrier. I, meanwhile, waited at the Navy base for transportation to my battleship. This was a forward combat zone, and living conditions were primitive. We were living four and five in an open hut, with the toilet in the middle of the road—which was normal. No one was complaining. But one evening, when I was taken by jeep to the other side of the island for a morning flight to my ship, I realized there was a difference between First and Second Class. At the air base—in contrast to the shore station—the barracks were clean, the food was excellent, and there were even inside toilets. That night I even saw a movie! In the morning I went aboard the special plane with my laundry over my arm—there was no time for it to dry!—and my orders in my briefcase.

On the plane I was seated beside the only other passenger, a fellow naval officer. His name was Gene Tunney. The undefeated heavyweight champion was traveling through the islands of the Southwest Pacific to raise the morale of the troops and talk about his physical-fitness program. During the flight he gave me a "pep" talk on the evils of drinking and smoking. I said I didn't smoke, but I *could* stand a drink. I didn't see any possibility of getting one, however, as I was assigned to a battleship and I understood that alcohol was prohibited on all Navy ships. We had a spirited discussion—with me defending cigarettes, which I do not use, and alcohol, which I was not going to be allowed to use. (Not until we were getting off the plane did Commander Tunney notice the chaplains' cross on my uniform. Only then did he realize that perhaps I had been pulling his leg a little bit.)

As the plane approached the island of Efate for a landing, I was treated to one of those once-in-a-lifetime sights. Lying to in Havannah harbor, with her head to the wind, was my great beautiful battleship.

Captain Allan E. "Hoke" Smith, commanding officer of the *South Dakota*, welcomed me aboard, and I began my combat life as chaplain on a ship that was already a battle-scarred veteran. She was a tremendous ship—680 feet long and 35,000 tons—and had been put in commission a few months after Pearl Harbor. There were 2500 officers and men aboard (one third were Catholics), and with them I was to participate in twelve combat operations.

I replaced the Methodist chaplain, Claypool, author of *God on a Battleship*, who left within a few days of my arrival. From that time until the end of the Gilbert-Marshall operations, I was the only chaplain aboard. Then Chaplain Newell Lindner, an Episcopalian, came aboard, and for the ensuing year we had a pleasant time, despite heavy combat. He was most cooperative, and we worked together without any difficulty. When the weather was good, Chaplain Lindner and I would hold our services on the fantail. Since we were in combat waters most of the time, this was sometimes hazardous. But we could get more men together at one time on the open-air fantail than in the cramped crew's mess compartment below decks.

The executive officer was Commander E. J. Taylor, who became admiral and has just retired as Dean of

Engineering at the University of Ohio. Commander Taylor always checked both services and attended the Prottestant one himself. I had Mass at eight, and on occasion a large number of Communions would slow me down a bit. Chaplain Lindner's service followed mine, and to help him get it started on time I would lend him a hand in setting up his equipment. He would always do the same for me. For instance, if he discovered that I was being delayed in the chaplain's office by confessions prior to Mass, he would have everything ready for me by the time I arrived. "I've never seen two chaplains work so well together," Commander Taylor often remarked.

This was the case, too, after Chaplain Lindner left and the Reverend Harold Post of Greensburg, Pennsylvania, came aboard after his cruiser, the *Honolulu,* had been torpedoed. Chaplain Post, a Presbyterian, was a man of considerable personal prayer.

One day during a battle the *South Dakota* picked up a young naval aviator who had been shot down by the Japs. He was dying when we got him over the side of the ship. His religion could not be immediately ascertained, but to be on the safe side I gave the last sacraments. Assisting me was a marine private from Sacred Heart parish in New York, named John Small. The flyer died, and arrangements were made for him to be buried at sea later in the day along with several other dead. My marine friend was at the burial service. As the flyer's body was slowly slipped into the water in its canvas coffin, Johnny Small whispered to me: "He's the fellow you gave the Last Rites to this morning. Why is Chaplain Post burying him?" I explained that we had not learned the young man's religion—that was why. Johnny still looked puzzled. "We have a special deal," I said to him in a low voice. "If we can't find out a man's religion, I put a ticket in his right hand, and Chaplain Post puts one in his left. When he gets to St. Peter, he holds out his hands and says: 'Saint Peter—which one do you want?'" Johnny thought that over for a moment. Then, out of the corner of his mouth, he said: "That's not a bad deal, Padre."

Six days before the *South Dakota* herself was hit, we, with several other battleships, fired for seven hours straight at shore targets in the Marianas. With our sixteen-inch main batteries and our five-inch secondary ones, we pounded the islands, softening them up for troop landings. In the days that followed, we kept up the tempo—and the enemy increased its own, sending all available surface craft and planes into the area. On the morning of June 19, a large number of Japanese planes attacked our task group. At 10:49 A.M. we were hit. A 500-pound bomb detonated on the first superstructure deck and blew a hole all the way down to the wardroom deck. The bomb landed only twenty-five feet from where I stood, creating havoc in the wardroom which was my battle-dressing station. My cabin, just down the passageway from the wardroom, was blown off the ship. All of my uniforms were burned up or were filled with holes from bomb fragments and bits and pieces of the ship's structure that were sent flying in all directions. Most of my chaplain's equipment was destroyed, including my "Mass kit." My personal chalice was snapped in two by a piece of the bomb. (I eventually had it repaired by a goldsmith in Rome.) Twenty-three of my shipmates were killed instantly, and four of the forty-two wounded died later.

The Japs paid a big price. On that one day alone 402 enemy planes were shot down, and the battle came to be known throughout the fleet as the "Marianas Turkey Shoot."

Incidentally, this was the first of a series of significant events in my lifetime to occur on June 19. It became a fatal date for me, not always a happy one, but one which brought me something to remember at three major periods in my life.

During this whole Marianas campaign my table companion had been Governor Harold Stassen, a member of Admiral William F. "Bull" Halsey's staff with the rank of commander. Governor Stassen had come aboard to look over the *South Dakota* as a possible flagship from which the admiral would direct his famous fast carrier task force. Governor Stassen was on the bridge when the bomb hit, and he witnessed the funeral at sea, around four that afternoon, with the officers and men remaining at their battle stations while we buried the dead. The governor, by coincidence, was to leave a few days later to attend the Republican National Convention. As did the other officers, I asked him to use his influence to get the ship back to the States because many of the men had been overseas a long time. What effect this had, I do not know, but within twenty-four hours after the governor had reported back to Admiral Halsey we received orders to proceed to the Puget Sound Navy Yard at Bremerton. For two months that summer I was in the States while my ship was being overhauled and repaired.

The *South Dakota* rejoined the fleet in time for the "strikes" on Okinawa, which were carried out on October 10, 1944, and until a month before the Japs surrendered in the following year I remained aboard her.

In between combat operations the ships in our fast carrier task force would steam into Ulithi, a horseshoe-shaped atoll of islands, for a few days' rest. I was sitting on the landing dock at the Ulithi lagoon one day, waiting for a boat to take me back to the *South Dakota,* when my old commanding officer from the ship came over to say hello to me. He was now Rear Admiral "Hoke" Smith and commanded a cruiser division. The admiral put his barge at my disposal and with his two-star admiral's flag flapping in the breeze I headed for my ship in first-class fashion. By this time I was a full commander, with three stripes. As we approached the *South Dakota,* the officer of the deck saw the coxswain of the admiral's barge raise three fingers, and he interpreted this to mean "three stars." Now the only three-star admiral in the area was Halsey. I never saw such confusion as when, from the admiral's barge, stepped not Three-Star Halsey but a three-striper chaplain—me! The O.O.D. had "run out" sideboys, Captain C. B. "Swede" Momsen (the commanding officer) had rushed to the quarter-deck from his cabin, and all hands in sight were at attention. I noted the look of dismay on the O.O.D.'s face as I came over the side and saluted the national ensign. I thanked them for the gracious reception, but no one paid any further attention to me. I kept on walking. The commanding officer was busy talking to the young jaygee who was O.O.D., and he was using language that it was best for a chaplain not to hear.

My tour of sea duty ended in July 1945. That month I was back in the United States, at the Great Lakes Naval Training Station, a huge shore installation with 100,000 men. When I arrived there, it had thirty-five chaplains, and for the time being I was senior chaplain. About a half dozen of the chaplains were Catholics, and the rest were of various denominations. After the war ended, the news came that those with a certain number of points—based on length of service and overseas duty—could be released to civilian life. I had had fifty-nine months of Navy duty—fifty-six of them overseas, including twenty-two of them aboard ship. Within hours after this news was received, the senior Episcopalian chaplain (a minister named Lipscomb) and I put on our combat ribbons and decorations and called on the commanding officer, advising him of our desire to return to civilian pursuits. A week later I was back in Winchester, where I had started my Navy career. I was the first Paulist chaplain released from service.

After reporting to Father Stark, my Superior General,

I returned to Tennessee and the trailer mission which I had set aside to enter the Navy in 1940. Trailer work was no longer being done. For all intents and purposes it had ended with the advent of World War II when troops by the thousands used the back-country area as training grounds and bivouacked in its hills. This type of activity, I learned, was now used only to a limited extent. What trailer work remained, I was told, was now being done, mostly in the summer, by Paulist Fathers who felt it was an excellent way to reach large numbers of people gathered in vacation areas, such as Lake George (in New York State) and in housing developments, like those in Baltimore. After the war, it seemed that the interest of the priests in this type of work was gone. Although several efforts were subsequently made to revive it, the enthusiasm which had been put into it by the priests of Tennessee was also gone. (Today, as a matter of fact, the Paulist Fathers have no trailer-chapels on the road.)

My stay in Tennessee, therefore, was short. I was there only a week when Father Stark called me to say that I was being transferred to Los Angeles. The Paulists there needed help and had been promised the first Paulist chaplain to return from war service. So for the next ten months I enjoyed Los Angeles as the assistant pastor.

Los Angeles had changed in the eleven years I had been away. It was no longer the little country-like area I had first known. It had grown fast—new roads, new houses were everywhere. The boys and girls of my band had grown up, too. One after the other they came in to welcome me back and to bring me up to date. A number had married. Some of the boys were buried in the Pacific. One of my fifers, Ronnie Burke, had been shot down in a flight over Germany. Billie Dean, one of our Protestant boys, had become a Catholic and was a medical student in St. Louis. A son of Joseph I. Breen, who had been appointed in the thirties to enforce Hollywood's motion-picture code, had lost a leg at Iwo Jima; another son, a tank captain in Germany, had been wounded four times and was much decorated. Doug Holtby, who once had hopes of being a great runner, had an arm mangled in the Battle of the Bulge.

I heard from my old friends from the garment industry, too. When Doug Holtby was married, for instance, his ushers and the best man were young men who had been his military companions. One of the young captains introduced himself and said his father wanted to be especially remembered to me. This fine specimen of an officer turned out to be the son of my old friend Joe Zukin—one of the most difficult of the manufacturers in his plant; a gracious man to meet on the street, and a magnificent host in his own home.

One night I had to ask Father Arthur Miller, the pastor in Los Angeles, and Father Louis O'Hara, one of our missionaries there, for advice about three letters which the mailman brought me. One of the letters was from Father Joseph McSorley, a friend of mine from New York. The subject of the three letters was the same: Father Stark, my first pastor, was going out of office as Superior General, and I was being suggested as the logical candidate to succeed him. Father McSorley had several projects in mind for which he asked serious consideration and a declaration of my point of view as a condition of his support. He felt it would be of help to Father Stark if I stated my mind in the matter. Father Stark himself had said nothing. I showed my two friends the letter from Father McSorley. After they both had read it, Father Miller said: "Well—what do you think yourself?"

I told them that I would like to help Father Stark in any way possible. But, I pointed out, in all fairness, that I had been away for five years and knew little about community affairs. I told them, too, that my own thoughts

2. Father Cunningham, as Chaplain, in the uniform of a Commander, United States Navy.

1. Father Cunningham just before he joined the Navy in 1940.

3. Father Cunningham on duty in the office at Santa Susanna's. (*Italikon*)

4. Father Cunningham with a couple he has just married at Santa Susanna's.

5. Father Cunningham with Roman orphans. (*Riccardi*)

6. Father Cunningham with a German orphan girl who has just been adopted in Rome. *(Farabola)*

7. A First Communion in St. Peter's.

8. Father Cunningham with First Communion and Confirmation class at St. Peter's. *(Del Vecchio & Scala)*

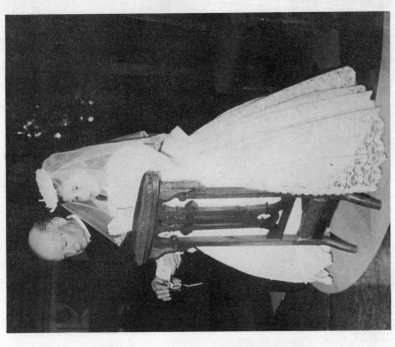

9. After a wedding at St. Peter's. (*Giordani*)

10. Father Cunningham accompanies a youngster making her First Communion at Santa Susanna's.

11. Richard Cardinal Cushing entering Santa Susanna's to accept the church as its titular Cardinal. Father Cunningham, in cope, at left; Father William Michell, C.S.P., Superior General of the Paulist Fathers, in center. At right of Cardinal is Bishop Thomas J. McDonnell, co-adjutor of Wheeling, West Virginia.

12. Richard Cardinal Cushing accepts Santa Susanna's as his titular church. At left: Father William Michell, C.S.P., Superior General of the Paulist Fathers; at right, Father Cunningham.

13. Pope Pius XII with Santa Susanna Guild and parishioners at audience, May 22, 1958. Father Cunningham is at right of Pope. *(Felici)*

14. Father Cunningham is received by Pope Pius XII. *(Felici)*

15. Father Cunningham receives a rosary from Pope John XXIII.

16. *Below:* Father Cunningham is received by Pope Paul VI.

still lay in the direction of the Tennessee trailer mission. For that matter Father Stark himself, when I had asked him if I could remain in Tennessee when I got out of the Navy, had said that in another year things would change and the new Superior General would probably allow me to get the trailer mission started again.

My two friends gave me the same advice in almost identical words. Father Miller put it this way: "You are not seeking the position. Why not leave the matter in the hands of God? Do not refuse to be a candidate, but at the same time refuse to do anything which could bring about your election." I followed this counsel. Since I had not even been chosen as a delegate to the Chapter which would do the electing, Father Miller felt that I had very little chance indeed of becoming Superior General.

He was mistaken. The day after the Chapter opened in New York, Father Stark called me on the phone to notify me that I had been elected, and that I was to come East immediately. I flew to New York from Los Angeles overnight and, right after my arrival, took office as Superior General of the Paulist Fathers. As Father Stark was cleaning out his desk, my eye caught the date on the calendar. It looked familiar. There it was again—June 19.

The next six years, as Superior General, were not pleasant ones because these were days of reconstruction and reorganization, and it was a period of considerable travel. Most of the Fathers recognized the fact that I had been away a long time and had little knowledge of the administrative side of the community.

One of my early calls was upon Archbishop John Joseph Mitty of San Francisco. In my first meeting with him I told him of how he had helped Navy men with his various gifts during the war, and he seemed pleased that I knew this. The Archbishop belonged to the rough-and-ready school and spoke his mind forthrightly—often vehemently. He was not a diplomat by any means. "We will get along fine," he said to me. "If you don't throw me any curves, I won't throw you any." But not long afterward I had to recall this remark to his mind. I was back in the San Francisco area on another visit to our Paulist houses when he sent word that he wanted to see me. As I walked into his office, he took a copy of the Paulist annual report from his desk and, thrusting it into my hand, declared: "This is away out of line with the costs of running other churches in the diocese." He began reeling off figures and said, for example, that the average monthly cost for supporting a diocesan priest was $150 while ours was—if I remember correctly—$255. He also seemed to be disturbed that we had $15,000 budgeted for the Paulist choir.

The Archbishop's criticism caught me short. So I said: "Your Excellency, I recall a statement you made about no curves. But here you are throwing this pitch at me from away out in left field. Give me a little time to check on this matter, and I'll come back to see you." Two weeks later I was back, with all the information in hand. "Your Excellency," I said, "I have here comparable studies, and it costs us less to support a man in San Francisco than in several other places in the country. In New York, for instance. . . ."

But he interrupted me.

"I don't want to hear any more. Leave your studies here, and I'll look at them some other time. But I know if you didn't have the right answers you wouldn't be back here to fight with me."

That was the end of the discussion. We had no further difficulty with the Archbishop. On several future occasions we met and enjoyed each other's company and talked about the old days in the Navy. (On his last visit to Rome he was not well and seemed to realize he had not long to go.)

In addition to making visits around the country, I also had to go to Rome frequently. My first visit to Rome took place a little over six months after my election. I wanted to visit Rome as soon as I could in order to reorganize our house there and get some firsthand information about postwar conditions in the Eternal City.

Our Church of Santa Susanna's in Rome had had its own war experiences. When World War II broke out, our two priests there returned to the States. But no one else had moved into the church in the meantime until the American army, fighting its way up the Italian peninsula, arrived in Rome. With the war nearly ended, Father Stark, the Superior General at the time, was able to renew the contact of the Paulist Fathers with Santa Susanna's through the help of President Truman. At a Democratic party dinner in Philadelphia, Father Stark had met J. Francis Doyle, a prominent Democrat, and this gentleman relayed to Mr. Truman the problem about our church in Rome. As a result, permission was obtained for Father Wilfrid Hurley to go into Rome (an occupied city) with the American army and report to the Vicariate that the Paulists were back. Since Santa Susanna's was serving the Allied armed forces at the time, and was being used by English-speaking chaplains, the Vicariate did nothing about it and did not seem to be in any hurry to welcome the Paulists back to their church. I found out later that the Vicariate officials were actually less than happy about our return, feeling that the Paulists, in a way, had "abandoned" the church when the war started—and had gone home—while other American clergymen in Rome at the time had stayed at their posts "for the duration." Father Thomas Lantry O'Neill, pastor at the church, was in the United States on community business when the war broke out and was unable to return to his post. Father Edward Peters, his assistant, had received word to come home. A few

days before Italy declared herself on the side of the
Axis he left the city, leaving the church in charge of
Monsignor DeDomenicis, who was to say Mass for the
Cistercian nuns. He was Italian and acceptable to the
Italian government. The community and Father Peters
had expected the return of Father O'Neill and learned
too late that his passport would no longer be honored
for the duration of the war. Other American priests remaining in the city were connected, in one way or another, with Vatican activities and enjoyed a certain immunity. Father Fred Heinzmann at the Maryknoll House
told me that the German authorities called on them just
once, looked over the house, and gave them no trouble.

I was anxious to make sure that everything was now in
order and that Santa Susanna's, as they say in the Navy,
was ready to go on active duty again as the American
national church in Rome.

On my first visit to Rome I had the memorable experience of having my first Papal audience. It was a
private one, and I was accompanied to it by Father
Hurley. In the presence of Pius XII I was moved profoundly, and it took me two or three days to get my
feet back on the ground again. We talked for some
twenty-five minutes, with the conversation centering on
the United States. He was very much concerned about
what the United States was going to do in the postwar
era and told me that my country was the hope of the
world, that everyone was looking toward the United
States for leadership.

Just a few days before my arrival in Rome, Pope Pius
had delivered a Christmas message which had stirred
the hearts of people everywhere—coming, as it did, after
a devastating war. The late Father James Gillis, the
world-known Paulist writer and speaker (and editor of
the *Catholic World*), had praised the Papal message in
his weekly column, and many prominent people had

sent him telegrams telling of their agreement. I had
carried some of these telegrams with me to Rome. During the audience with Pope Pius, I said that many of our
important American statesmen were very much impressed by his Christmas message, and His Holiness
seemed very happy to hear this. I took from my briefcase
five or six of the telegrams sent to Father Gillis and
handed them to the Pope. His Holiness read them carefully. "Mr. Herbert Hoover, I know—Ambassador Hugh
Gibson, I know," Pius XII said slowly, and went through
the names on the other telegrams in the same way.
Then, puzzled, he looked at me and—pronouncing the
word with a "*j*" sound, as in "Jill," instead of a *g* sound
as in "gill"—he asked: "But this Gillis—who is?"

A few days later at breakfast in New York with Father
Gillis I was telling him about my trip to Rome and,
casually, I said: "The Holy Father was asking about
you."

"He was?" Father Gillis said sonorously. He always
spoke in an impressive deep voice.

I repeated the conversation.

"Ye gods!" Father Gillis exclaimed. "A lifetime of
devotion to Holy Mother Church, and my epitaph from
His Holiness is: 'This Gillis—who is?'"

Yet even before the war Father Gillis was no stranger
on either side of the Atlantic, and he had ruffled some
VIP feathers in both places during his long career of
preaching and writing in defense of the Church. He was
anti-Roosevelt (almost violently) and anti-Mussolini.
President Roosevelt smarted more than he admitted
under the constant criticism of Father Gillis, and a
Bishop told me that this was indirectly responsible for
his removal from the *Catholic Hour*. Mr. Roosevelt had
been extremely helpful in the situation in Mexico where
the Church was being harassed, and he indicated to
grateful members of the hierarchy it would be appreci-

ated by him if something could be done about Father Gillis and his attacks.

The criticism of Mussolini, meanwhile, had reverberations at Santa Susanna's. Father Thomas Lantry O'Neill, who was in charge of our Rome church before the war, informed Father Harney (Superior General at the time) that friends of the Italian leader were very much upset. From the Apostolic Delegation in Washington, about the same time, came word that Father Gillis should stop denouncing Mussolini. The instruction was delivered verbally to the Superior General by one of our priests. Upon being apprised of this, Father Gillis offered to resign, but Father Harney refused the offer, telling him to continue to write what his conscience dictated. "If we have to go down," the Superior General said, "we shall all go down together."

As Superior General of the Paulist Fathers I met Pope Pius a number of times. During this period—and later when I had audiences with him as pastor of Santa Susanna's—I found him to be a friendly, but reserved Pontiff. Yet he had an almost concealed sense of humor, which was demonstrated to me at the time of Father Gillis' golden jubilee. I was arranging an honorary doctor of theology degree for Father Gillis, and the Apostolic Delegate, Archbishop Amleto Cicognani (now the Cardinal and the Vatican Secretary of State), suggested that I request that it be conferred by the Angelicum, the Roman university of the Dominicans. This was significant because the care and purity of Church doctrine has been traditionally entrusted to the Dominicans.

Since the Angelicum is a Pontifical university, formal approval of the Pope had to be obtained for the degree. The various papers, therefore, were submitted to Pope Pius, including a biographical sketch of Father Gillis and the number of degrees he already had. As His Holiness read down the long list in my presence, he glanced at me with a bit of a smile and asked: "What is Father Gillis doing—making a collection of degrees?"

I was given the award for Father Gillis and told to have the scroll prepared. It was done by one of Rome's finest Latin scholars, but when it was presented to Father Manuel Suarez, the late Master General of the Dominicans, he refused to sign it. The friar had found two mistakes in the Latin. He kindly offered to have it redone and sent to me in New York. But already knowing the dilatory tactics of some of our Latin friends I politely declined the offer and spent the day getting the scroll adjusted to the proper Latin. The next morning I took it back to the Dominican Master General for signature. He not only signed it but made a special stop in New York, on his way to South America, to present the degree personally to Father Gillis at a solemn Mass in the presence of Cardinal Spellman.

A day or so later, at breakfast, Father Gillis said in his best Pontifical tone: "I should like to ask you, Father Cunningham, is there any significance in this degree being granted by the Angelicum?"

"Yes, there is," I said. "Only three such degrees have been awarded in the last 100 years—and if you do not recognize the significance of the Dominican degree, then I am sure it is lost on everyone. It is the Church approval—granted by Pius XII—on your work and preaching through the years."

Yet I think he was more impressed a week or so later when at a community dinner—to the surprise of himself and of those present—I presented him with a Papal honor, *Pro Ecclesia et Pontifice* ("For Church and Pope"). In the presence of all I said this had been obtained for him by the Apostolic Delegate to the United States (the present Cardinal Cicognani), from whom Father Gillis had told me had come the original word to "lay off" Mussolini.

Chapter 5

ROMAN PARISH

When it had been suggested that I be a candidate for Superior General, I had not known what to say and needed advice. At the expiration of my six-year term as Superior General, I was asked if I would accept the position of pastor of Santa Susanna's (and Procurator General of the Paulist Fathers) if I was elected to it. I replied: "Certainly."

I was elected, and from that day began what seems to me to have been the happiest years of my priestly life.

The election was in 1952. The exact date, of course, was June 19—a red-letter day, for fair.

When I first saw Santa Susanna's, the four statues on the front of the church were browned with age and so covered with dirt they were practically unrecognizable. Eighteen years later, when I left Rome, the statues of St. Susanna and the three other saints in the niches on the façade were less recognizable than ever. In that long interval I never did succeed in having the front of the church cleaned—all because, early in my service as pastor, I had made a mistake and used the wrong word with Italian authorities.

I had been able to carry out a comprehensive restoration program inside. I even arranged for the removal of a fifteen-foot fig tree that had found a convenient spot to grow in at the very top of the church front. But the fine Baroque façade remained masked in the grime of centuries.

I wanted the front of the church to present a clean

fresh appearance and had made application for permission to sandblast it. The Fine Arts Commission practically swooned. Any other word than "sandblast" would have been better. *Sandblast,* in such a case, is an evil word, I quickly found out. The façade of Santa Susanna's is of travertine marble, this marble is soft and porous would disintegrate if sandblasted. My choice of words ended any possibility of cleaning the front of the church. My Italian friends in this field started to talk about other subjects, or walked out on me, whenever I mentioned doing something about the façade of Santa Susanna's.

Even for Rome, Santa Susanna's is a very old church. It is on the site of the home of Susanna, a Roman virgin, who was beheaded at the order of Emperor Diocletian on the eleventh day of August in the year 290. Susanna, the daughter of an early-day convert to Christianity, had consecrated her virginity to Jesus Christ by vow. When the Roman emperor designated her as the bride for his son-in-law, Susanna was faced with the choice of accepting Diocletian's wish—and thus break her holy vow—or suffering death. She chose death. The day after her head was chopped off, Pope St. Caius visited her home, where the martyrdom had taken place, and said Mass there—beginning the devotion to St. Susanna. Of the 400-odd churches in Rome, Santa Susanna's is one of the forty-seven designated as Station churches—which means that in the Middle Ages it was one of the churches visited by Popes on successive days in Lent. Santa Susanna's day was the Saturday in the third week of Lent. On that day every Roman missal throughout the world carries the notation: *Station at Santa Susanna.* Records from the fifth century identify the two priests assigned to the church at the time and refer to it as the Titular Church of Caius, just as today it is known as the Titular Church of Cardinal Cushing. As Jim O'Neill (the present head of the N.C.W.C. news bureau in Rome) wrote some time ago, Santa Susanna's has close ties with ancient Rome and modern America.

When the Paulist Fathers were offered a church in Rome in 1921, Santa Susanna's was one of three churches available. It was being used, only on occasion, by some Armenian priests. Father Joseph McSorley, our Superior General then, selected Santa Susanna's. When I asked him one time why the Paulists had been given this opportunity to go to Rome, he told me that the Cardinal-Vicar (the Vicar-General of the Pope, who is the Bishop of Rome, in directing activities of the diocese of Rome) had the impression that Americans in Rome were increasing in number. Just as there were Italian priests in New York looking after Italians, the Cardinal-Vicar felt there should be American priests in Rome for their own nationals. Father McSorley indicated that even at that time Roman officialdom expected many more Americans to come to Rome, both as residents and visitors. Since the Paulists were an American religious society—and the first one founded in America—it seemed logical to the Vatican that they should be offered an opportunity to look after American citizens abroad, as well as at home. The Paulists came to Santa Susanna's on January 10, 1922. (That happened to be the same year I entered the Paulist seminary.)

My six years as Superior General, from 1946 to 1952, were invaluable preparation and training for the demands that would be made upon Santa Susanna's by the growing number of pilgrims and American residents who would visit the church during the following twelve years when I would be its pastor. On my visits to Rome on community matters I had met the important officials in the various congregations as well as the American priests living in the city. I studied Italian at Berlitz in Rome with Father William Lynahan, another Paulist. I learned about the churches by visiting different churches, a pagan shrine, or some one of the various antiquities of the Eternal City each day and soon was familiar with many of these beautiful and often hallowed places.

Prior to one of my early trips to Rome as Superior General I had been in California on business, and while there I visited St. Paul the Apostle parish. Whenever I was in Los Angeles it was a "must" for me to drop in at the parish school which had been built since my days there. During the war the youngsters in the second grade had adopted me as one of the beneficiaries of their prayers. By this time they were now in the sixth grade. Their eyes bulged when I mentioned that I would soon be going to Rome. Little Mimi Hutson, who was a special friend in those days, got up from her seat and asked if I would give Pope Pius the regards of her classmates and herself. Sister Carmelita, the teacher, gave me a picture of the children to take with me. Some weeks later I had a private audience with Pope Pius. After my business with the Holy Father had been concluded, he continued to talk about the United States and various personalities. I said: "If I may, Your Holiness, I would like to tell you that the children in the sixth grade of St. Paul the Apostle school in Los Angeles are praying for you and say a decade of the Rosary each day." I showed him the picture of the class.

"That is what we need," he said. "The prayers of the children." He looked at the picture, carefully examining the little faces. With the picture in his hand, His Holiness said: "Do not wait until you get home to tell them I send them, and their parents, and teachers, my very special blessing and thanks. Please, today, send them a cablegram."

I know that my cablegram was put in a special frame on the classroom wall!

Pope Pius XII—unknowingly, probably, to himself—

was at that time creating an entirely new image of the Papacy. His willingness to receive people in audiences, his friendliness, the impressiveness of his bearing, and the feeling of sanctity which one immediately sensed in his presence impressed all who met him. Never before in the history of the Church had so many people seen the Pope, or received his blessing. Never since have so many been received in private or special audiences. Never before in the history of the world, either, had so many gone forth from general audiences in St. Peter's basilica, or from private receptions in the Papal halls, with the feeling that in very truth they had been in the presence of a holy man.

Each audience with him was always a special memory for me. I think he himself remembered one audience.

I had been invited to his summer residence at Castel Gandolfo and, taking advantage of the opportunity, I arranged to take all the Paulists in Rome with me. One of our priests, a very pious man, was not too well and was uncertain whether he should come along, but finally decided to join us. When the Holy Father came into the audience room, I introduced each Paulist in our group. As I presented our sick priest who was looking at His Holiness in awe, he said, probably knowing of the close relationship between the Holy Father and the Cardinal Archbishop of New York, "I am one of Cardinal Spellman's twelve apostles." The Holy Father looked at him and, then, at me. Whereupon, giving each of us in the group a medal and his blessing, he terminated the audience at once. We did not even have our picture taken! I was absolutely furious because I had not been able to say a word to His Holiness about the two projects which had brought me there. The Pope, of course, felt that we had a mental case on our hands—so out he went, leaving me standing in a state of frustration.

I did not say anything at all until the evening, when

my emotions were under better control. At dinner I asked this good father what he meant by telling the Pope he was one of Cardinal Spellman's twelve apostles. He said everyone knows who they are. "I'm stupid," I replied. "Tell me who they are." He went on to explain that for two years he had been one of a dozen priests of the archdiocese of New York who assist at the blessing of the oils in St. Patrick's Cathedral on Holy Thursday. The priests chosen for this service are called the twelve apostles, he told me.

"Do you think the Holy Father understood this?" I asked.

"Why, of course! *He knew.*"

"Then he must have thought one of us was Judas," I said, "because I have never seen a private audience terminated as was ours. You really blew it sky high."

Several times later in audiences with Pius XII—and he was always gracious!—I had the feeling that, as His Holiness looked at me, he was wondering what had ever happened to the twelfth apostle—Cardinal Spellman's, that is. (Actually, he is in good health and still carrying on his apostolic work and remains a good friend.)

Just prior to the Holy Year of 1950, while I was on a visit to the Eternal City, Archbishop Martin J. O'Connor, the rector of North American College, took me to lunch. Archbishop O'Connor is one of the truly great Americans in Rome. During the many years I came to know him there he, more than any one single person, represented the American Catholic Church to the Vatican and to the Italian government. At lunch we talked about the approaching Holy Year. The number of Americans who would come to Rome at that time, as well as the growing size of the American colony in the city, would require more men at Santa Susanna's, he predicted, than the two we had there. The Archbishop said Santa Susanna's should participate more actively in Rome's

civic, tourist, and religious life. The problems involved
in arranging for tourists to attend Papal audiences were
becoming more difficult. Santa Susanna's, instead of helping in this situation was doing nothing but sending people
to the North American College. We were not carrying our
full responsibilities, Archbishop O'Connor said. I promised
him we would do better.

Upon my return to New York, I mentioned the need
for more priests to Father Thomas Lantry O'Neill, the
prewar rector. He knew the situation from previous Holy
Years and felt that perhaps the situation was being
exaggerated.

But it was not. We were in a new era of opulence, of
quick transportation, and of a desire by Americans to
see the old countries of Europe. Archbishop O'Connor
had not at all exaggerated the problems that were to
face Santa Susanna's during Holy Year. He had shown
great foresight. I myself remained in Rome for the four
busiest months. The year started slowly. January and
February were quiet. But by the first of March the
American pilgrimages were coming into the city by the
hundreds. We had six priests at Santa Susanna's and
still could not keep up with the demands made of us.
The burden put on us by the numbers thronging the confessionals at Santa Susanna's was particularly heavy because of the conditions required at that time for the pilgrims to gain indulgences. To gain a plenary indulgence,
for instance, a pilgrim had to visit four major basilicas and
go to both confession and Communion every day. In the
Marian year, four years later, the Vatican changed this
so that an indulgence could be gained by going to Communion every day, but confession was required only once
a week.

Each trip I made to Rome convinced me more and
more that a complete restoration of the interior of the
church was needed. The decorations had not been

cleaned nor had there been any painting done in nearly 400 years. I often discussed this matter with Father Wilfrid Hurley, who was in charge of Santa Susanna's in the early postwar years. But things moved slowly. First it was the Holy Year that held us back. Then there were the usual delays. But I knew what had to be done, and when I took over as pastor I started the work.

Technically, I as pastor was second in command of Santa Susanna's. The theoretical pastor is the Titular Cardinal, and at the time of the start of the restoration work this was the late Edward Cardinal Mooney of Detroit. Because Santa Susanna's is a national monument, the Titular Cardinal is represented by a designated member of the Italian clergy who takes care of all the relations between the church and the government. This representative, or legal rector, was (and still is) Monsignor Salvatore Capoferri, a Papal master of ceremonies and a never-failing friend.

Any pastor in planning work in his church is faced with the problem of financing it. Besides that traditional problem, I had a unique one—I had to get government authorization for any repairs, reconstruction, or rearrangement work on the ancient church. Everybody seemed to be involved.

The Fine Arts Commission and the Commission for National Monuments approved the over-all restoration plan and agreed that we could proceed. My idea was to do it over a number of years, carrying out a part of it each year. The Fine Arts Commission gave me the names of three qualified contractors. Through Monsignor Capoferri I made arrangements for a meeting with one of them who had an excellent reputation, and the three of us sat down to discuss price.

In transactions of this nature in Rome it soon becomes so very apparent that you need an Italian intermediary. An American finds it distasteful to haggle about price.

But an Italian never expects to get his first price and, therefore, adds ten to twenty per cent to what he anticipates receiving. The sanctuary was to be the first phase of our restoration program and the contractor had submitted a *preventivo,* or estimate, of $10,000. The carefully prepared estimate was lying on the table in front of the three of us, but no one seemed to pay any attention to it. We were talking pleasantly about Santa Susanna's, and how old and beautiful it was, and what a fine idea it was to have it restored. Then, casually, as if he was doodling, Monsignor Capoferri picked up a pencil and, driving a line through the "$10,000" on the estimate, put down "$7000." The conversation, meanwhile, continued. It was all very cordial, and no mention at all was being made of the price. Now, apparently, it was the contractor's turn for "doodling." He made a line through the "$7000" of Monsignor Capoferri's and wrote "$9200." For the next five minutes we talked about how long the job would take, and how it would be necessary to interfere as little as possible with the church's regular routine. When Monsignor Capoferri took the next step in this price-fixing ritual, I noticed he had upped his figure to $7800.

No one said a word. But at that precise instant both Monsignor Capoferri and the contractor knew that the price eventually agreed upon would be $8500. A few minutes later, when the contractor wrote "$8500" on the piece of paper, the Monsignor looked at me and nodded his head. The agreement was complete!—and we all went out for a cup of coffee.

As promised, the work was finished a week before Christmas, but the scaffolding was still standing in the sanctuary. Although the workers had faithfully assured me they would come and take it down, it was still there the morning of Christmas Eve. Our sacristan, Giovanni, an old-time army man who knew how to get things done, sent out distress signals to four or five of his firemen friends. They arrived shortly. The dismantling was not done skillfully, but it was effective. The firemen did not seem to realize that dropping two-by-six planks onto a marble floor from a height of fifty feet can be damaging. Four or five pieces of our lovely flooring were cracked beyond repair. But the firemen got the scaffolding all down, and we were ready for Christmas.

All the paintings and frescoes in the sanctuary had been restored except the oil painting over the main altar, which showed the martyrdom of St. Susanna. To restore it would have cost $500, and I refused to pay that. I did not like the picture in the first place, and I had wanted it taken down during the restoration work, secretly hoping that they would never be able to get it back up again. But it turned out the painting had been attached with wooden pegs to the brick wall which had been built in the year 850. That did not end the matter, however; the painters were distressed that I would not let them restore the painting. Shortly after Christmas two of the dozen or so in the crew came to me and said they would do the restoration job for nothing, and on their own time, if I furnished the paint. It took them about a week, and the paint cost me fifty dollars. When they had finished, they came in to thank me for giving them the opportunity to do the restoration. I handed each of them $100. Anyone who loved art so much should be worthy of his hire. Since then a most cordial relationship has developed between us.

You can never be quite sure what you are going to find when you begin to work on an old church. I learned this in the second year of the restoration program— when we started in on the six giant frescoes which tell the story of Susanna of the Old Testament (Romans call this Biblical heroine "the Chaste Susanna").

Using a strong solution of caustic soda, the restorers

washed down—one after the other—the *Susanna* frescoes
which had been painted on the walls in the nave by
Baldassare Croce in the sixteenth century. Sometimes it
was hardly necessary for them to do any painting because the cleaning itself so perfectly restored the original
colors. They knew, too, that anything subsequently
painted onto a fresco had little chance of surviving.

All went well until they came to the painting of
Susanna in the Bath. She was covered with a cloak from
head to foot. But as they washed down the fresco, the
cloak began to disappear! (Some 150 years ago the
Church had gone through an era of modesty, or Puri-
tanism, and gowns were painted on the nude feminine
figures, while trousers were put on the men.) The
restorers called me up on the scaffolding immediately to
point out the approaching disaster. Representatives of
the Fine Arts Commission had arrived. "What do we
do?" I was asked.

"Keep on cleaning," I said.

—and off came Susanna's gown.

She stood there in the bath—on the church wall—
almost in the nude. In doing the fresco, however, Croce
had portrayed Susanna very modestly. When the cleaning was completed, the painting was viewed by seven
different commissions, photographs were taken, and
there was a lengthy discussion. Finally, a Fine Arts
Commission official asked:

"Now what do we do? Put the gown back on?"

Through our very good friend Monsignor Capoferri, I
replied: "I think if this is the way Croce painted her,
this is the way we should have her."

"We think so, too," a commission spokesman said.
"But you Americans are so unpredictable."

That was only the first of a number of surprises that
turned up in the restoration work. I learned why great
care is necessary in the restoration of a church—especially

a Roman church. Sometime afterward, in working in the basement, we uncovered a mosaic floor that obviously had been part of the third-century home of our St. Susanna. Another time we found a magnificent sixteenth-century tile pavement under the flooring of the St. Lawrence chapel (the flooring had been a source of irritation to me because it looked like black asphalt, and as you could plainly see it did not fit in with the décor of the chapel). Even in the smaller restoration projects of later years we still had our surprises—and some were on the grim side. Our office, for instance, was separated from one of the confessionals in the church by a two-foot wall. If someone rang the confessional bell outside of confession hours, the priest on duty in the office had to make a roundabout walk through the sacristy and into the church. I thought it would be handy, and save time, if we made a back entrance to the confessional through the wall so that the priest could walk into it from the office. The workmen, as they began digging into the wall, came upon an open coffin with a skeleton standing up inside it. That finished the door to the confessional! I immediately had the wall sealed up again, and Santa Susanna's priests continue to take the long way around from office to confessional. Up until a century ago, I found out, it was the Italian custom to bury people in churches.

No matter how small the job was, I had to get government permission. Quite a while after the main restoration work had been completed, I decided to do something about the four-century-old front steps. They were worn smooth by age and were particularly dangerous for high heels. Several of our people had already fallen. Besides the Fine Arts and National Monuments commissions, I also had to obtain permission from the street, police, and traffic departments. After an official inspection it was decided we might put in five new marble steps, but

I was told that two other steps were not sufficiently worn to warrant removal. The job was to be completed a week before Christmas, but work did not begin till the morning of Christmas Eve. I could see disaster signals going up because it was obvious the marble itself had not yet arrived. Phone calls indicated the truck with the marble had left Viterbo at 6 A.M. that morning for its two and a half hour run into Rome—and here it was mid-morning. There was no indication of any accident en route either. Finally, at noon, the truck driver showed up at the church without the load of marble and, also, without his truck. He explained that on reaching the Rome city limits he had paid the time-honored local taxes and had been passed on. But when arriving at Porta Pia, less than ten blocks down the street from Santa Susanna's, he was told by the police he would need a special permit to take his truckload of marble along the Via XX Settembre. At eight o'clock that evening, in the pouring rain, they were still working on the steps. But they had them ready for midnight Mass—the five new steps, and the two antique ones!

Some things, like the cleaning of the façade, I never was permitted to do—even partly. Our confessionals to this day are just about as old-fashioned as you will find. They are 400 years old, and are the open-air type. I restored them as much as I could, installing foam-rubber kneelers and new electric wiring, for instance. But the authorities would not permit me to replace them with more up-to-date ones. Modern-style confessionals, the Fine Arts Commission people said, would destroy the beauty of the church and its artistic symmetry—and I know they were right.

Restoration work in a church like Santa Susanna's is never complete. There is always something to be done. But by the beginning of spring in 1955, I felt that I had accomplished something. The major part of the restoration program had been finished less than three years after I became pastor.

Those early days of 1955 were busy ones. First there was St. Patrick's Day. Two days later came St. Joseph's feast day, a holy day of obligation in Italy. It turned out that the Feast of St. Joseph that year was also Santa Susanna's Lenten Station Day. The church was packed from early morning until after 8 P.M. For the Station Day we had opened the newly restored crypt, which contains a small chapel of St. Susanna. After having completed the restoration work upstairs in the church, I had turned to the crypt and had been restoring it for about a year. Now this work was almost finished, too, and it looked wonderful. There was a surprise for me also. On the wall above the Gospel-side stairway leading down into the St. Susanna chapel, the restoring artists had included as part of the mural a handsomely painted, framed inscription. I read the Latin words. They said the restoration work had been completed in 1955 by the Missionary Society of St. Paul the Apostle. The title *Procurator General-Pastor* was also written in Latin. What puzzled me for a moment was the name: *Jacopo* Cunningham. That was *me*. Jacopo is an ancient form of James.

The restoration program was naturally the biggest part of my efforts to give Santa Susanna's a fresh, clean look. But other things had to be done in the meantime—such as cleaning the windows high in the nave. I have no idea when they had been cleaned last—possibly when they were installed four centuries earlier. They were almost impossible to reach. But Italians, if encouraged, will always find a way! In trying to locate someone to do this job, I mentioned the problem to Giovanni, the sacristan. To my very great surprise, a few days later a detail of firemen came to see me. They asked $300 for the job. I felt this was a considerable amount of money to pay to clean a dozen or more windows, but I had no choice.

The firemen told me that they had read how Americans go by the law of supply and demand—and they were the only ones who could supply the service I was demanding. So I hired them, and they cleaned the antique leaded-glass panes without using a drop of water or a piece of cloth. They wiped them clean with page after page of old newspapers.

We used the firemen often, and no one seemed surprised to see them climbing up the front of the church or swarming over the roof. Santa Susanna's roof was a nesting place for birds—especially pigeons—and some of the seeds which they had transported from elsewhere would take root in places that were the hardest to get to, but which were perfectly visible from the street. The firemen were the ones who got rid of that fig tree for me that had been flourishing near the rooftop, and they regularly removed the garden of weeds that kept sprouting in the many cracks and crevices of Carlo Maderno's Baroque façade.

The price charged by the firemen was always high, but one reason for this was that my sacristan would get ten per cent commission from them. Anytime some special type of work had to be done—and I worked through the sacristan—I found I was paying a commission. I was not aware of this for several years. But employees like the sacristan, who earn so little, have no hesitation in finding people you need for specialized services and then taking a commission from them for having "lined up" the job.

A sacristan is needed at Santa Susanna's for only a few hours in the morning because, after the Masses are over, all he has to do is sit and watch the church. The priest on duty for the day opens the church in the morning, closes it at noon, opens it again at 4 P.M., and closes it in the evening. (We priests had regular duty days during the week. On Sunday we would divide the work as the spirit moved us.)

In the States a sacristan takes care of everything, from vestments to cleaning up. At Santa Susanna's all that is done by the cloistered nuns who live in the convent attached to the church. When the church is closed at noon and again at 7 P.M., the key to the front door is handed to the Mother Abbess. She then "extends" the cloistered area of the convent, and because no one else is around the nuns may then enter the church. The nuns put out the vestments for Mass, take care of the sacristy, and do all the cleaning. Any miscellaneous church work, such as the changing of candles, is done by the nuns or the priests themselves. If no one else was on hand to serve Mass, the sacristan would.

The first sacristan I knew at Santa Susanna's was Giovanni, the firemen's friend. He was already on the job when I had made my first visit as Superior General. Sometime around the end of the war he had walked in off the street. He told the army chaplain who was in charge of the church that he was a sacristan, and that he had worked in Santa Susanna's before the war. As far as I could find out, he was never hired officially. He just moved in and made himself useful. He proved to be useful, too. But he was also going to complicate my life just when the restoration program was finished and I was about to breathe a sigh of relief.

Giovanni was probably our most colorful employee. He was a former soldier living on a government pension and, when I first knew him, was in his early sixties. He stood about five-six and had eyes which could look very fierce and warlike. Actually he was quite gentle, until aroused. Then he would do nothing but shout—which is an old Italian custom. He wore military boots and a chauffeur's cap. But his mark of distinction—and his pride and joy —was a long sweeping handlebar mustache.

In taking up the Sunday collection, Giovanni had a greeting which went with the revenue. If a visitor put only twenty lire in the collection, Giovanni would give the person an Are-you-sure-you're-in-the-right-place look, and would glance down at the small coin with a bit of a sneer. The 100-lire piece brought a nod of recognition—a slight inclination of the head. For 500 lire, or a dollar bill, Giovanni had a smile and a much more recognizable bow from the hips. But if the donation was 1000 lire or more, he smiled broadly, stepped back into the aisle, clicked his heels slightly and gave a very impressive bow.

Giovanni always took good care of those he knew as generous contributors. Major General Frank Allen, Jr., was one of this highly regarded group. At the time, General Allen was in charge of the U. S. Military Assistance Advisory Group, but he had led the army of Occupation into Rome and was shot in the knee along the way. The wartime bullet wound always bothered the general, and he found it difficult to kneel on our wooden benches. As soon as Giovanni saw the general enter the church, he would rush into the sacristy and try to beat our generous contributor to the first or second row of pews with a pillow on which he could kneel.

I think Giovanni probably is responsible for the foam-rubber kneeling pads we have today. He always made such a fuss—and, I believe, sometimes embarrassed the general—that I began wondering whether something might not be done with the hard wooden kneelers. One morning I had just seen Giovanni's display of care and affection for the general—and the matter was on my mind—when some Jewish visitors from New Jersey came into the office with one of our friends at the Embassy, Alexander Matturri. A few days earlier I had arranged an audience for them with Pope Pius, and they were stopping by to thank me. My Embassy friend, Mr. Matturri, said

the gentlemen wanted to do something for Santa Susanna's. Since they were in the building and construction
industry, Mr. Matturri suggested they perhaps could help
with something in that line. I thought immediately of the
general and Giovanni and told them of our need for
kneeler pads.

Within two months the pads arrived from the States.
As a matter of fact they arrived during the week after
the Lenten Station Day which had climaxed the comple-
tion of our restoration program. Thanks to our Jewish
benefactors, Santa Susanna's had the first-foam-rubber
kneeling pads in Rome, if not in all of Italy, and praying
was given a comfortable assist.

On the Sunday after the pads arrived, I put some of
them in the church temporarily in order that our people
could try them out. But the very next day I had them
screwed right to the benches so that our light-fingered
"friends" would not slip into the church and take them
home as samples. It was something one had to think
about. The previous year one church lost half of its
lead shingles to a thief, and some months later he came
back with a truck to finish the job. They do some funny
things, but we tried to make it as difficult for them as
we could.

Not all the "funny things" happened to someone else,
however.

During World War II many Jewish people in Rome,
fearful of keeping jewels and other valuables in their
homes, brought them to the convent at Santa Susanna's
and asked the nuns to take care of their possessions until
the war was over, or until they came back to claim them.
It was rumored that these articles had been buried in
the basement of the church, which is like a small cat-
acomb. It was also rumored that some of these precious
things had never been called for, or claimed.

One afternoon, as I returned to the church office, the

Mother Abbess sent word that she wanted to see me immediately. She was in a highly disturbed frame of mind and told me right off that I would have to discharge Giovanni. There was abundant evidence, the Mother Abbess said, that Giovanni or one of his friends was entering the church when it was closed in the early afternoon or at night, when the nuns were not in it. She said the intruder was digging up two of the cemeteries in the basement.

I made an inspection at once, and even I could see the evidence that there had been some digging.

When Giovanni was dismissed, he said he was going to get a Red Communist lawyer to make trouble for us. But the reason for his discharge would have stood up before an Italian court. He settled for a lifetime pension of sixteen dollars a month, which added to his army retirement income was sufficient for him to get along. This was a voluntary arrangement on our part. Social security and the welfare benefits, now taken for granted, had not been in existence when Giovanni entered the employ of the church. For that matter, even when his successor was hired, there was no listing of "sacristan" as a social security classification under Italian law. The closest to it was "domestic." Therefore, for Giovanni's replacement we made no social security arrangements either. That seemed neither necessary nor possible.

Giovanni's successor gave Santa Susanna's another distinction. He was replaced by a woman. She was a pious Italian woman who had been coming to Santa Susanna's for many years, and she knew the Fathers since the prewar days of Father Thomas Lantry O'Neill. On Giovanni's departure this woman asked if she could help out temporarily. Things went so smoothly that we let the temporary employment become permanent. Later, whenever I mentioned social security to her and suggested that she see my lawyer to apply for coverage, she would say she was not interested. The situation was somewhat similar with Josephine, our cook-housekeeper in the rectory. She was already in our employ when I first came to Rome. In response to an inquiry of mine, I was told nothing could or should be done about social security for Josephine because she was a church employee. This turned out to be completely erroneous. Josephine herself did not do anything about it, but when an inspector came around one day and asked Josephine why she had not applied, she said: "Oh—I don't have time to be going to those offices and waiting in line all day. I've got too much work to do." When I eventually awoke to the fact that I was subject to heavy penalties for not providing for her the various insurances required, I approached a lawyer and it took us almost two years to bring the papers up to date so that I could pay the past social security charges. They came to a little less than $400. But since I had initiated the case I did not have to pay any penalties.

It cost a lot more than that to get "all squared away" on the social security and related questions involving the woman sacristan. She was with us about seven years and then abruptly quit. In a memorandum that ran several pages she claimed back compensation of approximately $5000, covering various things such as holy days of obligation on which she had had to work, paid vacations which she had not taken, old-age benefits, hospitalization, and a number of other items. I talked to the Vicariate about this because the matter involved sacristans everywhere, and its lawyer and mine sat down to work out the details of a settlement. We settled for approximately $1200—which I did not begrudge her as I had been at fault in not providing this welfare coverage to her as an employee. From then on, our new sacristans worked only three hours a day. Under Italian law, if workers are part-time, they do not come under this extensive umbrella of social security. These experiences taught me that I had to have a lawyer on permanent retainer fee. It is impossible to deal with an employee of any kind without the asistance of one. You must have a lawyer and a witness. You're a foreigner, and your word doesn't stand up in court anywhere nearly as well as an Italian's.

Some of our problems were solved very early—such as our transportation. We never had to buy a car at the church. Always some Good Samaritan stepped in to provide us with one. The first benefactor was Colonel Frank B. "Buck" Harding, who was with our Air Force at Naples. He decided to enter the Beda seminary (for late vocations) and, arriving in Rome in uniform and with his Fiat-1400, was dismayed to learn he could not retain the car while studying for the priesthood. So he asked me to take it off his hands. I am not sure, but I may still owe Father Frank B. Harding of Our Lady of Lourdes Church in Bethesda, Maryland, the one dollar I was to pay to make the transaction legal.

The car worked fine for quite a while. Then one day, as I was driving to the airport, I had to make a quick stop. As I did, the steering wheel pulled itself loose and lifted off in my hand. I put it back very cautiously, turned around, and went back to the garage. A few days previously a visitor "passing through" had left a donation which he told me to use as I wished. Over to Fiat I went with the old car and the check. With the gift I was able to arrange a trade-in and to provide our church with a new car.

My second car was doing very well until, at a Communion breakfast in the church patio one Sunday morning, I had to put out a group of gypsies who were "roughing up" some of our people and being a bit difficult. The gypsies left, but not before uttering sinister words and making all kinds of signs and signals to indicate that I was the world's worst person and had really come under their condemnation. They promised to put a "whammy" on me, and they made it clear that if I knew what was good for me I would stay out of their Frascati area. I forgot about the incident until some Sundays later when I invited my teen-age grandniece, Marla, and several of her friends to lunch with me in the hills of Rome. As we reached the long uphill climb at the border of Frascati, the gypsies' "evil eye" went to work. I made four attempts, but the car just would not go up that hill. I had a garage man in the area examine the car, and he said it was all right. I tried again, but I still could not make that Frascati hill—so we had to return to Rome.

Sometime afterward I was telling Al Bloomingdale and his wife, of Los Angeles, of the gypsy "whammy." (What actually caused the car to balk on the hill, I found out, was a defective carburetor.) A day or so later the Fiat agency called me and asked what color car I wanted. I protested that I had a car and had not ordered a new one. There must be some mistake, I told them. But they insisted a new car had been ordered for me. It turned out that Al Bloomingdale (the head of the Diners Club) had come in and given them a check for a new car for me—all I had to do was pick out the color.

Another time, when a parish family was returning to the States, the man—who was in the oil business—had his nearly new Plymouth station wagon checked over from top to bottom prior to selling it. His prospective buyer, at the last minute, said he would buy it only if the price originally agreed upon was cut in half. The man said he'd rather give it away than do that—and he gave it to me! I explained I had no need for the car, but if he would let me pass it on to a convent or hospital I'd accept it gladly. This he agreed to do. With that I called Monsignor Andrew Landi, of Catholic Relief Services, who at the time was sending orphan children to the United

States for adoption and could use extra transportation—especially a station wagon. One thing we had all learned in Rome was to suspect motives. But I assured him that it was a good deal, and that I was accepting the car and the power of attorney to dispose of it. He took the car, and two years later when it no longer was needed in his work he sold it. His New York superiors, to whom he had explained the car's history, authorized him to return to me half the sales price.

Chapter 6

PEOPLE IN MOTION

The cloistered Sisters at Santa Susanna's never once changed their fee for all the work they did in the church and sacristy day after day. It was always the same: 2000 lire a month. That comes to about $3.20.

I have no idea when that fee was set. For all I know, it might go right back to 1575 when the Cistercian nuns, having been granted title to the sacristy and its revenues by Pope Sixtus V, moved into the convent that was between Santa Susanna's and the new Quirinale Palace. It was a spacious and beautiful convent. A well in the gardens had been designed by Michelangelo. In those days 350 nuns lived in the cloister. Their garden and most of the convent eventually became the property of the Italian government, and now the Noble Guards of the presidential palace are lodged in quarters which were once part of our nuns' cloister. Though a tenth of their former numbers, the nuns have remained a vital part of Santa Susanna's life.

They help support themselves by needlework and by making vestments for priests as well as clothes for lay men and women. For a bride they will produce a complete trousseau, apart from silk underclothing (they refuse to work on *that*). They also turn out excellent men's shirts and need only a sample to duplicate it in every detail. Alexander Matturri of the Embassy had a shirt he was particularly fond of and ordered a half dozen just like it. The left sleeve on the original had been a little too long, and his wife had taken a tuck in it above

the elbow. The six new shirts came out the same way—
each with a beautifully built-in tuck in the left sleeve.

I had the privilege of talking face to face with the
Mother Abbess and Mother Prioress, but others talked
through a grille in the *parlatorio,* or speaking room. Certain extern Sisters, such as the doorkeeper, could speak
to workmen and to those coming to have things made.
None of these outsiders entered the cloister, however. For
people having a dress fitted or a suit made, the nuns
had an accordion-like wooden screen which extended from
the wall on the convent porch, and formed a makeshift
but serviceable fitting room. The Sisters left the convent
only to vote, although in later years they also were given
permission to visit a doctor or dentist.

Each year on my birthday the Sisters presented me
with a beautiful set of Mass vestments. They also made
all the vestments for the church. We would furnish the
material and pay them for their work. There are probably
few churches in Rome that have as many sets of vestments—and as fine ones—as Santa Susanna's.

These holy women themselves led a most frugal life. Not
wishing to interfere in their traditional arrangement of
charging such an absurdly low fee for their maintenance
work, I sought to make up the difference by providing food
and other help regularly. Following in Father Wilfrid
Hurley's footsteps, for instance, I bought them meat or
chicken, as well as table wine, for one "holiday" meal a
month—and for all feast days and holidays they had
something special. On Thanksgiving Day, even, I made
sure these Italian nuns had turkey and all the trimmings.
To feed nearly three dozen nuns I would have to get
quite a few turkeys because the Italian variety is smaller
(and tougher) than our own.

My shopping was made easier, in a way, with the advent of the supermarket in later years. I became quite
familiar with the clerks in the supermarket at the Olympic

Village. Whenever my driver, Palermo, and I arrived, they would greet us cheerfully and, no matter how many people were waiting, one of the clerks would come to us at once and say: "Something for the nuns today, Father?"

"Yes. Eighteen chickens."

The Italian housewives around the counter would smile and bow, as I did my own selecting. The chickens came neatly wrapped, and this always fascinated the nuns. They had never seen anything like that before. Each Sister got a half chicken. We always brought home an extra one to take care of any guest the Sisters might have, or to make sure that if one of them became sick she would have chicken soup for three or four days. With the chickens bought, I would go over to the beverage section and buy six half-gallon bottles of wine. It might be a white Zoave, or a Chianti, or a Valpolicella. The price would be about fifty cents for two quarts. The wine came in bottles like those we used to have in the States for homemade root beer—the kind with snap-down porcelain caps. Once, without my knowing it, the supermarket changed things around during an inventory and, on entering, I started in the direction I always took for the wine. The manager saw me. Calling out to me across the entire store, he said: "The wine is not over there any more, Father. It is down this way now."

What might have been scandalous at home was just a routine purchase in Rome!

The boy carrying the chickens and wine bottles out to the car would always refuse the tip—with some regret probably. Palermo at times would have to insist on his taking it, saying that I would feel badly otherwise. Back at Santa Susanna's the white-gloved *vigile* (traffic officer) in the piazza would signal us to park in the No Parking zone in front of the church, and he would stand beside the car till it had been safely unloaded. In summer I would have ice cream sent in to the nuns at lunchtime. This was a great treat.

When the nuns went out to vote, many of their relatives met them at the convent door and walked with them to the voting booth. Afterward they would stand chatting and making their final good-byes in the convent patio. I would be watching from the side door of the church office. I used to wait until the Mother Abbess was just about to shoo the nuns back into the convent. Then I would say: "Just a moment, Mother, please. I was having some ice cream brought over." She always looked at me tolerantly as if suspecting in her heart that I was a born conniver and that nothing could be done about it. Within a few minutes the boy from the coffee bar across the street would bring the establishment's whole supply, including cups and spoons. This interlude was a welcome bonus because it gave all of them a little more time together.

Doing something for the nuns was one investment which paid off many hundreds of times. The nuns were helping us with their prayers, and their prayers were powerful. We used to say they could "pray a hole through a ten-foot wall," and we had ample evidence of this power. We rarely had a second collection at Santa Susanna's (and never seat money!), but we started an annual fuel collection for the nuns. It would be on a Sunday in the August holiday period. Until the last few years, when we persuaded them to install electric heating, the nuns bought wood with the fuel money—and used it for cooking! The inside of their convent was like an icebox. For $100 they could buy enough wood to get through the season very nicely—in their way. We always announced the fuel collection to our people as an investment. If they gave a little something, we would say, we would be happy. If they did not give, we would feel sorry for them because they would be missing out on the prayers of the Sisters—and the prayers of the Sisters are second to none.

It has always been my experience that nothing is lost which is given to charity. It was almost a principle of life in Rome: whatever you gave away came back to you very shortly with compound interest. The nuns at Santa Susanna's have a saying: "There are two sisters, *Dare* and *Ricevere*—give and receive. If you give with one hand, you receive with the other." Whenever I gave them something, they would thank me and I would say: "Oh, that's all right, Madre. It will come back."

"*Veramente*, Padre," the Mother Abbess would say, nodding her head in agreement. "That's so very true."

From their choir, hidden behind the main altar, the nuns sang for daily High Mass and for Sunday-afternoon benediction. At benediction the nuns would make the responses of the Litany in Latin but the priest, in the reciting, would use English, even if there was no one in the church. We never did anything in Italian, so as not to discourage Americans from coming. Even before the Council, we made a very special effort to see to it that services which did not have to be conducted in Latin were in English.

I wished, if possible, to have the most excellent services in all Rome and at the same time keep before the people that Santa Susanna's was an American church. Archbishop O'Connor helped us greatly by allowing North American College students to assist us at Easter and Christmas, on Thanksgiving Day, and on other special occasions. These young Americans studying for the priesthood would handle all assisting functions, from deacon to torchbearer. They came in teams and were all approximately the same height—which was tall. At the end of Holy Week one year a little old Italian woman came up to me and, her voice filled with awe, asked: "Father—where did you ever get those giants who conducted the services?"

"*Signora*," I said. "They are from the North American College on the Janiculum Hill."

She smiled understandingly and said: "Ah! That wonderful air on the Janiculum!"

Monsignor Andrew Landi of Brooklyn usually said the Solemn Mass on Thanksgiving Day, and we always had a special preacher. One year Bishop Charles Mulrooney, another Brooklynite, preached the sermon and proposed that our American holiday be made a Holy Day. Santa Susanna's was always packed on Thanksgiving Day. All American priests and nuns in Rome were invited to join our parishioners and, after Mass, the guild ladies served coffee and doughnuts to everyone on the patio. It was a far cry from a Thanksgiving Day dinner back home, but it gave all Americans—priests, nuns, and laity—a chance to meet. We would then close the church for the day and go out to play some golf. That was a special feature of Thanksgiving Day for me.

Whether it was a feast day or not, we always had nice flowers on the altar. I have a peculiar quirk about high altars. I dislike seeing one without flowers. In Rome, where flowers are so beautiful and so inexpensive, I made sure our altar was always properly adorned. My own relations with the Communist group in Rome developed during my visits to the public flower market to buy flowers for the altar. When the market people began to know me a little better, communism often cropped up in our conversation, and I took pains each time to say something about it.

On one occasion, two of the men engaged in a bit of an argument with me—telling me communism was going to take over Rome, and they would be the leaders. So I asked them: "Who is your best customer for flowers?" They said I was. "Well, where do I get the money?" I asked. "Oh," one of them answered, "you have a rich uncle—Uncle Sam." "No," I said. "I get the money from the American tourists who come to Rome. With it, I buy the flowers." They were listening to me carefully. "Have you ever seen Russian tourists in Rome? No? Well—when the Communists 'take over,' there will be no more American tourists, and no one to buy your flowers. In Russia they don't buy flowers for church altars. And how will you feed your *bambini?*"

With that a few women who had been in the background came forward, and one said: "You are right, Padre. These men are stupid. Life has never been as good as now."

I noticed that when I stood up to these men who spoke for communism—and fought back—they regarded me as a strange priest. No Italian priest would stand on the corner and argue with a Communist, these flower men explained to me. Italian priests, I learned, are not trained for such give-and-take, and the Bishops want no trouble. If the priests did stand up and fight, they might find themselves in the Regina Coeli prison (like one Italian priest friend I met there).

From that point on, I got along very well at the flower market, and during my subsequent years in Rome I was always well received there. I did not convert them to my point of view, but I know they gave me up as a lost cause. The men with Communist sympathies were less eager to engage in controversy, and the women began to ask for missals and rosaries. Even the men were less hostile and much more friendly whenever I fought back. Italians love somebody who will argue—no blows! but lots of animated conversation.

Santa Susanna's was governed by the same rules of the Roman Vicariate as any other church in Rome. The single exception is that, because Santa Susanna's is a national church, it does not have the usual parish boundaries. The parish reaches to wherever Americans are in the Roman area.

In 1952, when I became pastor, about 10,000 Americans were in Rome on a permanent basis. As United States aid and military programs were gradually eliminated, this figure shrank. Today there would be between 6000 and 7000 Americans in Rome on a more or less permanent basis, and of these 800 to 900 are priests, nuns, brothers, and seminarians. At certain times we have had as many as 250 American families coming to Santa Susanna's regularly, but in later years the "hard-core" figure was 125 families, or 500 to 600 persons. The number could change anytime, though. The largest single group of parishioners was from the Embassy, and the military personnel. When transfer time came around, a sizable number of our parishioners might be moved to other posts and their replacements would not necessarily all be Catholics. It worked the other way, too—we sometimes gained parishioners by the personnel transfers made by our American government. I found out very quickly that approximately one third of my parish would change every year.

A large number of American medical students came to study at the University of Rome at the time of my arrival as pastor, and many of these young men and women were devoted parishioners of Santa Susanna's. I arranged for several of my Jesuit and Dominican friends to give the medical students lectures on ethics, and I also spoke to them myself. The students found the medical ethics lectures helpful. One non-Catholic, however, balked at first, saying he did not see why he had to listen to priests talking about Catholic ethics. I told him there was no problem if he thought none of his patients would be Catholics. But if he expected to treat Catholics when he became a doctor, he should try and understand their religious and moral points of view. He agreed with me.

I was particularly impressed with the concern these

young people had for each other. One of the students—
and I must say he and I never did see eye to eye—was
riding a scooter in downtown Rome one day when he
was killed by a bus. His wife was Japanese and she had
four children, whom she was bringing up as Catholics.
She had trained them well, and they were beautifully
behaved. Her husband's death left the poor woman without funds and in desperate condition, and the other
medical students rushed to her aid. I helped her and
her little family get back to her sister's home in San
Diego, and even now, years later, she still writes me,
expressing her gratitude.

Among my "permanent" parishioners were families of
the most diverse backgrounds. Often one of the adult
members was an America (usually the wife), who was
married to an Italian. This was the case with Elizabeth
Driscoll Tine, from Reading, Pennsylvania, who married
an Italian stockbroker and raised her two children in
Italy. Another bi-national parish family was the John
Scotts. He was an American Negro army sergeant who, on
retiring from military service, married an Italian woman.
They have four lovely children. Mr. Scott operates a dry
cleaning establishment, and his wife is wardrobe mistress
at a motion picture studio.

I am sure Bishop Fulton Sheen will not forget the
family of Dick Liu, a Pan-American jet expert. Bishop
Sheen was to preach for us one Sunday and was kneeling
on the first kneeler in the sanctuary saying his preparatory prayers before the sermon. I interrupted the Bishop
to ask if he would mind moving a bit so that some people
could take the seats to his left. His Excellency's eyes
seemed to get wider and wider as the Liu family filed
past him, with Mrs. Liu leading the way (holding the
baby in her arms) and trailed by her six other little
Hawaiians—the last one carrying the baby's bottle.

It was good to see someone like Bishop Sheen in the

pulpit. The pulpit I had bought for Santa Susanna's some years ago looked like it was designed for preaching. There was a positive homiletic look about it. I am prejudiced on the subject of preaching because for almost all the time I was pastor I taught Sacred Oratory to the young seminarians at North American College. (I would tell them two things were to be remembered in a sermon: start with an anecdote to get attention and interest, and do not use technical, theological language—speak so your mother will understand you.) In my opinion a pulpit gives the preacher the best opportunity for the presentation of his message. Yet its appearance should not be so gaudy, or glamorous, as to distract the people. Our pulpit was built in Todi, the birthplace of the man who wrote *Stabat Mater,* and is modeled after the one in the cathedral there. The pulpit in the Todi cathedral has always been my ideal. It is dignified, conservative, and functional. I liked the one in the cathedral at Pisa, too, but it was marble. Since our church is finished in marble, however, we had to have some contrast and our pulpit is carved from wood.

It got so that hardly a Sunday went by when we did not have someone special preaching for our parishioners. On another occasion I asked Bishop Sheen to preach and, uncertain of his schedule, he said he would let me know a few days later. Meanwhile, I had visited the Jim Murray family (good friends of His Excellency's) and I told them he would be preaching on the following Sunday. "You shall have the first pew," I promised them. By Wednesday, however, I had not heard from Bishop Sheen, so I alerted Father Paul Maloney, my assistant, to be prepared. "If the Bishop does not preach, you will preach," I said. About twenty minutes to ten on the following Sunday the Bishop walked in, and I took it for granted it was my invitation that had brought him there. The Murrays were there, too, and I escorted Mr. and

Mrs. Murray and the girls to the front pew as I had promised. After Mass I spoke momentarily to the girls as they were on the way out. "You thought I was fooling about the front pew," I said, with a big smile.

"Oh no, Father," one of the girls said, looking very solemn. "We knew you were not fooling."

Whereupon Mr. Murray joined us. "The Bishop had dinner at our home last night," Mr. Murray said, "and the girls told him we were going to hear him preach at Santa Susanna's this morning. That was all news to him obviously, and he said he was doing no such thing. During the week, the Bishop told us, he had tried to get in touch with you to tell you definitely he wasn't coming." Pointing to one of his daughters, standing listening to the conversation, Mr. Murray said: "At that she spoke up. 'Oh, Your Excellency,' she said to Bishop Sheen. 'You must. Father expects you—and we have the first pew.'"

The women were forever saving the day for us at Santa Susanna's! They were the vital force in parish life. I don't mean to downgrade the men by saying that. The men were always available for special projects (the bazaar, ushering), and in emergencies they responded like firemen. At seven o'clock some quiet night in the middle of the week, for instance, I might hear from Cardinal Spellman that he was passing through Rome and would like to say Mass in Santa Susanna's at eight o'clock the next morning. To make sure there was a fine turnout for His Eminence, I would call one of the men parishioners on whom we could depend in an emergency—such as Commander Tom La Forest in the naval attaché's office. Tom would press the "panic" button, and before midnight the whole American colony would have the word!

But we could not keep a parish men's group together the way we would in the States. The lives of the men were so diversified. Whether they were at the Embassy or in non-governmental work, they had occupations which kept them involved and committed from morning to night. A number traveled considerably, and this made it all the more difficult for them to make specified dates for meetings. James Wagner and Arthur Sheehan in their immigration work might be in Portugal one day and northern Italy a few days later. Colonel John Nealon, in the air section of the Military Assistance Advisory Group, had to fly a great deal. Henry Manfredi, a veteran U.S. government agent overseas, was always on the move. Charles Siracusa, now the Crime Commissioner in Chicago, headed the United States Treasury narcotics office at the Embassy for a long time. One week his duties would take him to Beirut; the next week he would turn up in Turkey or Syria, working with Interpol.

An old-time Navy shipmate of mine, Jimmy Attee, joined the ranks of our mobile parishioners. Without any warning, Jimmy walked into Santa Susanna's one day and told me he was a clerk in Charles Siracusa's office. He was the same old Jimmy, except now he was married and had a wonderful family. Jimmy was one of the finest boxers I have ever seen, and he had a philosophy of life which makes him very self-reliant. On the *South Dakota* we once had an intership boxing tournament. The officer from the other ship warned me about one of the boxers in his group, saying he had done a great deal of boxing as a club fighter in private life. "He will be too good for anybody you have," he said to me and suggested that his man could put on an exhibition match instead of a real bout. Before they even got near the ring, I told Jimmy the other fellow was a "pro," and we could make it a contest or an exhibition. "Let's make it a real bout, Father," Jimmy said. "No matter how good he is, he is only one man." It ended in a draw, and when it was over the sailors on both sides gave the two men a standing ovation.

I don't know to this day whether Jimmy's wife was aware of his peculiar type of work, or if she knew why, as a "clerk" for Mr. Siracusa, he had to travel so much —being away three and four weeks at a time. Since he will never go back to that area again, I can say Jimmy was an undercover operator in the Middle East for the U.S. narcotics division—and an outstanding one. He did a very sterling job. I admonished him on several occasions to be careful, and I remember his answer. It was always the same. "If they come at me, Father," Jimmy would say, "they'll come at me one at a time." Jimmy, like so many of our men parishioners, could hardly be a member in good standing of any men's society at Santa Susanna's. He never knew where he would be from one day to the next!

So the Women's Guild was one of the mainstays of the parish. Much of our activity, from a parochial standpoint, revolved around these women. They were the ones who took care of our annual one-day bazaar and the monthly Communion breakfast. After the parish Mass on the first Sunday of the month, the ladies served American coffee and doughnuts in the patio, and it was a chance for all the parishioners to get together. At one of our early Communion breakfasts—in December 1954—the youngsters ate so many free doughnuts they cleaned us out. This proved to be not unusual. The following Saturday the ladies put on Santa Susanna's first bazaar. Everybody worked on it. The decorations for the booths made a hit with one and all. They were done by Mrs. John Roberts, a Christian Scientist.

Nowadays the bazaar is held indoors, in the seventeenth-century Barberini Palace, a couple hundred yards down the street from Santa Susanna's. But in the beginning we had it in the patio under a canvas tent—in circus style. At the 1957 bazaar I got a good idea of what a circus goes through during the season. For three or four days before we had had high winds and bad rain. We had planned the tent so the water would run down the sides. But you know how these things are—everything is perfect on paper, but something is forgotten. In this case it was the pivotal center pole: the one which was to hold up the tent. The rainwater, instead of running off, collected at the center. The tent top sagged so much in the middle it looked like an elephant was sitting on the roof. Fortunately by opening time the rain stopped, and we succeeded in getting rid of the water. In circus fashion I scattered several bags of sawdust on the ground so that the feet of the guild ladies and their guests would not get wet. The bazaar was a lot of work that year, but it was a big success. The next afternoon (Sunday) I slept like a dead man for over three hours, and Josephine, the cook-housekeeper, had to come and knock on the door to see if I was all right.

Everybody was welcome at our bazaar, but now and then someone would try to take advantage of our hospitality. One year I thought I recognized coming in the door a couple of Italian young men I had seen before—and under less appealing circumstances. I went up to one of them and asked if we had not had the pleasure of meeting elsewhere. He smiled and raised the cigarette in his hand. Suddenly it dawned on me. The visitor was one of the pickpockets from Regina Coeli! He freely admitted that he had indeed partaken of my cigarettes there. I pointed to the plain-clothes man near the doorway and, pleasantly but firmly, said, "Look, my friend. That is the Marshal of the Security Police, and these are my people."

The pickpocket was understanding.

"Padre, we would not think of bothering your people." Bowing courteously, he and his partner left immediately.

They had not left empty-handed, however. Ten minutes later a Beda College seminarian came up to me to report he had brought a 10,000-lire note to spend at the bazaar, and, when he had reached for it, it was gone. I told him it was too late because the pickpockets were also gone. "But since they are 'our boys,'" I said, "I shall reimburse you."

Whatever background the pastor has, he may be quite sure he will be able to use it. When I arrived in Rome I was still a registered pharmacist in the state of Connecticut, but I felt confident I would never need my pharmacy for anything. I found out differently when Antonio Palma was dying. Mr. Palma, a registered pharmacist from New Jersey, had founded the Squibbs pharmaceutical house in Italy. As he was on his deathbed, his daughter came to tell me that it was very difficult to make him aware of his condition, and he had consistently ejected Italian priests who had called on him to bring him the Sacraments. Would I give it a try? the young woman asked. I had previously spent a half hour talking over pharmacy in the old days with him. When I told him I had come to hear his confession and that I planned to bring him Holy Communion the following morning, he said he was not prepared. "Let me tell you, as one pharmacist to another," I said—he laughed when I said that—"you are going to have to go to Communion sooner or later, so let's make a little inventory of your conscience right here and now, and try to settle up accounts." On that basis he went to confession. There must have been ten members of the family saying the rosary in the next room all the time I was with him—and I am sure it was their prayers that settled the matter so easily. But his daughter was amazed. "How did you do it?" she asked. "I talked to him," I said, "about something he wanted to hear—pharmacy." The old man welcomed me next morning when I came to bring him Holy Communion and to anoint him; not long afterward he was buried from Santa Susanna's.

My years behind the drug counter came in handy time after time. When the Mother Abbess of our convent was sick with a leg infection, the doctor said she needed *American* penicillin. Dr. William Finkelstein of Waterbury rushed some to me at once. Fiore Petricone, formerly the Drug Commissioner of the State of Connecticut and a Torrington druggist, every year sent me a package of drugs via a friend—and they were always put to good use.

The Embassy people were always an active part of our parish family. Because I had been a Navy chaplain, I had especially close relations with the people in the offices of the military attachés. One privilege I had, as a former naval officer, was the use of the Army post office, and at the suggestion of Captain Bill Marshall, the naval attaché at the time, I used his office as my mailing address. This APO privilege made it possible to get packages into Rome without going through customs, and a number of people knew I had it. However, I consistently refused to let other people use it in my name.

Then one time I made an exception. Two good friends were having their son Peter baptized in St. Peter's, and the mother of the man (the director in Rome of an international insurance company, and a golfing companion of mine) told me she wanted to send a package to her son on her return home to Rochester. I explained I was not allowed to receive packages for other people, but said that if she sent me a small package with my name on it, I would understand it was to be delivered to her son. She said she would send one small package. I gave the matter no further thought until one morning, a month or so later, when Captain J. O. "Jack" Miner (now admiral), and the naval attaché, called me on the phone. "In the name of heaven, Padre, what have you done to us?"

"I don't understand, Jack," I said—and I really didn't. He asked me if I would please come over immediately. The way he said *please* sounded like he was desperate. I hurried over to the Embassy.

My "one small package" had arrived!

The clerks in the post office greeted me like a leper. I could understand why. One part of the package had burst between the first and third floors of the Embassy. This was the part that contained 100 rolls of pink toilet tissue. Some of the rolls had been retrieved and were stacked in different parts of the naval attaché's office, while others trailed through the halls and stairways like decorations for a party that had been caught in a storm. The floors of the naval attaché's office were coated with a white powder, and several of the sailors were vigorously brushing their blue suits. I asked one of the boys what the powder was. After placing several adjectives before the word "detergent," he explained this was what was left of another part of my package—fifty pounds of soap powder —which had taken off like a cloud when placed, not too gently, on the office "deck" (as they say in the Navy). There were several other parts to my "one small package." As best as I could, I collected them and, after making two trips by car, finally got them all to Santa Susanna's. To say the relations between the pastor and the naval attaché were strained is to put it mildly. But Jack Miner was a good friend, and the storm blew over.

Ever since the time the Paulists first took over Santa Susanna's, there has been a friendly link between the church and the Embassy. In the old days, I have been told, the Embassy occupied a building alongside of Santa Susanna's—the side opposite the convent—but that next-door building disappeared in Mussolini's street-widening program. Today the Embassy is in a luxurious palace on Via Veneto that once upon a time served as the residence for Queen Margaret of Savoy.

Ambassador James Clement Dunn had been transferred to another post when I took up permanent residence in Rome, but I had met him during my earlier visits. He was the very essence of the poised, well-trained professional of the State Department. Following in his footsteps was Ellsworth Bunker, who in more recent days became Ambassador to the Organization of American States and was active in the Santo Domingo "troubles." Ambassador Bunker, a highly regarded businessman, was with us in Rome only a very short time before being transferred elsewhere. His successor was Clare Boothe Luce. Of all our Ambassadors during the nearly two decades that I knew Rome, I think it was Mrs. Luce who made the greatest impact on Italian life and customs. She was a hit right away. Upon her arrival in Italy—with only six weeks' preparation—she thrilled the Italian people by speaking to them in their own tongue. To the work to which she had been assigned she gave of herself unstintingly. She once laughingly told me two Ambassadors were needed—one to work; one to play.

Mrs. Luce arrived in Rome as Ambassador in April 1953 in my first year as pastor. She was a lovely, well-groomed lady and talented in just about every field. She was a Catholic, and I had hoped that she would make Santa Susanna's her parish church in name and in fact. The Ambassador and her husband, Henry Luce, made a handsome couple when they came to Santa Susanna's for Sunday Mass during the first weeks after her arrival in Rome. She was the center of all eyes, and there were always a couple of photographers hanging around, hoping to be able to get a candid shot of her at Mass.

It was not long before the Italians began to crowd her a little and, so, when I knew she was coming to Mass, I would arrange to have some of our own people in the pews around her. On this one particular Sunday I felt we were well covered. Jules Hammond and his wife, Dolores, were behind her and two marines, not in uniform, were in the pew in front. I ushered the Ambassador and her husband into their pew, but since I was going to preach I spoke to my first assistant, Father Thomas McMahon. "Keep an eye on them, Tom," I said, "and don't let any of our photographer friends get near them." With that I headed for the sacristy, put on my surplice, and went into the pulpit.

No sooner had I gotten into the sacristy—I learned later —than the photographers made another attempt to get into the church. Once again they were put out by Father McMahon, and he was returning to the head of the aisle to keep an eye on things when an old friend came in. It was Bricktop, the American Negress entertainer.

"Hi, Father Tom," she said. "How about going to confession?"

"Sure, Brick," Father McMahon said. "I'll be right there."

He went over to the confessional at the side of the church and entered it.

A photographer dashed down the aisle and took two fast shots of Mrs. Luce kneeling beside her husband, who was reading a missal. Mrs. Frank Kelley, the wife of the New York *Herald-Tribune* correspondent, was an eyewitness. Benitia Kelley was British and had an accent to go with it. Later she reported: "And there was Henry in full prayer!"

I, of course, was not aware of what had been going on. After Mass, as I escorted Ambassador Luce and her husband to their car, she just about took off all the hair left on my head. She was very upset and told me in no uncertain terms she disliked coming to a church where one had to dodge photographers. I had to get the photographic plate back immediately.

I did try to get the film back, but was not successful. It was printed a few days later by one of the Italian papers. (I had the impression all the time that Mr. Luce was not upset, because he gave me a little grin, as if to commend the ingenuity of the photographer.)

But that ended Ambassador Luce's visits to Santa Susanna's for Sunday Mass. Not until the last two Sundays of her stay in Rome did I see her again at my church. In referring to her absence, Ambassador Luce—diplomatically, I thought—would tell me that she and her husband felt more could be accomplished if the Italian people saw her going to various churches in the city for Sunday Mass. Many of our parishioners were disappointed, as were many tourists who called up to ask what time Ambassador Luce was attending Mass.

Our social relations were most cordial. I was often invited for dinner to the Villa Taverna, the Embassy residence. Many times at receptions Ambassador Luce would seek me out and introduce me to some of her State Department personnel. "Go to work on this man," she would say with a twinkle in her eye. "He'd make a fine Catholic." I officiated at the marriage of two of her staff members—Wharton Hubbard, her executive assistant, and Joan Webster, a secretary. I am sure Wharton Hubbard's bride has never forgotten her baptism. She had received preliminary instructions and wished to be baptized and received into the Catholic Church prior to her marriage. She, Wharton, and myself had had many talks together. Her parents had arrived for the wedding, and the evening before it was to take place I arranged for Joan to be baptized. She preceded her parents into the church, and as she walked into the sacristy I was just about to come out. She grabbed me by the arm and said: "Padre, I am scared to death."

"Oh, you'll be all right," I said, and she was, of course. But what she remembers most, I am sure, is our conversation after the baptism ceremony.

"This is *it*, Padre?" she asked me.

"You're in, kid," I told her. That impressed her father. It was not the Latin salutation he half expected his daughter to receive as she finished her baptism, but a colloquial greeting from New York's West Side.

On one occasion when I was Ambassador Luce's guest my lunch companion at the Villa Taverna was Mrs. Joseph Kennedy. Her son, Senator John F. Kennedy, had just made his first unsuccessful drive for the vice-presidential nomination at Chicago, and I told her that I felt he had put up a magnificent fight. Mrs. Kennedy replied that she had not known he was going to try for the nomination; otherwise, she would have stayed at home to help him.

After lunch, all of us were shown around the house and grounds. The Embassy residence used to be the summer home for the Roman seminary, and seminarians would go there for vacation. A marble plaque in a ground-floor room recalls this ancient history and the villa's association with the "Apostle of Rome," St. Philip Neri. The plaque's inscription translates something like this: "In these fields in the golden days of yore Philip Neri played with and taught the young men of Rome." There are several acres of gardens, with cypress and ilex trees and all kinds of flowers.

In the gardens Henry Luce pointed out a piece of statuary which had been there since the Villa Taverna's seminary days. The statue was headless, but the original tall Papal hat had been replaced on its shoulders. Henry Luce good-humoredly referred to it as a Pope who had lost his head during the Reformation, but not his miter. He went on to say that no one had ever been able to identify the statue. Prince Marcantonio Pacelli (the nephew of Pius XII), who had attended the luncheon with his wife, the Princess, gave it a cursory glance and, using the coat of arms as his main clue, immediately put a name—Clement XII, I believe it was—on the headless Pope.

When Mrs. Luce became sick, there were long discussions in Rome about the cause of her illness. Up to the present, I still have never heard a satisfactory conclusion. Like everyone else in the city, Josephine, our cook-housekeeper, was concerned about the health of the American Ambassador and on several occasions asked me to pass the word to the Embassy about the need for carefully washing the fruits and vegetables. Josephine felt quite sure that Mrs. Luce did not have her domestics thoroughly clean these items, especially the lettuce. Ambassador Luce's illness was reported to be arsenate of lead poisoning, resulting from the flaking of paint from the ceiling in the Villa Taverna. Some doctors in Rome felt this could have possibly happened and one—and he was a respectable doctor—gave me an illustration of how children sometimes get this kind of poison in their systems by licking a newly painted chair or the railing of a porch —the way little boys and girls often do. It seems that no one was completely satisfied with the information given out, but there is an old saying (and I have never found it to fail): "In Rome all things are possible."

I was always very much impressed by the cordiality of Henry Luce and by the obvious affection he had for his beautiful wife. If ever I saw a man proud of his wife, and who expressed his appreciation for the job she was doing in every look and gesture, it was Mr. Luce. Because of his extensive business interests in the United States, he spent only a few months a year in Rome, coming in for a week or ten days at a time. When in town he would attend the monthly meeting of the American Club, which was founded during the first year that Mrs. Luce was in Rome. Henry Luce addressed the club's first meeting, and he was present when Ambassador Luce was our guest of honor at the meeting prior to her departure from Rome at the end of 1957. A record crowd of some 300 members were present that day.

Two days before our meeting, Dick Spater, the club

president and Trans-World Airlines district sales manager, called me to say: "Father, we're over a barrel. The American Women's Association and other groups, I understand, are giving some token of regard to the Ambassador as a going-away gift. What are we going to do *ourselves?*"

I was still trying to think when he said: "You get something, Father."

She wore a fine gold bracelet with charms, I had noticed, and it seemed to me that possibly a medal with St. Clare, her patroness, on one side and St. Francis on the other might be the answer. I searched Rome inside and out next day, but no such medal could I find. I did find one of St. Clare—about the size of a penny—and another medal, of the same size, of St. Francis. But there were two medals, instead of the one I had planned. But there was no choice. Time was short, and we had to have something.

Ambassador Luce had a prepared speech which had already been released to the press and, upon introducing her as our speaker, Dick Spater presented her with these two tiny medals. From where I sat at the head table they looked smaller than ever. But as I watched the presentation I saw her face light up instantly. She was obviously moved and very much pleased. Henry Luce, too, seemed to be genuinely affected, and nothing would do for him but that she immediately take off the charm bracelet and have the two medals attached.

The prepared speech was forgotten! Instead, Ambassador Luce gave a splendid twenty-minute extemporaneous talk on St. Francis and St. Clare, and what they meant to her and to the beautiful Italy she loved so much. The thing I remember particularly about this talk was a statement she made. "Italy," she said, "is a nation of lovable but frustrating people."

It was a fine affair and the members of the American Club certainly succeeded in their purpose—to honor an outstanding lady and her religion.

Chapter 7

THE UNEXPECTED IS THE USUAL

I had just finished saying my six-o'clock Mass one week-day morning when the phone in the office rang. It was a transatlantic call. I could tell from the quick, insistent ringing which sounded particularly loud at that time of the day. The caller gave his name, and I recognized it immediately. He was a Midwestern pastor whom I had known both at home and in Rome.

From the way his voice came through, you would think he was in the next room.

"I am sitting in my office here and it is past midnight," the voice on the phone said. "I have with me a lawyer, a doctor, and the father of a little girl who is going to have a baby. She has no husband because we have just discovered that the man is not free to marry. Like her, he comes from a good family, and there will be scandal and heartbreak if she remains at home. Can you take care of her over there?"

"Yes, Monsignor."

There was a momentary pause as if the transatlantic connection had been broken. Whereupon the Monsignor's voice was again heard. "Is that all you are going to say?"

"Well—you asked me, Monsignor, if I could take care of her and I said Yes. Why don't you have the girl's father write me a letter saying when she is coming, and I'll handle the rest!"

I met the girl at the Rome airport. With me was my driver, Palermo, himself the father of four children. On the way out I had explained the situation to him. His only comment was a sympathetic *poverina*—the poor little girl.

She was a typical American girl, except now she looked frightened and tense. I tried to put her at ease right away by saying everything had been arranged, and there was nothing for her to worry about. She would have prenatal care, I told her, and I had lined up a job for her as secretary to the Mother Superior of one of the religious congregations in Rome. She was to work, as long as she could, up to the time of the baby's birth. About a month or six weeks beforehand, I said, I would like her to let me know what she wanted done—keep the child or have it adopted. I remained silent for a few moments so that she could absorb all this information. Then, as casually as I could, I said that on the way into town my driver would stop with her at a jewelry store and buy a ring.

The tension in her face seemed to relax.

"Thank you very much, Father," she said. "I have a ring. My aunt gave it to me before I left."

In the months ahead she was very cooperative. That is the way it always is. Once one of these kids knows you are on their side and that you are not going to "blast" them, they will cooperate and do just as you say, gladly. Telling them that they should not have done this is not going to help anyone. You have to recognize a *fait accompli*—you have a pregnant girl on your hands and you are not going to change it. So you accept the situation as it is, and it is up to you to do your best to help out with kindness and charity. These girls do not need to be criticized or challenged at this point. Most of the time they are embarrassed and extremely humiliated and are even fearful of asking help.

In this particular case, the girl decided not to keep the child, and I went ahead with plans for the adoption. There was a wonderful American couple in Rome at the time who had no children and they became interested. Without the girl's knowledge, I arranged for the wife to observe her while paying a call on the Mother Superior to inquire if she could help the nuns in any way. She was impressed by the girl's manner and general appearance, and she and her husband decided to take the child at birth. This is a gamble, because one never knows what will happen.

The girl went through everything without flinching. She had the child (a handsome blue-eyed boy!), registered the birth with the Italian government, and then when the baby was only a little more than a week old went with me to the Embassy to get him his own American passport—with a picture, too. The mother signed for the passport. Then we were ready for the next, and final step. The following morning, after all the preliminary paperwork had been taken care of, she held the little baby in her arms for several minutes and then slowly put him back in the hospital crib. It was to be good-bye forever. Together, the mother and I kept an appointment I had made with a notary and an experienced, kindly lawyer. The lawyer was to be a witness. Before these two men, the young woman gave up her child. First one, and then the other, asked the same questions. Did she know what she was doing? Did she do it of her own free will? Did she realize all that was involved? Each time she replied affirmatively, and with great courage. Before we returned to the hospital, the adopting parents by arrangement had already arrived to pick up the child and take him home. They left a note for the young girl, wishing her God's blessing. The note was with a dozen American Beauty roses.

The baby has grown up to be a fine young fellow, and a source of great joy. I was able to follow the growth of these babies over the years, and it was wonderful to hear couples talk with such delight about a child they had adopted. One adopting mother, who later died, had told me what a blessing the little boy had been whom she and her husband added to their own family of two children. After her death I was at the airport with her husband as he prepared to take the body of this very fine American woman back to the States for burial. The three children were there, too, but they were to remain behind in Rome. As he kissed one after the other of the children good-bye, he said something to each. It remained for the adopted youngster among the three to cause him, almost, to break down. "Pray for Mummy," he had said to the ten-year-old boy.

"Mummy is all right," the little child answered. "She does not need our prayers. I shall pray for you."

It was never any problem to deliver a European youngster to adopting parents waiting in the States. Someone was always going back home and would gladly take the little one with them out of the goodness of their hearts. When Monsignor Andrew Landi and his Catholic Relief Services later took over this activity, a small fee was given to the person acting as escort to a child coming to the States for adoption. On one occasion I was escorting a four-year-old boy to New York. On the flight home my little fellow became terribly sick, and all his clothes had to be changed. He had only the one suit, too. The stewardess took his clothes off and hung them near a blower to dry. She then wrapped him in a blanket and propped him up alongside of me. It was not long before he felt more secure and, shedding the blanket, he began walking up and down the aisle in his shorts!

Three wonderful nuns were incomparably kind with girls who were going to have babies. There was, of course, Mother Johanna, the efficient helpful administrator of Salvator Mundi Hospital. Another was Mother Martina, a gracious elderly Irish nun who had a "professional deafness." She heard only what she wanted to hear, but she was never too busy to lend a helping hand. The third nun who aided us in these, and other, matters was Mother St. Joseph. I sent a young girl to her one day for a place to live, not knowing that housing was the least of the young woman's problems. It ended up with Mother St. Joseph, myself, and the girl calling on Mother Martina, who made the arrangements. Before the girl entered the hospital ward, Mother Martina managed to find a ring to slip on her finger so that busybodies would not ask questions. "And you will call yourself *Mrs.* while you are in this hospital," Mother Martina told the girl.

Mother St. Joseph, a generous Englishwoman with a beguiling smile which showed her Irish background, was in charge of an orphanage and a *pensione* at her St. Thomas of Villanova convent. She took an active part for a number of years in helping us in our bazaar, and we helped her with her orphans. Mother St. Joseph was one of our chief sources of assistance for housing. When Pius X was canonized in 1954, for instance, she set up a dormitory for nine clergymen for whom I had made reservations. I was thankful because, with all the pilgrims in town for the canonization, there was not one bed to spare.

Only three of the clergymen showed up! That cured me. From that time on, I tried to follow a policy of putting people in direct contact with hotels. It is incredible how many times (after you have made reservations) people do not arrive, change their plans, or come a few days later—without letting you know. Perhaps they think it makes no difference. They do not seem to realize that even though they are only one person, I had to commit myself a hundred times a year. The reason we have been able to get reservations so many times is that the hotel people knew they could depend on my word. If the travelers did not call or write me by a certain time (to confirm their arrival plans), I would notify the hotel to go ahead and release the rooms. (A hotel, on its own, would not dare release a room if the reservation had been made by a priest. That was fine up to a point, but if the people did not show up, the priest often had to pay for the room.)

Easter was our busiest time. "You rarely see any joy in the face of the clergy at Easter," one parishioner remarked. A parishioner told me one year that my "Happy Easter" greeting at the door sounded like a snarl.

I recall one Easter Sunday in particular. Just as I closed the church after midnight mass, a GI arrived from Germany with his little pigtailed daughter in blue jeans. There was positively not a place in Rome—that I knew. I set them up in chairs in the Grand Hotel lobby and then, after my six-o'clock Mass—four hours later—I managed to find room for them at a convent. The rest of that Easter morning was one thing after the other until about one o'clock in the afternoon when I locked up the church. I was promising myself that finally I would get a little sleep when, on the way out into the patio by the side door, I bumped into three GIs in uniform. They were obviously down from Germany on leave for Easter. One of them was bubbling with enthusiasm. "Hi, Padre," he said. "Where does a guy get to confession around here?"

I glared at him.

"Would you come into your parish church at home at one-thirty Easter Sunday afternoon and ask that?"

"No, Padre, I wouldn't. But this is Rome, and I've been saving up for Rome."

I couldn't refuse them. I said I wouldn't open the church again for the President of the United States but, if he wanted to go to confession right there in the patio, I would hear him right now. As we sat down on the wooden bench in the sunny courtyard, he said:

"Any place at all, Padre. Any place at all."

Our friends in the hotels—the managers, the desk men, the concièrges—directed many visitors to Santa Susanna's. Other visitors came with notes from their pastors or clerical friends. Their first question always was: "When can we see the Pope?"

There are as many channels to an audience with His Holiness as there are clergymen in Rome. Some people will "shop around" at two or three different sources to find out who is going to get the best ticket for them. This is especially difficult when you have requested tickets for a group of fifty or sixty persons, only to find out at the last minute that two other people have asked tickets for them also. This leaves an empty space in the audience program, with your name as sponsor—and that is not helpful when you are looking for audience tickets the next time.

We have had sad experiences, too, with people who regard His Holiness as one might the Taj Mahal—as if they could go and see him any time they wished. I would tell people the audience was on Wednesday, and they would say they had plans for that day but would be glad to go on Thursday. Something like this happened with some New York banker friends. Because a mutual friend wanted special treatment for the New Yorkers, I arranged a special audience for the seven in this group after considerable effort. With some sense of triumphalism, I called his friends at the Grand and said the audience was set for the next day at 9 A.M. It was a bit of a shock to be told: 'Thanks very much, Father, but we can't go tomorrow because we have plans for a tour of Rome."

At times it worked the other way, too. One November weekend in 1954, Ed Gorman's daughter and two of her friends came into Rome. Ed, who is general manager of the Fidelity and Deposit Company of Maryland, was a fellow hand tennis player and we were friends from

the New York Athletic Club. Acting like a "big shot," I
told Ed that no matter when the girls got in I would see
to it they had an audience. It turned out that the Sunday
they were in Rome was the first Sunday that year there
had been no audience. The Pope was ill and in retreat,
and the girls had to leave two days later without seeing
him.

When Pope Pius resumed audiences the following May,
I had fifteen of our visitors at the first special audience
he had given in months and I also had had good seats
for our people at the general audience a couple of days
earlier in St. Peter's. A young lady from Los Angeles
who was to go to the general audience told me she
would love to have a special memento. Pope Pius had a
custom—discontinued by Pope John—of giving his white
skullcap, the *zucchetto,* to a person at an audience who
presented him with an exact duplicate. Before accepting
the new cap, the Pope would look inside to see if a small
chalice was reproduced. If it was not, he would touch
the *zucchetto* to his head and smilingly return it. I suggested to the Los Angeles girl that she buy a *zucchetto*
and see whether he would give her the one he was wearing. He did! According to eyewitnesses, she just about
swooned. I received a letter from her later, telling me
all about it. She had me to thank, she said, because I
had practically forced her to stay an extra day in Rome
for the audience, instead of going on by bus to Assisi
with her friends. She missed Assisi, but caught up with
her friends at Florence—and, in the meantime, had acquired the special memento her heart had been set on.

We never had any trouble on clothes for an audience.
Everyone knew how to dress. On occasion a woman forgot a hat or veil, but we always had several mantillas
on hand. At first I had bought expensive handmade ones,
but when we lost them all the first year I replaced them

with fifty-cent ones, and never lost a one. They all came back.

For the summertime audiences at Castel Gandolfo we ran our own fleet of cars. That is, Palermo and other professional drivers with their own cars would take pilgrims to the audiences. These drivers were men of family and were always meticulously dressed. Some days we had as many as thirty-five cars making the trip out into the hills of Rome. I worked out this special car service after two old ladies came in to see me one day and said they could not afford the thirty-dollar cab fare to Castel Gandolfo. Under the arrangement, Palermo and the other drivers brought pilgrims out to the Pope's summer home for $2.50 apiece, with four in a car. The cars would leave from Santa Susanna's, and as a last word to the departing pilgrim I would say: "You pay the driver when you get in the car." I had to begin doing this after I found out that a number of people had taken the ride out and then disappeared. They probably just forgot. But the drivers are poor men, making an honest living as best they can, and losing these fares meant a lot to them and their families.

A car pilgrimage got off to a stormy start one summer morning. I was sending a group of fifteen people to a special audience at Castel Gandolfo when a well-dressed woman approached me and insisted on joining the party. I told her politely that she needed a special invitation with her name on it, as this was a private audience, and explained to her how to get a ticket for the next day's audience. Immediately she poured forth a torrent of abuse and shouts for all to hear (and all of these people were embarrassed Americans). "If I had crossed your palm with ten dollars," she shouted, "you'd let me go." The rest of the day she went around Rome saying, wherever she could, that the reason she did not visit the Holy Father was because she had refused to pay for an invitation. Not until the end of the day, when she ran into Anna Brady at a tea party, did she get her come-uppance. Anna, a veteran American journalist in Rome, put this woman in her place.

People with limited time in Rome frequently try to do too much and consequently, among the older ones, we would have a half-dozen hospital cases every couple of weeks. On one day alone I visited three people in Salvator Mundi. We would tell visitors to follow the Italian style: tour in the morning, rest in the heat of the afternoon, and shop—if they wished—between five and seven in the evening. Until they collapsed they would not believe this was a good system.

Old friends from everywhere were among the visitors. I often thought Tom and Ann Fitzpatrick came to Rome yearly to bring me up to date on current stories. Tom, a part-owner of the Artists & Writers Club restaurant in New York, always had a vast supply. Martie Horan, the famous restaurant man of Paterson, New Jersey, visited Rome each year. Although he was not a Catholic, he regarded Santa Susanna's as his parish church.

I had many chances to "shoot the breeze" and swap remember-when? tales with old Navy shipmates. I met one of them one day as I was walking down the Via Veneto from the Hotel Flora. I had just left the sickbed of an elderly lady from Cleveland whom I had been instructing in the Catholic faith for several months, when I came across Dr. Ralph Emerson Duncan, the Navy medical officer who had shared a cabin on my voyage to the South Pacific to join my battleship. I had not seen him since we parted company at the base camp in Espiritu Santo. He was sauntering along, enjoying the scenery. On his coat, I noticed, was a Masonic symbol. He did not recognize me because now, instead of a Navy uniform, I was in my Roman clerical clothes—cassock and wide-brimmed hat. I walked up to him and took him by the coat lapels. "Duncan!" I said. "What are you doing in Rome? Spying for the Masons?" I thought he would have a heart attack right there. He still did not recognize me. I had to take off my hat before his face broke into a big smile of recognition. We had a very pleasant visit, and also on other occasions when he was in Rome.

Now and then I would recognize a name on the list of those who had applied to us for audience tickets. That was the case with a retired admiral named Hutchinson, who was living in Florence. When he came in for the audience tickets, we looked at each other and I asked him had he ever been with the "submariners" in Panama. He had indeed! "And you," he said, "are the one who took my daughter on her first date." I remembered his daughter, a fourteen-year-old youngster as bright as a button. Although not a Catholic, she belonged to a so-dality of our Navy juniors at Coco Solo. One day Com-mander "Buddy" Weber, the commanding officer of the air station, had asked me to entertain a group of South American naval cadets who had just come into port on their training ship. I hastily arranged a dance for that night, and the daughter of this future admiral came to visit me in the library that afternoon and asked me why she could not come to the dance. I told her she was not old enough. "With my hair up, I am a grown woman," she said, "and I want to go to the dance. Will you take me?" The same question had been asked a few weeks earlier by Admiral Dale Price's teen-age daughter, who wanted to attend a dinner at France Field, and I had learned to say: "If your father and mother say Yes— I will take you." Shortly afterward I received a phone call giving the parents' approval. The dance was in the BOQ lounge, which had only two exits. Each time a visiting cadet and his charming young hostess started to leave for a walk in the beautiful Caribbean moonlight they found two or three Navy fathers at the door who very graciously pointed to the handsome interior of the Bachelors Officers' Quarters, indicating that the lounge was to be their area of operation. I can remember standing talking to two of these cadets and hearing a bright young voice whisper in my ear from behind: "Stinker— that's what you are, Chaplain!"

Not only former officers came to see me at Santa Susanna's but also enlisted personnel. Eddie Maykut, an ex-marine from New Britain, Connecticut, reminded me of a recreation party I was in charge of one time in the Ulithi lagoon, on the absolutely barren, tiny island of Mog Mog. Beer, which had been under strict lock and key aboard ship, was being brought ashore for the men, and Eddie was the head of the working party. As I was checking out the supplies, I asked Eddie how many cases of beer he had. He told me, "Fifty," and I asked him to count again please. This time there were forty-eight. We looked at each other and finally he said: "What do you intend to do about it, Chaplain?" Eddie, sitting in my office at Santa Susanna's, smiled when he recalled what I had said. "Nothing," I had answered, according to Eddie. "The damn stuff always tastes better if you steal it."

A regular visitor for several years during my early days as pastor was a gallant old gentleman from the Argentine named Sir Henry Lynch. When he introduced himself the first time, I said there had to be some good in him because my mother's name had been Lynch. Sir Henry had a great devotion to the Blessed Mother and had visited her shrines in many parts of the world. We became good friends, and just before spring in 1955 he arrived in Rome again and came in to see me. This was going to be his last visit, he said. He was seventy-seven then. The old gentleman told me, however, he still had some unfinished business with the Blessed Mother. He wanted to visit her shrine, Our Lady of Good Counsel, at

Genazzano, fifty miles from Rome. Would I go with him the next day? I said I'd like to, but just did not have the time. Sir Henry looked at me tolerantly. "You can't be too busy for the Blessed Mother," he said. "You just have to give her a little of your time."

"All right," I said. "We'll go tomorrow morning."

We attended Mass at the shrine, visited for two hours with the Augustinian hermits, and stopped along the road for lunch in a hilltop restaurant. We arrived back in Rome about four-thirty, as the late-winter sun was spreading a golden brown across the rooftops and cupolas. "My boy," Sir Henry said, "you have made this a glorious day which I shall always remember. I shall not see you again, but I will remember you in my prayers, and I am sure our Blessed Mother will amply reward you for your graciousness to an old man."

Of all the personalities I met in my years in Rome, Sir Henry Lynch stands out as one to be remembered for his character, spirituality, and especially for his unashamed devotion to the Mother of us all.

For a completely different reason I have never forgotten a visit made with the late Bishop Thomas Markham of Boston. He had come to Rome for the ordination of a nephew, and after lunching with us at the rectory asked me to make a final tour around Rome with him, as he was leaving in the morning. So we began our *giro*, as he called it, of the places he considered most important to him in Rome. We started with St. Peter's and went from there to St. Paul's Outside-the-Walls. Then, on our way to St. John Lateran's, the Bishop thought he would like to see Cardinal Spellman's titular church, Sts. John and Paul. It was still broad daylight when we arrived there, but the sacristan was closing the doors and did not wish to allow us to enter. When I told him my guest was a Bishop, he relented and led us to a small gathering at a side altar.

Not until that moment did I realize we had stumbled, unknowingly, into an exorcism.

A Passionist Father was about to read the ancient rite of casting out the devil over a middle-aged woman who was said to be "possessed." Four stalwart companions held her. We were told the Pope was praying for the priest to whom he, as Bishop of Rome, had given the required permission for performing the exorcism. Padre Pio also knew of the case and was adding his prayers. The good father himself who was to do the exorcising had prepared for the ordeal by a week of spiritual exercises.

This was an exciting experience. As the priest began reciting the long series of prayers in the centuries-old ritual, the woman screamed, cursed at him, and practically tore herself away from the people who were using every bit of strength and ingenuity to hold her. The poor woman's arms seemed to come out of their sockets as she did two or three somersaults—with the four women companions hanging onto her arms vigorously. When the old Father blessed her with Holy Water, she spat at him and began to scream louder than ever.

"Silence in the name of Christ," the priest intoned in Latin. The woman subsided. He had gone only a few sentences further in his prayer when again the woman started shrieking. This time, more vigorously than before, the priest once more ordered: *Silentium in nomine Christi.* With that the woman seemed to have recovered some consciousness, for she looked at a picture of the Blessed Mother behind the altar and cried out pathetically: *"Madonna, Madonna!"* At that, Bishop Markham turned to me to say:

"You have heard what takes place at affairs like this, haven't you?"

"You mean the betrayal of the secret faults of those who are present?"

The Bishop nodded and added: "I think we should get out of here."

I was never happier in my life to say "Yes, let's go." Leaving the exorcism rite (which I heard later was brought to a successful conclusion), we went to St. John Lateran's. As we knelt before the Blessed Sacrament, we were two thoughtful and chastened clergymen. It is one thing to read about such happenings. It is quite another to find yourself suddenly involved in one of them.

Written tributes, from many of our writer friends, along with the word-of-mouth kind, brought visitors and kept them coming in increasing numbers to Santa Suzanna's. Their requests varied from where they could find a good dentist who spoke English to how they could arrange a visit to a Rome fashion house to buy remnants. Most visitors wanted to know where to buy religious articles, but sometimes they had a very special medal in mind, or an accessory for a Knights of Malta uniform. Bishop Fulton Sheen once needed us to help him hunt through the antique shops for a rare *lavabo* used in the ceremonial washing of hands. On one transatlantic crossing Jimmy Thompson, an old friend from the New York Athletic Club who was not coming to Rome this time, asked me to buy some scarves for him at the Laura Aponte shop on Via di Gesù e Maria. I was probably the only clergyman who had ever entered the smart boutique.

We had mail requests, too, and they were as varied as the in-person ones. A professional man in Baltimore, whose wife had been stricken with cancer, wrote and asked us if someone could carry his spiritual request for help to Padre Pio—and one of us made this journey to the holy Capuchin's hilltop town near the Adriatic.

Often people wrote asking our aid in obtaining employment. There are three or four Italians for every possible job, we would tell them. But some came anyway. A problem we often faced was that of girls who wanted to prolong their visit by obtaining some kind of work. I had to tell them a secretary in Italy must be conversant in several languages (one of our own secretaries a few years ago could handle five). Besides, no American girl could support herself on the standard pay of an Italian office worker. A government job, with American wages and benefits, was one thing. But living on the Italian economy at Italian wages would not be the *dolce vita* the average American girl had in mind. I would tell these girls—as well as other visitors who had no experience in international living—about the night we ran out of American coffee at the rectory. The housekeeper went out and bought a pound can of Maxwell House down the street. It cost 2000 lire (about $3.20). At the Embassy our friends pay about a dollar for the same thing.

One "stranded American" or another was always knocking on Santa Susanna's door for help. Some came seeking jobs in the motion-picture industry, or in the journalism, art, or music fields. Many a would-be actress discovered that her age, ability, and personal charm could not compete with the attributes of Italian "extras." Some people come abroad without a return ticket—hoping for the best. Mothers with two or three children have left their husbands in the States to return to live with their parents—only to discover their old mother and father could hardly support themselves. Or it might be the unmarried mother-to-be who arrives without friends, money, or a job to have her baby here. Two young men artists went to Menotti's Two Worlds festival at Spoleto, figuring they could pay for their passage home by selling their paintings. They did not sell a one.

There were those who learned that a social security check would not stretch as far as they thought it would. A number lost their money in their travels or were robbed—or at least said so. Still others assured you a letter was on the way from home with a check, or that money was being transferred to them at American Express, or that the Embassy knew their case and had promised to help them. Vince McAloon, a fellow American Legionnaire and the head of the Notre Dame Hospitality Center, called me one Sunday afternoon about a stranded American who needed money urgently, but who gave his word he would pay it back in the morning when his own arrived. "Never trust them on Sunday," I told Vince. "You cannot check their story, and they know it. The Embassy, American Express— everything is closed. There's no mail."

One day there came into my office a young man attired like an American priest. He seemed so young I asked him where he had been ordained. Well—he had not been ordained, nor had he ever been in a seminary. He had come to Rome to study under the direction of an American priest who had just started a "seminary" of his own, and he and an ex-marine were the only "seminarians." Their seminary was a place on the outskirts of Rome, but they were not being fed, living conditions were not good, and they were very unhappy, he told me. The two "seminarians" now wanted to go home. Through the Embassy I contacted the brother of one boy and he sent him the money to return to the States. The ex-marine had no one to repatriate him, so I got him a boat ticket from Naples to New York. He said he preferred to sail from Le Havre so that he could see some of Europe while he was at it. "The only Europe you'll see," I said, "is between here and Naples. If you are not on that ship by four o'clock tomorrow, you're on your own."

He, like others, solemnly promised he would pay back the transportation funds as quickly as he could. But you knew as soon as you put the ticket in their hands that you had heard the last of them—and certainly hoped so!

Many of the "stranded Americans" were deserving and the Embassy, in most cases, will repatriate people. However, between the application and the actual departure there is a waiting period of four to six weeks, and that would mean they would have to be housed and fed in the meantime. That is where we at Santa Susanna's often came into the picture. Over a period of years we helped and repatriated many of the "stranded Americans" through a fund administered by John Fornacca of American Express and Reggie Perkins of American Export Lines. However, the fund eventually ran out because people did not pay back the money loaned. (In recent years another fund has been set up. When Mrs. Elizabeth Tine became president of the American Women's Association, she presented the problem to Mrs. Frederick Reinhardt, the wife of the American Ambassador. Mrs. Reinhardt loaned the Villa Taverna for a style show, and $1500 was raised. The new fund is under the supervision of the Catholic and Protestant pastors of the American churches in Rome, but the money is distributed by the consular section of the Embassy. We felt the Embassy was in a better position to make these people guarantee to return the loan.)

We had one very special repatriation situation—an old lady of seventy-two. She had a small picture, about eighteen inches square, based on St. Francis' "Hymn to the Sun," and she considered it very valuable. Her idea was to preside over a symphony orchestra, which was to play the music for this beautiful poem written by the saint of Assisi. Someone told her the Holy Father would be very much interested in her symphony, but there was no possible way for the woman to reach him as her only recommendation seemed to be her own personal enthusiasm. The woman's sole support, meantime, was a social security check. For a while she stayed with relatives, but soon her funds ran low. No matter how many times I tried to fend her off, she kept returning to tell me of her problem.

In the repatriation application the Consulate had listed her picture as one of her assets, whereupon Washington in its reply said to sell the painting and use the money to repatriate her. Well, even if there was a market for such a picture, it would not bring more than five dollars—ten at the most. This turn of events left the woman completely stranded with no one to help her, except Santa Susanna's. I persuaded Reggie Perkins to cable John Geehan, general manager of American Export Lines, for a "complimentary repatriation," and we got a free boat ride for her. She refused to take the train to Naples because, for some reason or other, she had acquired a large amount of baggage. So, in desperation, I hired a car and chauffeur. It was well worth it to have her gone.

You can never be quite sure in Rome of the people with whom you are dealing. At least twice I was "taken" for funds by *friends*. One was a convert. She had spent months taking instructions from me and had been such a considerate girl. After I had received her into the Church, she sent me a slip-on cashmere sweater—red on one side; black on the other. ("When you are playing golf," she said, "wear the red side. It is a danger signal. In the church, put on the black side.") So I was grateful to her. One day she came in and said she was in difficulty. Would I cash a check for $250? Of course! The check turned out to be written on rubber, and it bounced all the way back to North Carolina. So my golfing friends thereafter referred to my "$250 sweater," and I amortized it at the rate of fifty dollars a year.

You wonder how you can be so wrong in judging people until you find out later you are only one of many on the P. T. Barnum list ("There's a sucker born every minute").

Whatever you have done to the least of my brethren you have done unto me. These words would bother me sometimes when I had to face the never-ending line of beggars, professional mendicants, and just plan inept people who seemed to think we had a direct link to Fort Knox. It was impossible to take care of all of them—but where do you draw the line?

One of the facts of life which must be learned in Rome is that begging is a profession. The same people beg in the same area year after year. They are not "winos" or alcoholics. Many are the "professional poor" who regard begging as the normal way of life. But very shortly I discovered that I could not cope with the hundred or more beggars who kept coming at all hours during the day. Sometimes I would be instructing a convert in the office when two or three of them would barge right in to tell a long story which I knew was untrue.

So one day I decided to ask the beggars to send in their "head man." He and two others came to see me. We talked about the Roman tradition of helping the poor that had been started by St. Lawrence (Italians are much like our people in the hills of Tennessee— rarely do they go directly to the point). Finally I said we wanted to work out a definite day for alms dis- tribution that would be convenient to them, and accept- able to us, so that during the rest of the week we would not be running into difficulties. The "head man" sug- gested Friday morning, and I agreed to that. We shook hands on it, and during the ensuing years Friday morn- ing has always been our day for the poor.

As I dealt with the beggars and became more used to them, I developed a sixth sense. Often a complete stranger would walk into the office and, before a word was spoken, I would know it was going to be an appeal for money. I could spot a "touch" from the sanctuary.

I might be arranging kneelers for a wedding, putting the chairs in order, or setting up a "mike" for a Bishop who was to speak from the altar at the next Mass. And as I looked around and saw a visitor approaching, my radar would go into action and lights flashed TOUCH!

Rome, I learned, is a city of great contrasts. It is said every mentally disturbed person with a religious complex or motivation sooner or later arrives there, and I found that to be the case. A great many came to see me. Often such people, it was obvious, were mentally upset. But all had one thought in mind from which they never deviated: they wanted to see the Pope. So you had to make a quick decision. Did you have a saint on your hands, or a person with hallucinations?

A young woman entered the office one day and asked for me by name. She had a letter from Father John Gogarty of Glasgow. He had been a twice-a-week golf companion of mine when he was in Rome as vice-rector of the Scots College. Father Gogarty was a glorious raconteur, but he was not a practical joker—in fact, he could not be, because every practical joker must have a little touch of unkindness or meanness about him, and there was nothing of this in our good Father Gogarty. Yet I felt a little uneasy when this very ordinary-looking girl told me the Holy Father had sent for her. After a few moments of conversation, however, I learned that this was indeed the case. Her name was Winifred Ford, and at Lourdes she had been cured in a first-class miracle. Since then she had organized a society of people who had not been cured at Lourdes, and who were offering up their sufferings to God, through the Blessed Mother, for the spiritual strength and graces of priests they adopted in their prayers. This "Incurable of Lourdes" organization had become a life work of Winifred Ford, and it was why Pope John had sent for her.

The more you talked to Winifred Ford, the more you

were captivated by her inner glow. There was something that reached out. I had felt it once before as I had sat in the rear office of the St. Lawrence O'Toole bookstore in Lourdes, listening to Charlie McDonnell of Dublin tell about his miraculous recovery after he had been sent home from the hospital to die. Like Winifred Ford's, his cure was recognized as a miracle. What was the most impressive part of the miracle? I asked Charlie. He told me that all that day he had kept saying to himself that his name was being mentioned in the Kingdom of God in a conversation between Our Lord and the Blessed Mother. Charlie said he could see Our Blessed Mother interceding for him and saying:

"I have a young Irishman down in Lourdes that I'd like to cure."

"What kind of an Irishman is he?"

"Oh—run of the mill. Not good. Not bad. Just run of the mill."

"Are you sure you want to cure him?"

"I am."

"Well—go ahead and cure him, and don't be bothering me."

Charlie McDonnell and Winifred Ford have made it their life's work to manifest, publicly, their gratitude to God and his Blessed Mother for favors received.

On another occasion a young California woman, a convert, came in to say she needed a spiritual director. She was to be in Rome for probably two years and wanted me to help her. After a very few minutes I recognized it would be most presumptuous on my part to undertake her spiritual direction. One of the Consultors of the Discalced Carmelites at that time was an American—a man, mature and intellectual, and also a man of profound piety. I explained to the good lady my hesitation in this matter and while she was present I telephoned my Carmelite friend. Yes, he said, he would accept her. When I met him a few weeks later, he told me this woman was truly a modern-day saint—very close to God and far advanced in things of the spirit. You can imagine the shock something like this can be to a parish priest, like myself, who is busy in many activities —so busy, in fact, that often his own elementary spiritual life is neglected. I recalled how in our conversation on the day we met the young woman had said that she had been told to come to me and that I would select the spiritual director Our Lord had in mind for her.

Possibly a bit on the naïve side, I had asked:

"Who sent you to me?"

She only smiled.

Chapter 8

THE MANY FACES OF MARRIAGE

A two-star general having lunch in the New York Athletic Club with a friend of mine one Friday mentioned that he had a marriage problem. "Why don't you jet over to Jim Cunningham in Rome," my friend advised the general. "Whatever it is, he'll take care of it immediately." The general lost no time in following the advice. He was at Santa Susanna's the next day. I had just come off the altar after an eleven-o'clock wedding Mass, and I thought all I had left to do was close the office door when the general walked in.

He came right to the point: "I would like you to straighten out a marriage problem for me, Father." He told me his marriage had been performed outside of the Church because his wife had been married before. He felt sure this previous marriage of hers was not valid, but he did not want to discuss the matter with priests at home. The poor man had the impression that somehow between siesta time on that Saturday afternoon in Rome and the following Monday morning I could arrange for the solution of his problem. Just like that!

Rome has a magic name for many people, especially those with a marriage problem. In talking with friends at home they are told: "Oh—if you could just get this case to Rome! It would be settled in no time at all." But validating a marriage in Rome is not like putting coins in a slot machine. Often it has fallen to me to break the bad news to such people that it can take as long in Rome as it would back home because the same procedure is followed. Sometimes it is even longer because of the delay in getting documents back and forth. In the general's case, his problem was solved, but it took two months and the aid of a canon lawyer.

Now and then couples are sent—with high hopes—by a parish priest at home. I talked with a couple one afternoon who came to Rome to work in Italian motion pictures. He had been married before, and divorced, and had been taking instructions in the Catholic religion on the West Coast. She was already a Catholic. They had a letter from the priest who was giving him the instructions. The priest wrote that they were a fine young couple and had not had the time to have their civil marriage validated before leaving. "But I"—said this priest, who was a second assistant in a California parish—"hereby delegate whatever permission and authority you need to proceed with the validation" (that is, to put the Church blessing on an already existing marriage). Of all the documents necessary, the boy had only two: his marriage and divorce certificates. She had absolutely nothing. This was one more case where I had to sit down and explain the facts of life.

Some people have found that if they are living in Rome, and apply for validation of their marriage while there, attention is given immediately to their problem.

We had in Rome a very lovely American couple with three children. The oldest girl was making her First Communion and had been after her mother to approach the sacraments with her. The mother could not do this because she was not a Catholic, while the father—although a Catholic—could not go to the sacraments because his marriage was not considered valid by the Church. (In Rome, when a couple is married outside of the Church, the word used is not "excommunication." They are referred to as being *irregular*.) The mother was in tears. What can we do? she asked me. I questioned the couple. She was of Jewish birth, and this was her second marriage. The first one, to a Jewish man, had ended in divorce. This seemed to be a case where the "Pauline privilege" could be used—a situation where two non-baptized persons divorce and never intend to go back together again. As a matter of fact, the woman's first husband had already remarried, and happily. The woman told me she had wanted to become a Catholic for some time, but her husband, for the past dozen years, had been transferred from one post to another and it had been hard to do so. As in all these cases, I talked first with an official of the Vicariate, who did not say no to my plan.

Within ten days I assembled all the necessary documents, including a statement from her first husband. My plan was to baptize her after giving her some final instructions. She was already completely versed in Catholic teaching and practice and had been attending Mass at Santa Susanna's regularly. I told her that after she was baptized there could be no marital relations while the "Pauline privilege" application was being made. I telephoned her husband at the Embassy and explained this to him, too. After she was baptized, I submitted her case to the Vicariate. The marriage tribunal was definitely unhappy. "You had no right to do this—to go ahead and baptize her," an official said.

"As a non-Catholic she has no standing in your court," I replied, "and she has a case to present to you. She could not present it otherwise."

Looking at me sternly, he said: "We shall decide who has the right to present cases before us." He paused for a few moments—as if to control his temper—and then asked: "Does she speak Italian?"

"No, Monsignor, but my secretary does." Within an hour the woman and my secretary were before the tribunal. The interrogation lasted for two hours. The next morning there was a phone call from a tribunal official

—the "Pauline privilege" had been granted. The reprimand from the Vicariate official was more than wiped out by the woman's oldest girl, who came skipping up the aisle the following Sunday while I was ushering people to their places. "I have a great surprise for you, Father," she said. "Mother and Daddy are going to Communion with me today. Isn't that marvelous?" Her whole face beamed and the sight of her happiness reassured me I had pursued the right course.

Rome has a magic attraction, too, for people wishing to get married. Necessity often helped in the decision to choose Rome. Because Christian marriages are not permitted in Saudi Arabia, for instance, Americans working in the oil fields there would make the long journey to Santa Susanna's, knowing they would feel at home. No matter what the reason was for the choice of Rome as the place to be married, all couples liked the idea of getting a wedding gift from us in the name of the Pope (a white rosary for the bride; a medal for the groom).

Many times young American women have told me they were thinking of marrying an Italian boy. They expected that the Italian boy would have the same background, mentality, and code of ethics as the boy at home with whom they went to dances. They are shocked and completely unwilling to believe the conditions they must expect if they marry into the normal Italian family abroad. An Italian girl marrying an American boy makes a wonderful wife. Because of her affection for home and family there is no difficulty. But the American girl marries not just the man, but his whole family. It is difficult for American girls to believe that an Italian woman, under the domination of her husband, comes pretty close to being a second-class citizen. On a number of occasions I have had these girls talk to some of the American women who have lived abroad a long time and are married to Italian husbands. I always recommended caution. I would quote an old Italian saying: *"Chi va piano va sano e va lontano*—The one who goes slowly goes safe and sound, and goes far." I would also suggest that they keep another principle in mind: never settle a serious problem on the other fellow's home grounds.

I could not officiate at a marriage in my own church without getting a delegation (permission) from the pastor of San Camillo's, which is the "parish church" for us and about ten other churches in the area. This was a time-saving administrative practice worked out by the city government. Instead of having to deal with the more than 420 public churches in Rome, the civil authorities needed to concern themselves with only the thirty or forty "parish churches."

Once all the documents needed for a marriage were made out, I would have one of our civilian drivers take the couple on the rounds of the various offices. We called this the *giro matrimoniale,* or "wedding tour." It started at the Ministry of Foreign Affairs and ended at the Vicariate. In between was a stop at the municipal *Anagrafe,* where the couple registered their intention to marry. Two witnesses were needed for this. Many times the couple did not know a soul in Rome. In the corridors there were always students and others ready to be professional witnesses. For fifty cents they would swear they knew you for five years. The problem of the publication of the banns was easily solved by Dr. Marsico, who was in charge of the Matrimonial Office for Foreigners. He was an old friend and very pro-American, and streamlined things when both parties were Americans. The couple would wait in his office while he went to the one next door. In a loud voice he would announce to his colleagues that there were two Americans who wished to marry and give their names. *"Molto bene*—very well," Dr. Marsico's colleague from next door would say.

That took care of the banns!

It was called a "verbal pronouncement." All the papers needed for the marriage, therefore, could be processed in three or four hours. It was even quicker if the marriage was to be in St. Peter's rather than Santa Susanna's. Because St. Peter's was in the independent state of Vatican City, no Italian documents were needed—only the religious ones. Italian regulations were so complex I recommended that people be married in St. Peter's, rather than Santa Susanna's.

When the late Domenico Cardinal Tardini was appointed archpriest of St. Peter's, things tightened up for a while. Cardinal Tardini prohibited marriages in St. Peter's for everyone. No one seems to know why he did this, but it could have been because some of the marriages were said to have been invalid. (This could be. Of the marriages I myself had in St. Peter's, I think, two were invalid. One was an army sergeant who had a notarized statement from the Bureau of Vital Statistics in his hometown that his first wife had been killed in an automobile accident. Some three years later he came to me with a letter from the parish priest at home saying his first wife had turned up. It was finally worked out somehow—just how I do not know—because I saw him several times in Germany, where he was with the Air Force, and he said everything was fine. I also had a letter from his second wife who said that all was satisfactorily settled. My other questionable marriage concerned a couple who arrived just before Christmas one year with glowing letters from a priest in New York. Acting on these letters, I arranged for them to be married on Christmas Eve, which is an especially difficult time with us—and they went on their way. Three or four days later I received a letter from the same priest who had sent the original recommendation. This couple would be arriving any day now, he said, but we were not to marry them. He explained that after finishing a course of instructions and baptizing the groom-to-be he had discovered that the man, a Lutheran, had been married before—and the marriage was valid! Well—this Rome marriage had already been performed, and nothing much could be done about it. I wrote the bride's parents, but nothing further was heard.)

The American government added to our marriage problems at the time of the Olympic Games in Rome. When the latest Foreign Service manual arrived at the Embassy that summer, it was discovered in the fine print that consular officials no longer could issue a *nulla osta* for Americans wishing to be married abroad. (This document, officially confirming that a person is free to marry, was required by the Italian government before the marriage could take place.) There was turmoil. I appealed to Cardinal Spellman, the head of the far-flung American military diocese, and to Cardinal Cushing, as titular pastor of Santa Susanna's, to help our citizens for whom marriage overseas was made impossible by this regulation. Almost immediately I received reassuring letters from John McCormack, the House Democratic leader, and from State Department officials. From then on, Americans took a juridical oath at the Embassy that they were free to marry, and this statement was stamped with the official seal and the words *nulla osta* were included. This was not the same as the original form, but the Italian government was willing to accept it, and after some hectic weeks things were back to normal again.

The *nulla osta* problem sometimes cropped up, however, in cases where one of the parties was not an American. For one reason or another, a non-American often could not get a *nulla osta* from his government. Bishop Eustace Smith, the American Franciscan in Beirut, sent me a young couple one time who were confronted with this problem. The young man, an American, had no trouble, but the girl was an Arab Catholic from Aleppo, in Syria, and her Embassy in Rome refused to give her a *nulla osta*. If Cardinal Tardini's ban on marriages in St. Peter's was not still in effect, there would have been no problem. They could have been married there without a *nulla osta*. But now there seemed no way for them to get married. They looked brokenhearted indeed, but their eyes lighted up when I said there was a way out if they wanted to try it.

"We have an enclave in Italy, the Republic of San Marino," I said. "I know a lawyer and a judge there. No *nulla osta* is needed. You have enough documents as it is. In twenty-four hours you can be married civilly. This will be a legal marriage, and will be so recognized in Italy, both by the Vicariate and the government. But it will not be a valid Catholic marriage. However, if you go up there and get married, you can come back here the next day and I will get the marriage validated. In the meantime, though, you will not be able to live as husband and wife."

They followed my suggestion, and it worked out fine. I had five of these cases in a half-dozen weeks.

When I turned up with the sixth case, a Vicariate official stopped me short. He questioned the procedure. "What can this couple do to get married?" I asked. He shook his head, meaning *nothing*. "But they have a right to get married, don't they?" He agreed with that, but said there was no way. Yet the San Marino procedure I had developed was a way.

This sixth couple happened to be Chinese and lived in Hong Kong. She was a model for a dress designer and he was a businessman. These remarkable people were both over six feet tall, and the short Italian women would cluck over them—coming up and touching them. The couple had papers allowing them to travel, but no actual passport. That was the trouble. To get a *nulla osta* from their Nationalist China Embassy they needed passports.

After my somewhat heated exchange with the Vicari-ate official on this case, Monsignor Marcello Magliocchetti, head of the Marriage Tribunal, sent for me. He told me that the Cardinal-Vicar was very displeased with me, and with all these special recommendations I had been mak-ing.

"Monsignor," I said. "I have come to you beforehand each time, but you said there was no possibility. I know there is a loophole in canon law that I might use, but this does not entitle me to civil documents. This couple, being international people, need to have their marriage valid in the eyes of the state as well as the Church so that they can get passports and other official documents as man and wife. (The loophole I referred to applies in a situation where someone, such as a GI in Germany, having been refused permission by his commanding of-ficer to marry, could exchange marriage vows with his fiancée in front of two witnesses, and the couple could declare themselves married. Then they would go to the parish priest and ask that the marriage be inserted in the church register.)

Monsignor Magliocchetti laughed, and once more said that the Cardinal-Vicar was displeased. But he went on to say that the Cardinal told him that if I came again I should go to St. Anne's Church, the parish church of Vatican City—rather than the Basilica of St. Peter's—to have the marriage validated. I did that gladly. The slight by-pass avoided Cardinal Tardini and his tight rules governing the Basilica.

There were other reasons why a couple would get married first in a civil ceremony. In the case of a mixed marriage, for instance, the non-Catholic member might have refused to sign the required promises, and a Catho-lic wedding therefore was not permitted. The essential promises for the non-Catholic party concerned the marriage; it was to take place only before a Catholic priest, and this was to be the sole ceremony; and the children —they were to be brought up as Catholics. These were signed by both parties to the marriage. A third for the non-Catholic alone was that he or she would not interfere in the religion of his or her partner. This was the situation with a couple who came in one morning. They talked to the priest on duty and he had them return in the afternoon to see me. They wanted their marriage validated because the wife was anxious to get back to the sacraments. But the man would not sign the promises. He told me he was a lieutenant with the United States Army Engineers, and his word was his bond. I listened to him for about five minutes, and then I said: "Let me tell you something, son. In the Navy I had the equivalent rank of lieutenant colonel when you were born, so don't try to pull any of this stuff on me that you are an officer in the Army. Does the Army take your word when you want to do anything? How many papers do you have to sign every day of your life—for housing allowance, and even to go on leave? Does the Army recognize your word as your bond? No sir, it does not. It wants your name on the paper. Now if you are willing to bring up your children as Catholics, and not interfere with your wife's religion, then you should have no hesitation to put your name on the paper. If you don't want to sign, then it means you are not in good faith—and please get out of here, and don't waste my time."

He looked at me steadily for a moment and then said: "This is the kind of language I understand. I should have met you a few months ago."

We got down to business. Within twenty-four hours, by means of cablegrams to the States for baptismal, confirmation, and other certificates, we were able to get the papers cleared, and the Vicariate took my word they were free to marry. I had the marriage validated and have heard from them every year since. That was four or five years ago. This case worked out well, but only because I understood the man and was able to get to the root of the problem. Each couple is unique and you have to "weigh them in" and decide whether they are sincere—and you should try to do something for them—or whether they are time-wasters who just want to talk.

My marriages ranged from those that presented no difficulties to those replete with vexing problems. The first one was a mixed marriage, and in my last one the young girl was a Catholic herself but her parents were not. Both marriages were in St. Peter's. (The Tardini ban had lasted only a relatively short time.) In this last marriage I performed in Rome the girl was marrying a young man from Chicago who was soon to graduate from medical school. She had come to Europe with her parents, but was unhappy about being separated from her fiancé. Her parents asked me if it would be all right to cable the boy and suggest they marry in Rome—rather than wait till the fall, as planned—and honeymoon in Europe. "Certainly it is all right—and possible, too," I said. The boy arrived within the week, and I arranged the wedding for the Chapel of the Choir in St. Peter's. I told the Basilica workers about the couple and how much in love they were. "They want flowers on the altar," I said, "but keep it to five dollars as they don't have much money." When I saw the altar on the wedding day there must have been $100 worth. I was alarmed, but not as much as the father of the bride. He asked the groom how much he had allowed for flowers. "Five dollars," he said. "Right, Father?" I said that was right. I did not tell them what I had found out: the workers had borrowed the flowers from other altars in the Basilica. If the couple had returned to St. Peter's ten minutes later, they would have seen the flowers back on the original altars. But by then the newlyweds were already off on their honeymoon!

My first marriage at St. Peter's seemed to set the tempo for the subsequent crises which, somehow or other, had a way of hovering over some of our Roman weddings. The girl (from South Bend) was marrying a boy at the Embassy. Her parents arrived a few days ahead of time and the mother was obviously concerned about her daughter, a Presbyterian, marrying a Catholic. She also was very much interested in where the wedding was to be, and I took her to St. Peter's five or six times to check on everything. Even then she did not seem completely satisfied. "Lynn, what *does* your mother want?" I asked. The girl's answer was straightforward enough. With a smile she said: "Really, Father, she wants a Presbyterian wedding in St. Peter's."

We had the wedding scheduled for the morning of April 25 in the Chapel of the Canons. That happened to be the Feast of St. Mark, and the canons were to make their traditional procession, chanting prayers for good crops. At the last minute the time of the canons' ceremony was changed. Then it was changed again. Meanwhile, there were problems on our side. The wedding papers had been forgotten. Irritated Basilica officials said the wedding could proceed if I gave my assurance that all the documents were in order. But now the groom had disappeared—he had taken a cab to get the papers. When we were just about set once more, there was a flurry of excitement about the matron of honor's short-sleeved, low-cut dress. She had to find her coat and put it back on. Otherwise, I am afraid, our good friend Archbishop Francesco Beretti (pastor of St. Peter's) would have had a stroke if he had seen her. At last, everything was organized. Then, just as the organ began with "Here Comes the Bride," into the Chapel of the Canons walked a couple dozen, unhappy-looking old men, chanting the litanies. This meant another delay. Finally the ceremony took place, and I was just wiping my brow when the bride's father came up to me. "Young man," he said reproachfully, "do you know I came 5000 miles to give the bride away, and I never had the opportunity?" In all the excitement, he had been forgotten!

The canons of St. Peter's dramatically intervened in another wedding of ours—one of the most gala of all. It was the marriage of Alexander Matturri of New Jersey, the Italo-American Conciliation Commissioner with the diplomatic rank of Minister, and Dorothy Santopadre of Chicago, an opera singer who had made her debut in Rome as Mimi in *La Bohème*. The wedding had been set for the Chapel of the Choir, but Dorothy, on seeing the Altar of the Chair at the far end of St. Peter's, asked why she could not be married there. I explained that it was a "reserved" altar and could be used only for certain very special occasions. Monsignor Giulio Rossi, who had replaced Archbishop Beretti at the Basilica of St. Peter's, was doing his best to be helpful. Overhearing Dorothy's request, and my answer, he said: "Why, of course, you may be married there."

That was that. The invitations were printed, and the Ambassador and most of the Roman colony were invited. Then, about ten o'clock on the Thursday night before the Saturday wedding, Monsignor Rossi called me to say the canons would not allow the wedding at the Altar of the Chair. I said it was too late in the evening to argue about a matter like that, but I would see him in the morning. When I arrived at the Basilica's parochial office the next day, you could cut the gloom with a knife. What is more important than anything else in Roman life is *la bella figura*—and the old Monsignor sure had lost face! He could do nothing about it either. So I called upon Monsignor Joseph McGeough, of the New York archdiocese, who was in the Secretary of State's office. (He now is Apostolic Delegate to South Africa.) Monsignor McGeough is noted for saying very little—and that very slowly—and for acting with still more reserve. But he jumped right into the breach. "I'm not going to make a federal case out of it," he said, "but I'll do my best." His intercession did the trick. Monsignor Sergio Guerri, who among his many responsibilities was chief administrator of Vatican property, said he would make an exception in this case if we promised never to ask for the altar again. Monsignor Rossi, meanwhile, was so grateful at "saving face," he went all out. He seemed to be related to half the Basilica staff, and they were as happy as he was. We were treated to special carpets, robes—the works! The rector from the American Episcopal Church sat in a special chair, with private kneeler, only a few yards from the altar.

Sometimes I came back from these marriages a nervous wreck. I felt like that when the daughter of a famous American admiral was being married at St. Peter's. I was already vested and ready to start when she said that she did not think she wanted to be married. "Just what do you mean by that?" I asked, and she repeated the statement. "O.K.," I said. I took off my vestments and went out to make an announcement to the people in the chapel. "We have a little problem here, folks," I said, "so please bear with us just a few minutes." I then told the girl she had five minutes to make up her mind. "If you really do not want to get married, decide it now, so that no one will get hurt," I said to her. "But if you go ahead with the ceremony, and then later decide you should not have married, then everyone will be hurt and you will have a real problem."

The groom was absolutely crushed.

I knew the girl, so I said: "Tell me, Mickey. Why don't you want to get married?"

"Well—Mother and Father are not here. I believe it would be better to get married in the States."

"Mickey! Your fiancé has many friends, but your father

is not one of them. He will never come to the wedding, no matter where it is." I looked at her. "Do you love this boy?"

"Yes, I do, Father."

"Will you marry him eventually?"

"Yes, Father."

"O.K., Mickey," I said. "I'm going to punch you right in the nose if you don't go ahead with this marriage right now." Evidently my threat and my whole demeanor convinced her. She went ahead with the ceremony, and the marriage "took." There are four children.

The wedding of two of my best friends, Jim and Francesca Wagner, actually had to be called off at the last minute. Jim, a cousin of Mayor Robert F. Wagner, Jr., of New York, and Francesca, a beautiful and intelligent girl, had made extensive preparations for their marriage at Santa Susanna's. Jim was attached at the time to the United States Air Force detachment at Ciampino airport and had applied to Wiesbaden, through his commanding officer, for permission to marry. On his wedding papers it was recorded that the permission had come through.

Ten minutes before the nuptials were to begin, the "C.O." from the Ciampino detachment came into the sacristy from the patio entrance. The marriage could not go on, he declared. "Now, just a moment, Captain," I replied. "The marriage *is* going on, and I am the one who is going to officiate." Then he told me that in going through Jim's file that morning he saw he had made a mistake. Instead of giving permission for the wedding, Wiesbaden had sent a routine request for further information. Since the captain planned to make a career out of the Air Force, I told him it would be better if I handled this, and I sent him back to his base. When he left, I broke the bad news to the people in the church that the wedding had to be postponed until official permission was obtained. This made sense to American GIs present, but none whatsoever to the Italians. They were not quite sure what kind of trick this was. I contacted Wiesbaden, through some of my chaplain friends in Heidelberg, and within forty-eight hours cabled permission was in my hands. That Saturday evening, upon receipt of the cable, I called Jim and Francesca, and they were married at our ten-o'clock Mass the next morning. These two fine young people have recovered from that shock on their wedding day—but none of us would like to undergo such a disaster again. Jim later returned to Rome with Francesca and, after working for Monsignor Andrew Landi at Catholic Relief Services, had an opportunity for an Embassy position. Francesca was our secretary for a while, and their boy, Steve, was a bonus from the marriage for Santa Susanna's, because he became one of the finest altar boys we had ever had.

One day Margie Stern, the daughter of my friend Mike Stern, the well-known journalist, came to see me to say she was going to marry an Italian boy and would like the wedding at Santa Susanna's. I made plans for a mixed marriage, since she was Jewish. Then, out of a clear sky, Margie told me she wanted to be a Catholic. "Margie," I said, "with the wedding a week away and all preparations made, how come now you're bringing this up?"

"But, Father," Margie says, "I don't want to be married as a non-Catholic. I want to be married at the altar with Mass."

"Who's pushing you, Margie?" I asked. "Your boy friend?"

She said no one was. She reminded me that she had gone to Marymount for four years and knew the Catholic religion. With a smile she recalled, too, that she had once played Bernadette in a school play.

"O.K., Margie," I said, "but who's pushing you now?"

"Well, maybe Mother, indirectly. 'You're going to be with Catholics all your life,' Mother said, 'and your children will be raised as Catholics.'"

"O.K., Margie. Your father and I have been friends for years, and I'm not going to hurt him. I'm going to call him up and see what he says."

"Father Jim," Mike answered, "whatever Margie wants Margie gets."

I asked again, this time more specifically. "Do you approve or disapprove?"

"Anything Margie wishes, I approve of," Mike replied.

It was one of the most beautiful and colorful weddings —this marriage of Margie. It was on a Saturday noon. Monsignor Landi said the Mass, and I performed the ceremony in Italian and English. The sanctuary, on both sides of the altar, was filled with the parents and relatives of the bride and groom, and close friends including some of Mike's associates from the motion picture *Cleopatra*, which was being filmed in Rome at the time.

Not until then had I ever realized, quite so clearly, the deep meaning of the Catholic wedding prayers. Here, in the words of the universal Catholic marriage ceremony, the God of Israel was invoked, and this little Jewish girl, like Catholic brides everywhere, was being blessed in the name of Abraham, and of Isaac and of Jacob, and being commended to Rachel, and to Ruth, and to Sarah—all saints of the Old Testament!

Despite the American Catholic schools in Rome, there were always some children who, for one reason or another, had not made their First Communion or been confirmed. In recent years we turned over the preparation of these children to the Sisters at the Holy Child convent— but well on into my second term as pastor I used to instruct the First Communion class myself on Saturday mornings. I would not only teach them their catechism but take them through all the steps—even showing them how to enter the church and stand at the altar. Why does a pastor do this? Because he likes to!

Many people want to have their children make their

First Communion in Rome, and Americans would come with their youngsters from Germany, Naples, or some other military or diplomatic post in Europe. They would even come from the States. It was no problem to arrange for a First Communion in St. Peter's. The only thing needed was a letter from me. To get this, they had to have a baptismal certificate and a statement from their parish priest that they had been instructed. If they had not already received instructions, I would arrange for them.

Confirmation was no problem either. A Bishop was always readily accessible at St. Peter's, and each Sunday there were at least two groups in the Basilica for confirmation. Those to be confirmed would go to the sacristy and present a letter which I had given them. This would have all the needed information in it—birth date, baptism date and place, names of parents and sponsors, country of origin—and a statement that they had been thoroughly instructed. Each would then procure a candle from the sacristan. Kneeling before the confirming Bishop for the sacrament of confirmation, they held the candles in their hands. As he confirmed each one, the Bishop would take the candle and hand it to an altar boy who, in turn, would place it on the altar.

Many times confirmation would be administered en masse, as for a group of GIs from Germany or sailors who had come up from Naples. Alma Herger, the long-time director of the Rome USO, called me once about a group of some seventy-five to 100 sailors from the Sixth Fleet, and I made arrangements for Bishop Primo Principi to confirm them. Alma acted as godmother for all the sailors, placing her hand on each young man's shoulder as the Bishop went down the line confirming them one after the other. One Navy chaplain for whom I arranged such a group confirmation gave me a huge bag of coins for the Bishop. The sailors had collected the coins from nine different nations as their ship completed a mission to as many countries bordering the Mediterranean.

Weddings, baptisms, and confirmations were always joyful occasions, but often I was obliged to be the bearer of sad tidings when I had to tell a mother of the death of her son or participate in the funeral of one I knew well. There is no *easy* way to "break" the news of a loved one's death. There was no easy way in the Navy when I had to tell a Cleveland woman her chaplain son had been killed in action. There was no easy way to tell the Baroness Josephine Pomeroy Marincola di San Floro that Gianpaolo, the younger of her two boys and an aviator in the Italian Air Force, had just died in an air crash. Pete, the other son, and his wife had come to the church office to tell me I would have to break the news to his mother. They asked me to do it as easily as possible. The Baroness took the news like the real lady she is. Tall and dark-haired, she was one of the many American women in Rome who were married to Italian husbands. She came from New Jersey, and several members of her family had been distinguished American diplomats. The Baroness became our secretary after Jean Fennimore left, and she was beloved by all our parishioners. I have never heard a harsh word pass her lips, nor have I ever heard her utter a single complaint. Every year she volunteered for the harrowing task of being a nurse on the White Train that carried the sick and dying to Lourdes. She was a most charming woman.

We had Gianpaolo's funeral from Santa Susanna's. The family had asked for a simple service, and no music. But I disobeyed their orders and was glad I did so. Since the boy was of noble blood, a piece of black cloth was placed on the floor and the coffin rested on that, rather than a catafalque. His sword and Air Force dress cap were on the coffin, and sixteen of his fellow aviators in uniform—with mourning bands on their arms—stood at attention during the Mass, never moving a muscle. But there were tears in their eyes. I went to the Campo Verano cemetery for the burial. The Italians have a way of tearing out your heart. As we stood waiting for the mason to brick up the wall opening, the girl whom Gianpaolo was to marry in two months walked up and placed alongside of the coffin the letters of some four years that he had written her. This was the ultimate gesture. Everything was finished. Truly, I remembered the words spoken when Our Lord was being placed in the tomb—words heard by another mother who walked sorrowfully away after the death of her Son: *Then they closed the tomb, and all withdrew.*

The death of Mary McGurn was a shock to the whole Roman community. Mary was the wife of Barrett Mc-Gurn, the famous *Herald-Tribune* correspondent, and mother of their three children. A convert who brought to her Catholicism all of the civic virtues of a New Englander, she was the soul of kindness and was always available to help. Mary founded the Girl Scouts of Rome, for example, and when the Overseas School needed a teacher desperately she stepped in and taught. In apparently fair health she had checked into Salvator Mundi one Friday night to have some X-rays taken the next morning. That Saturday evening she was to give a dinner party for a young woman teacher at the Overseas School, who was going to be married. About seven-thirty in the morning Mary called the nurse. "Get the priest immediately," she said. "Don't bother about the doctor." She died while Father Cormac Coyne, the hospital chaplain, was giving her the last sacraments.

Because Mary had been such a wonderful parishioner, we had the special drapes brought to the church which are used for funerals of eminent clergymen. The morning of the funeral was particularly overcast, but as I started the eulogy—just exactly when I started it—the sun broke

17. Memorial Mass for President Kennedy in St. John Lateran Basilica at which Father Cunningham served as archpriest to Cardinal Spellman, the celebrant. *(Felici)*

18. Father Cunningham, Cardinal Spellman and Archbishop Joseph McGeogh leaving the Grand Hotel in Rome.

19. Francis Cardinal Spellman, celebrant of the Memorial Mass for President Kennedy at St. John Lateran Basilica; and Father Cunningham as archpriest. Posted on the pillar above the Cardinal's head is the document from Paul VI granting permission for the American prelate to use the Papal altar for the Mass. *(Giordani)*

20. Father Cunningham with American army chaplains to whom he is giving a retreat at Berchtesgaden in Germany.

21. At North American College in Rome. The group includes: Father Cunningham, left; Archbishop Martin J. O'Connor, center; and Bishop Frank Reh, the president rector, right. *(Felici)*

22. At Irish College in Rome. Left to right: Father Cunningham, Cardinal Agagianian, Eamon de Valera, and Monsignor James Chambers, vice rector of North American College. (*Agenzia giornalistica Italia*)

23. Mother Ramazzotti, director of Girls Town in Rome, greets Father Cunningham. She is a nun who is authorized to wear civilian clothes in her work. (*Wide World Photo*)

24. *Above:* Ed Sullivan, his manager, and Father Cunningham look at picture of St. Genesius in St. Genesius' Chapel in Santa Susanna's which Ed helped to restore.

25. *Right:* Actor Edmund O'Brien and his wife enjoy Father Cunningham's Roman attire.

26. Bricktop, the famous night club entertainer, a Roman parishioner and daily communicant. *(Moya's Photo Studio)*

27. On steps of Santa Susanna's, left to right: Father Cunningham, Georgiana Young Montalban, Ricardo Montalban's brother, and Ricardo Montalban.

28. Father Cunningham receives cup for winning Anglo-American golf tournament from Alexander Matturri, president of the American Club in Rome. *(Fotvedo)*

29. Blessing the offices of an American stock broker in Rome.

30. Father Cunningham in American Legion cap and the Rev. Charles Shreve, rector of St. Paul's Episcopal Church in Rome, at Memorial Day services in the American military cemetery at Nettuno.

31. Father Cunningham in Luxor, Egypt, in civi[l]ian clothes.

32. Father Cunningham with boy and girl cad[d]ies on the golf course near Tokyo.

33. Father Cunningham at mission in Morocc[o] with Navy Chaplain Father David Casazza [of] Newark. *(U.S. Navy)*

34. Archbishop Martin J. O'Connor awards Papal decoration to Father Cunningham. *(Wide World Photo)*

35. Father Cunningham being congratulated by parishioners after receiving Italian government award. *(Farabola)*

36. Father Cunningham prays at the grave of a fallen G.I. at the American military cemetery in Nettuno. (*Publifoto*)

37. Father Cunningham in the pulpit of Holy Spirit Cathedral in Istanbul. (*Ifa Hikmet*)

through the clouds and poured almost blinding rays on the catafalque and the drapes on which her coffin had been placed. It was almost as if God was saying he wanted no sadness or gloom over Heaven's gain.

Chapter 9

BEYOND THE TIBER

During 1958, America lost two distinguished prelates, when first Cardinal Stritch and then Cardinal Mooney died. I was particularly affected by the death of Cardinal Stritch, for many years Archbishop of Chicago, as he was an old and dear friend of mine. America had been honored when Pius XII appointed Cardinal Stritch as Secretary of the Congregation for the Propagation of the Faith. This was the first time that an American Cardinal had ever been elevated to the Roman Curia, and it was with considerable interest that all of us in Rome had awaited his coming. We had followed the accounts of the farewell ceremonies in Chicago and at the pier in New York. But then, some twenty-four hours before his ship was due at Naples, Monsignor Ernest Primeau, the rector of Rome's Chicago House (and now a Bishop of Manchester, New Hampshire), received confidential word from the Cardinal's assistants that they were concerned about His Eminence's health.

Monsignor Primeau and I went to Naples, and Reggie Perkins of American Export Lines arranged for us to get aboard ship some fifteen minutes ahead of the journalists and well-wishers. Cardinal Stritch was an old friend. After all, he did come from Tennessee, the land of my trailer mission, and when I, as Superior General, used to visit him in Chicago I would hear him lapse into the Tennessee type of talk. As Monsignor Primeau and I greeted His Eminence in his stateroom, it was obvious that he was a sick man. His hand was purple and swollen.

He had thought this was from so much handshaking before leaving the United States, but the cause was far more serious—a blood clot. The condition of his arm got worse aboard ship, and gangrene had set in by the time he reached Naples. Monsignor Primeau asked that I hold the entrance door to the Cardinal's suite and not let anyone in until it was decided what to do. After about ten minutes of keeping the door closed on distinguished visitors—one kept telling me he was the Archbishop of Naples (and he was!)—I sent word to Monsignor Primeau that I could not hold the crowd back any longer. With that, Father Peter Shannon, a Chicago priest, came to tell me there would be a press conference in the lounge. Father Shannon, now president of the American Canon Law Society, is built on "pro" football proportions. As the Cardinal came out to go to the conference, Father Shannon walked ahead of him to keep his path unobstructed, and a Monsignor was on either side so that no one could shake his injured hand. After the brief conference he was put on the train for Rome immediately.

The Italian doctors recommended amputation of his arm. Cables were sent to Chicago requesting the presence of doctors from there. One arrived so quickly he did not even have a passport. But it was evident nothing could be done to save the arm and the operation was performed. There followed days of grief and fear—days when His Eminence tried to say Mass with one arm. As he elevated the chalice at Mass one morning, an assistant of his broke down and wept. He died of blood poisoning shortly afterward on May 27.

Fifty-eight nations were represented at the funeral of Samuel Cardinal Stritch in the spring of 1958. But the two chairs and kneelers which I had reserved for American Ambassador James Zellerbach and his wife remained empty. Only then did I realize that I had not called him on the telephone to say that he was expected. My lapse was covered by the presence of Bishop William Arnold of the Military Ordinariate and his chaplain.

After the service I called Mathilde Sinclaire, the Embassy protocol secretary, who was always most cooperative. She felt the Ambassador's absence was her oversight. Ambassador Zellerbach was very distressed. He called me to ask that in the future I personally notify him of any function I thought he should attend.

Cardinal Stritch's death was a blow to American hopes to have a representative in the Curia at Rome. A few months later the whole Church lost its leader with the death of Pius XII. I saw him perhaps fifty or sixty times during his reign—but I have a poignant memory of him during an audience in his last months. I had set up a special audience for the twenty-five members of our guild. At the last minute the mothers wanted to know if they could bring their children. Whereupon the fathers wanted to know why they were being left out. Then Archbishop Martin O'Connor asked me if I would take along some American pilgrim friends because our audience was the only one that day. Of course! I was fearful of all the children—especially the little ones (the group even included a six-weeks-old baby). But they were all positively angels, and they looked in awe at this figure in white who started out his speech by saying: "So this is the Ladies' Guild of Santa Susanna's—each, it would seem, with a small family guild of her own."

He spoke beautifully to the group for about ten minutes. Then he came down and stood in the midst of the children so that a picture might be taken. Little Gale Connolly, seven years of age—she looked like a fugitive from a fairy tale—knelt just in front of him. She was aghast when her white veil fell off. I leaned over to pick it up, and the Holy Father took it from my hand, and put it back on her head himself. After giving everyone his blessing, he started to leave. On the edge of the group was four-year-old Maggie Mudd, whose father, Clayton, was in the Embassy political section. Possibly she felt she had not been getting sufficient attention from His Holiness for, as he moved by slowly with his white cincture dangling, Maggie reached out and gave it a tug. He stopped sharply, quickly—and looked around. The youngster raised her innocent little face and, wrinkling her tiny fingers in the appropriate gesture, said: "*Ciao, Papa*—Good-bye, Pope." Pius XII burst out laughing—the first time I had ever seen him so genuinely amused. But *Ciao* it was! The next time I saw him I was kneeling at his deathbed at Castel Gandolfo. Little Maggie Mudd had had the last word!

Just about an hour before the Cardinals were to enter the conclave to elect a successor to Pius XII, the Titular of Santa Susanna's, Edward Cardinal Mooney, died unexpectedly at North American College. It was a Saturday afternoon. Archbishop Martin O'Connor called Monsignor Ernest Primeau and myself with the news and asked us to come to the college immediately. Upon arrival we sat down with the Archbishop for a staff meeting. Monsignor Joseph Breitenbeck, the Cardinal's secretary, and some clerical friends of his were there, too. It was decided within ten minutes that we wished to return the body to Detroit on the seven-o'clock plane the following night. Monsignor Primeau was assigned to notify Eugene Cardinal Tisserant (who at that very moment was just about to enter the conclave) of Cardinal Mooney's death. It is understood in Rome that no Cardinal may leave the Eternal City—alive or dead—without permission of the Pope. Since the See of Peter was vacant, Cardinal Tisserant, as dean of the College of Cardinals, was acting in place of a Pope.

My task was to get the mortician, line up the transportation, and make all physical arrangements. With extreme difficulty I persuaded my friend Pierre Mattei, the undertaker, to come to the college. He came under protest. A

plane had crashed near Rome that morning, and he had
been on his way to identify the bodies. At my insistence
he had sent an assistant to the crash scene and had come
to the college. When I told him of our funeral plans, he
shook his head vigorously. "Father Cunningham," he said,
"you are completely out of your mind. What you are asking is impossible. This is a weekend. All Italian offices are
closed. This cannot be done."

I told him Ambassador Zellerbach was having the Consulate people work around the clock, if necessary, to prepare the innumerable documents required for shipping a
body. I asked Signor Mattei to have someone help him
get all the Italian papers in order. He looked at me,
dumbfounded. I realized the problem involved. The police
will not let a body be moved from the place of death for
twenty-four hours. Then, if embalming is necessary (as
it would be for shipment to the States), another twenty-
four to forty-eight hours are required, because this is done
in two stages. I was asking him to do everything in about
twenty-four hours—and on a Roman weekend!

The next morning I rode with Ambassador Zellerbach
to the North American College for the ten-o'clock funeral
Mass. Afterward I made a final check to make sure everything was all set. It was! The patrol of motorcycle police
arrived on schedule for its escort duty. I was hoping, of
course, that any minute now the necessary Italian documents would be ready. Then I discovered to my dismay
that we had not received permission to transfer the body
through Italian territory. Archbishop O'Connor approached Count Enrico Galeazzi. The governor of Vatican
City, in turn, with one of the prelates we used to call the
"political Bishops," went to work on this problem immediately. Within a half hour, on that Sunday morning, permission was obtained from the proper department to move
Cardinal Mooney's body through the streets of Rome to
the airport.

The body was already on the plane, the two priests accompanying it were in their seats, and the Pan-American airliner was prepared for its seven-o'clock departure—but I was still waiting for the papers which had to be given to the customs official. Those of us officially involved (the customs men, the airline people, and *myself*) were really sweating it out. As the minutes ticked by, I began to feel very uncomfortable. I had seen the interior of Regina Coeli (with its priest-prisoner sacristan!) and had no desire to spend any time there for thwarting Italian law or the country's customs regulations. About ten minutes before seven, my old friend Pierre Mattei roared up—out of breath, disheveled, and unhappy-looking. His first words were: "Father Cunningham! I have had a frightful day!"

Fearfully, I said: "You *do* have the documents?"

"Yes," he said, and with that handed them to me. A sigh of relief from four or five of us could be heard, I am sure, at Regina Coeli. I passed the papers over to a perspiring customs official (who still, whenever he sees me, regards me with suspicion). No sooner had the customs man waved to the pilot than the plane took off, carrying the body of the Titular of Santa Susanna's. Pierre Mattei, the undertaker, was unaccustomed to much conversation. But several times later I heard him refer to that incident, and he always described it as the "only first-class miracle," he had ever seen in Rome.

I was in Saudi Arabia, giving one of my mission conferences, at the time Archbishop Richard J. Cushing of Boston was nominated as a Cardinal. Having been around Rome long enough to know that if you wanted anything, you asked for it, I returned immediately from Saudi Arabia, called on my good friend Monsignor Salvatore Capoferri, and enlisted his help. I had decided to request Pope John to designate Cardinal Cushing as Santa Susanna's new Titular. By cable I asked the Archbishop if he

would be agreeable to this, and he replied that he would
do whatever His Holiness wanted.

The petition, listing the reasons for the request, was prepared and presented outside of the usual channels. It was
placed on the night table beside Pope John's bed. The
next day I was told His Holiness had agreed to my request. One never knows, however, until the Pope himself
at a formal ceremony designates the churches of which
the new Cardinals will be Titular. To our great joy, Santa
Susanna's became Cardinal Cushing's. We had a new Titular—and an American!—much sooner than I could have
hoped for.

The official announcement came after the Archbishop of
Boston was formally notified of his appointment as Cardinal. He, along with Cardinal-designate John O'Hara (a
personal friend from my Navy chaplain days) and Amleto
Cicognani (long-time Apostolic Delegate in Washington),
received the Pope's official messenger at North American
College. I invited Ambassador Zellerbach to attend the
notification ceremony. Father William Michell, our Superior General, had come from the States, and he and I
accompanied the Ambassador.

The notification ceremony began a busy week. Between
300 and 400 Bostonians—including the mayor of Boston—
had come along with Cardinal Cushing, and there was
something doing every day and night. The many priests
with him meant extra Masses each morning at Santa Susanna's, and a large number of communicants.

Cardinal Cushing's formal "taking possession" of Santa
Susanna's climaxed the week. Everything was closely
timed. The service was to begin at 5 P.M., and at 6:30
P.M. we would have a joint reception at the Grand Hotel
for Cardinal Cushing and Cardinal O'Hara (who was being inducted at his church the same afternoon). A quarter
of an hour before the service was to start, the North
American College porter called to say Cardinal Cushing

was just about to leave. So, five minutes before the hour, I formed a procession to march to the church door to meet His Eminence. It was a cold December night. For two days we had been trying to heat the church with our antique heating system—and had succeeded! At one minute before five, we opened the doors wide for His Eminence. Then we waited from five o'clock to twenty minutes to six, wondering what had happened to our Titular Cardinal and his police escort. I later learned that the good Sisters at the College, in sewing on his ermine collar, had attached it to the wrong garment (in the way a man's wife might mistakenly sew a shirt collar onto his undershirt), and the Cardinal had to summon the Sisters and have the proper adjustments made.

It was an historic occasion. It was the first time that an American pastor in Rome had welcomed an American Cardinal to his Titular church—and both of us were New Englanders!

There were to be two addresses—his and mine. I said I planned to speak about fifteen minutes. His Eminence replied that he would also talk about the same length. He did—informally. Then he began to read a prepared speech which was to go on another thirty minutes. We were now running almost an hour late. Halfway through our Cardinal's second speech, Cardinal O'Hara entered the church. He had gone from his own induction ceremony to the Grand, but found none of us there. His unplanned arrival created some difficulty because Roman protocol is peculiar about the presence of two Cardinals in the same church. However, it was too late to get him the screen that was called for, or make other arrangements. So our master of ceremonies did the best he could with the situation at hand and set a special kneeler in the sanctuary for Cardinal O'Hara. Sitting there in the sanctuary, attired in a heavy cope, I breathed one more sigh of relief. Just then Monsignor Capoferri, acting as Cardinal Cushing's representative, as well as the assistant master of ceremonies, leaned over to say something to me. After I answered him, he backed away—into two lighted candles which the acolytes had set on the floor. His beautiful, very frilly Italian lace caught fire and went up in smoke! Fortunately, the Monsignor suffered no serious effect because a quick thinking North American College seminarian ripped the surplice from his shoulders. We arrived at the Grand exactly one hour late—but we got there!

That afternoon I had received an invitation to visit Pope John the next morning. But Cardinal Cushing had decided to ordain a man from his diocese at that time, and there were many problems involving TV cameras and extra lights. When I called the *maestro di camera* at the Vatican to explain this, his answer was terse: "The Holy Father wants to see you, and that should be sufficient."

For the audience the next morning I had prepared an offering and, kneeling before the Holy Father, I thanked him for giving Cardinal Cushing to us as our Titular. As I handed Pope John the small envelope—he immediately passed it to an aide—he struck me affectionately alongside of the ear, and said:

"You Americans! However, since *you* did not ask for anything, I could refuse you nothing." This was his humorous way of indicating that he knew that I had asked Monsignor Capoferri to present my request—rather than making it myself—and thus had gotten something without asking for it.

After the ordination that morning, Cardinal Cushing took me by the arm and, in his most generous way, said: "What can I do for *you*?" I said: "Your Eminence, we need nothing. Everything is under control." That was true. The main restoration program had been finished, and only small work in two chapels remained. "Well," the Cardinal continued. "I'm doing something for everyone in Rome, and I must do something for my own church." I found, in the past, it is always wise to have a project, and I asked him how much he had in mind spending. He said, "About $10,000."

"If Your Eminence will make it $15,000, I can put in a choir loft over the main door and install a pipe organ for the honor and glory of God in memory of Richard Cardinal Cushing and the people of Boston."

"Fifteen thousand dollars you have," he said, laconically, and within fifteen minutes the check was in my hand.

His Eminence was generous to Santa Susanna's, but I diverted many of his gifts from the church to the restoration and repair of the nuns' ancient convent. Something had to be done about the convent (their living conditions were primitive—in fact, one nun died of pneumonia in choir while chanting the office). I would ask the Mother Abbess to get an estimate on the top-priority project on her list, but warn her not to tell the contractor who was going to pay for it (otherwise, the price would be double). Then I would write a letter to His Eminence and say the nuns needed such and such to do this part of the restoration.

Whenever I returned to the States, the nuns would have some little gift for me to take along to the Cardinal. Once it was a miter they had made for him. On the same trip I had also promised to bring some friends a peculiar type of tuber which looks something like a potato but is much more "aggressive"—in a garlic sort of way. I was warned these *tartufi*, or truffles, were odorous. But an Italian friend told me if I put three or four in a large tin box, covered them with rice, and sealed the lid with masking tape, I would have no difficulty. I did more than that. After sealing the inner package, I wrapped it in brown paper and again sealed it with the tape. I put both the miter and the *tartufi* in the same side of my suitcase, and they stayed side by side for twenty-four hours. Perhaps the Boston breezes took care of the Italian fragrance emanating from the Cardinal's hand-made miter. But my suitcase was so "odorized" it was a challenge, for a long time afterward, for every air spray I could find.

Earlier I mentioned I had been in Saudi Arabia. The reason for my visit there was that Saudi Arabia had become part of my "parish" sometime earlier when Tom Barger, the president of the Arabian-American Oil Company (ARAMCO), visiting me at Santa Susanna's one day, said something had to be done to take care of the religious needs of his personnel in the oil fields. At present, he said, it was a hit-or-miss affair, with clergymen coming now and then from Bahrein. With the help of Father Fred Heinzman, the American Maryknoll Father, and Archbishop Pietro Sigismondi, secretary of the Congregation for the Propagation of the Faith, Capuchin friars from Detroit were made available and put on ARAMCO's payroll as teachers. It had to be this way because a clergyman as such is not allowed in this strict Moslem country of Saudi Arabia, where Mecca is located.

Shortly after the first of these "teachers" arrived, I was invited to visit Saudi Arabia, also as a teacher. Special travel arrangements had to be made. I first had to get a letter from my superiors that I was to do Community work. On the basis of this letter, the American Consulate took away—temporarily—my clerical passport and gave me one in which my employment was listed as TEACHER and which showed me in civilian clothes. In that way I could enter Saudi Arabia (and similar countries) without complications. Technically, the clothes I wore for the passport photo were not "civilian." I had on the jacket of my old blue Navy uniform (without my braid showing) and the white shirt and black tie. Getting together a civilian wardrobe that would suffice for a month in Saudi Arabia was something else. I am sure parishioners wondered why I was looking the men over so carefully as they came out of Sunday Mass. I had an eye out for one my size who looked like he might have an extra suit (Colonel John Nealon and Walter McAdoo answered specifications). I ended up with two suits, a half-dozen shirts, and four or five neckties. My black shoes, it was felt, would do.

I was told not to bring my mission crucifix nor any indication of things religious to Saudi Arabia. But customs men, everywhere, know who is who. If a man is not wearing a ring—one of them once told me—ninety-five per cent of the time he is a Catholic clergyman. The Arab inspector at the Dhahran airport gave me a thorough search with his eyes. He noted that my passport said TEACHER. He found neither liquor nor cigarettes in my baggage (these are strictly forbidden), but he did see a heavy file of sermon notes. He passed me "through" immediately.

We called them mission conferences and had them in the camp theater—family-style. It was inspiring to see men, women, and children going to Mass, confession, and Communion together at six in the morning. We had to have it that early so that they would have time for breakfast before work. The oil people followed the Moslem customs of the country. Wednesday for them became the day of abstinence (instead of Friday), and Friday (the Moslem holy day) was the day for attending Mass or, in the case of Protestants, religious services. Sunday was an ordinary workday. On the first free afternoon I was introduced to the Dhahran Country Club golf course. There is no grass anywhere! The so-called "greens" were made with oiled sand which had been raked, and you played with red golf balls. One had to be a dedicated golfer to play the course. I played it!

Through the contact of our mission conferences over the years, many ARAMCO people came to Santa Susanna's to be married. One of our most beautiful weddings was a couple from India. Her name was Suzamma (the Indian word for "Susanna") Thompson. We had their nuptial

Mass on a Sunday. That is unusual, but we made an exception because they were all alone and knew no one. Mrs. Elizabeth Tine, in Christmas-tree fashion, telephoned three parishioners who in turn called three others. By the time of the wedding, Santa Susanna's was packed with well-wishers. The bride looked so beautiful and cute in her white sari. She was a graduate nurse, but seemed like a tiny child. As a matter of fact she became indignant when, visiting St. Peter's later, she was asked if she had just made her First Communion. "I've just been married," she replied, trying to sound very tall. We got about a half-dozen people together and had a wedding dinner for them at the Madison House that night. Suzamma wore a lovely sari of gold lace. They returned to Saudi-Arabia, living happily—he, working as a photographer. One morning, while she was feeding her baby, her sari caught fire on a candle. The baby escaped injury, but the poor woman died of the burns she suffered while trying to protect her little one.

A couple of weeks before Cardinal Cushing became our Titular I was appointed by Cardinal Spellman to the supplementary duty of Vicar Delegate for the Atlantic Fleet and most of the Mediterranean area (the title was changed the following year to Chaplain Delegate). In effect, I was the Chancellor of the American military diocese in my area and had special powers in regard to marriages, regulations for chaplains, and other basic matters. There were Army, Navy, and Air Force chaplains, and many were personal friends. Long before my appointment by the Cardinal, I had worked with these chaplains in many ways and had cared for their personnel visiting Rome. When newly appointed Monsignors among the chaplains came to Rome on a quick one-day trip to get their robes, I would take them to Gammarelli in the morning to be measured, arrange a fitting for them that afternoon, and have them on the way back to their post the same day. Within two weeks, with an assist from the air attaché at the Embassy, the robes would be delivered and "the Right Reverend Monsignor" would be properly attired for his ecclesiastical functions.

Before this, my work with the military chaplains, as a matter of fact, started as soon as I became pastor. No sooner had I arrived in Rome in September of 1952 than an invitation came from the chaplain's office of the United States Army headquarters in Heidelberg. Monsignor James Murphy (now a colonel), a Bostonian and a devotee of Francis Thompson the poet, invited me to give a day of recollection for the chaplains. During the following years I gave many of them. They would be once a month. The Northern Area Command chaplains would have their *Day* in Frankfurt—on a Tuesday. That night a headquarters staff chaplain would drive me to Heidelberg for a Serra Club dinner meeting. Then, on Wednesday, I would be driven to Augsburg (or Munich), and on Thursday I would repeat the day of recollection for Southern Area Command Chaplains. This way we would "hit" all chaplains—some even from France. The Air Force chaplains attended with their Army colleagues. The interservice cooperation was so good that a chance to address the Holy Name Society at the Air Force base in Wiesbaden was invariably on the schedule worked out by the Army.

I also gave retreats for the chaplains as well as missions for the personnel and their families. My first mission was at the headquarters chapel in Heidelberg. Father Dan Shea of San Francisco, really one of the greatest pastoral chaplains I have known, set up an intense schedule for me—several Masses to preach at each day, a full afternoon of instructions for the children, and then confessions and the mission sermon in the evening. He had done magnificent groundwork, and the turnout—from the commanding officer right on down—left nothing to be desired. Father Shea and Father Al McAlwee, a Pennsylvanian, liked to

bring in outside non-military priests to help the service-
men and their families feel completely at home in the
"Church Abroad." I often arranged for priests from Rome
to help the chaplains. There were mutual advantages.
The chaplain had a new speaker for his military families,
a different confessor for himself, and another point of
view on things spiritual. Young student priests in Rome
found it a joy and a delight to get into the work of the
ministry and away from seminary life for a few weeks, at
Easter and Christmas. In sending priests to help out the
chaplains, I was able—as Cardinal Spellman's Chaplain
Delegate—to grant them the necessary faculties for preaching and hearing confessions.

There were economic advantages, too. When funds were
low at Santa Susanna's, we could always depend on the
income from the military missions to help us over rough
times. On my last mission in Heidelberg, Father Shea
contributed the final collection to the Paulist Fathers. It
was just short of $1000. But he was dismayed to find
no five-dollar bills in it. He was more dismayed two
weeks later when he discovered that the man who had
taken up the collection had suddenly become affluent
and, after buying a scooter, had gone to Italy on a ten-
day leave.

We were treated fine. After my first visit to Heidelberg,
Agatha the housekeeper knew my appetite and my culi-
nary delights. She was a short, affable German *hausfrau*
who had looked after a long series of headquarters chaplains, including Father Charles Murphy, a fellow home-
towner from Danbury. After Italy, where steak is a rarity
and a good steak almost an impossibility, American food
was a delight. Whenever Agatha heard I was coming, wonderful American steak and delicious American ice cream
made my stay most pleasant. Even the chaplains who
lived there felt the treatment I received was not impartial.

At Berchtesgaden I had the simulated rank of major general and stayed in a fine suite of rooms, overlooking the Alps, in a B.O.Q. named "Big Red One" after the Army. Danburyite Father Murphy, who had invited me to give the Berchtesgaden retreat, said the chaplains wanted to present me with a set of Rosenthal china. All I could foresee was the difficulty of getting a huge box of porcelain through the Italian customs. Being almost ignorant of the gift's value, and having no use for china, I thanked them—but declined it. My sister-in-law has never let me quite forget that at least on this one occasion I failed to take advantage of a wonderful opportunity.

Between the two weeks of the retreat at Berchtesgaden I crossed over the border to Salzburg where Monsignor Cajetan Troy, a brother of one of our Paulist Fathers, was chaplain. I talked to his Holy Name Society at a Communion breakfast and helped with Sunday Mass. A fringe benefit was the hearing of Puccini's *La Bohème*. Since it was prohibited for me to attend the opera in Rome, it seemed a bit ironical to listen to a beautiful Italian opera sung by a German-language company.

In Germany, particularly, I often did more than straight mission or retreat work. One weekend, for instance, I filled in at St. Sebastian's, on the Frankfurt Military Post, for Father McAlwee, who was sick in bed with the flu, and I baptized four German babies. They had been fathered by American GIs who could not get permission to marry the German girls with whom they had been living. The German girl that the GI wished to marry was subject to a very intensive security check-up by the Army. On some occasions a girl might be accused of immorality, in the investigative report, and permission would be refused —in this particular case she was accused of immorality because she was living with an American GI who was the father of her child and he wanted to marry her. This situation presented a serious problem to the German pastors as well as to the chaplains—and to me as Chaplain Delegate!—for, according to Church law, everyone has a right to marry unless there is an impediment to a valid marriage.

No chaplain could condone these immoral relationships. They warned against them constantly. However, the first knowledge he had of the situation would be when the soldier appeared with the young lady asking for permission to marry. She would already be with child. Some of these cases would be settled by marriage after the man was released from military control in the United States. At other times a security check was reported favorably before the GI was returned to the States for discharge or change of duty. There was an economic problem involved. If married in Germany, the soldier could take his wife back as a dependent. If not, and he had to return to Germany to marry her as well as wait for clearance with its attendant expenses, he found the costs involved a major obstacle.

Since my Chaplain Delegate activity was confined to countries which bordered the Mediterranean, apart from France, my problems in this field were fewer than those faced by the chaplains of Germany and their very large groups of land-based personnel. I learned from several German pastors at the Council of the heartbreaking and unsolvable problem it was for them. Many of the girls and their children were left behind. Especially was this the case in Southern Germany, which was a fertile source of adoptions after the war. One of the pastors told me that in case of another war America "will need to send only arms and ammunition—the personnel are already here."

Most of my military work was confined to Germany, but it also reached along both sides of the Mediterranean. This was the extraordinary thing: an American pastor who made all of Europe, and parts of two other continents, an extension of his parish activity in Rome!

On the first night of a mission at NATO headquarters, outside of Naples, I was telling some stories of the Tennessee mountains to a half-dozen different national groups in the chapel. An American Marine major, seated in the front row with his wife, seemed to enjoy the stories so much that it made me wonder—they were not *that* funny. Afterward, he and his wife came into the sacristy and before I could say anything he said: "I am Major Kirby-Smith."

My reply made him start laughing all over again.

"What in heaven's name is a Kirby-Smith doing in a Catholic church?" (Next to Robert E. Lee, Confederate General Edmund Kirby-Smith is the most famous name in Tennessee, and the descendants are notably Episcopalians.)

"She is a Catholic," the major said, pointing to his wife, "and has been since she was born."

I explained that I knew the Kirby-Smiths at Sewanee, Tennessee, where the general had died, and was rightly accused by Dr. Kirby-Smith of using cut stone that had been stolen from him to build my church. He said the contractor was stealing it from his quarry. Yet he refused to accept my payment for it when I offered to reimburse him—and the stone stolen from General Kirby-Smith's descendant built most of my church in Alto, Tennessee. The major said the reason he had been laughing so much during my talk was that he could identify almost every one of the people I mentioned in my Tennessee stories. Later he invited me to his home. It had a bar, over which was a sign: *The Rebels Roost*. He went down the hall corridor, knocking on doors and shouting:

"Get up, children! We have a real Catholic priest from Tennessee!"

The little ones—aged from four to twelve—got up in their white-flannel nightgowns and threw their arms around me. They hugged me so much it was a week before I could get the white lint off my black cassock.

After working for the Army so many times, it was a most pleasant surprise when Father David Casazza, a Navy chaplain, came into the office one day and asked if I could do some mission work for him at his base in Port Lyautey, Morocco. Such an invitation had to be accepted immediately by someone like myself, who was born with the wanderlust and the constant desire to see new faces, places, and things. About a month later the Navy picked me up at Capodochino airport in Naples and, by way of Malta, flew me to Port Lyautey for the mission I was to give.

Port Lyautey at the time was a huge communications center. Approximately 700 people attended the mission. Since it was to be paid for by special Navy funds, Father Casazza requested me to announce there would be no collection. With the old-time missionaries it was traditional that between the sermon and the benediction a hymn would be announced and a collection taken up. So, on the first night, I gave the name of the hymn and then said I had been told to announce that there would be no collection. Everyone laughed. Each night thereafter I would— sadly—say: *No Collection*. On the last night, Father Casazza came to me and said: "The boys want you to announce a collection tonight. They feel that making a mission and going to the sacraments—without making some kind of a contribution—is not quite Catholic."

Turkey, another Moslem country, was also part of my jurisdiction as Chaplain Delegate in the American military diocese overseas, and it gave me an opportunity to be with the Air Force. Every year since my ordination I had been giving a mission somewhere, and in the year 1959— shortly after Cardinal Cushing's induction as our Titular —the scene of my mission was Turkey. The Air Force invited me there for three weeks of missions. I had to use "borrowed finery" because in Turkey it is forbidden to wear clerical garb on the street, and I left Rome dressed as a civilian for the flight to Ankara. It always seems to me that a priest never looks at home when he is out of his clerical clothes, and my gray suit and nondescript necktie did not quite fit the Pan-American stewardess' idea of what a man reading a breviary should look like.

Our mission in Ankara was held in the chapel of the Italian Embassy, which always had an open door for the Air Force chaplain, Father James Gribbon, and for the American colony. (Since the time of Ataturk, no Christian churches have been built!) The chapel was in charge of the Franciscan Fathers, who also had a school in the Embassy for Italian children. The friars did everything possible to make me feel one of themselves. After all, I was a Roman! Each night after the services we would have confessions. It was bitterly cold in this 3500-feet high city, and snow and ice covered the ground. As I walked into the priests' quarters the first night to get a heavy coat to wear in the cold confessional, the good Father Superior was on hand with a large glass of red wine. His instructions were: "Rest for five minutes as you drink this, and you will not catch cold during the mission." Nor did I catch cold!

From Ankara I went to Istanbul for a mission at the Karamarsel base, on the Asian side of the Bosporus. Simply by taking the ferry at Istanbul I had crossed from Europe to Asia. The Karamarsel base was still building, and there was mud everywhere. I suppose that week I brushed my shoes at least twenty-five times.

While in the Istanbul area, I spent a Friday (the Moslem holy day) on a trip to Nicaea, the site of the first Ecumenical Council in the year 325. From the Council's deliberations came the Nicene Creed we say at Mass each Sunday. It is a fairly large city and an archaeologist's happy hunting ground. I was particularly interested in one of the city gates because it was erected by the Emperor Hadrian, who condemned St. Eleutherius to death in the year 110—and the body of this martyr is in Santa Susanna's.

My mission in Turkey had started out with the Franciscans, and ended with them. I am sure all of the Air Force chaplains joined in my prayer of "God Bless Francis of Assisi" for establishing an order of men so hospitable to strangers in their monasteries.

St. Anthony's monastery in Istanbul was the place chosen by the Air Force chaplains to have the final dinner when I had finished my three weeks of missions in Turkey. An American military truck from the Karamarsel base backed up to the monastery door and unloaded the food, and an American sergeant arrived to prepare it. I am sure the good friars have very pleasant memories of all these unusual goings-on. All kinds of American food favorites—fresh from the PX—were placed on the table before the thirty priests. There were peanuts, cocktail sausages, and even potato chips. I feel certain, too, that at no other time in the history of the monastery had such a choice of beverages been on the table at one time—wine, Coca-Cola, milk, ginger ale, coffee, and tea. There was also a pitcher of water—but, obviously, not for drinking purposes.

It was interesting to see the priests wearing collars and ties. But the Apostolic Delegate came and went with his Roman collar on, although he had it hidden behind a huge scarf. Halfway through the meal, the Apostolic Delegate remarked that the "missionary" (that was *me*) had not arrived as yet. Father Robert Mossey, the Karamarsel chaplain, pointed to the other end of the table, where I, in a gray suit, was having a good time with the friars.

Despite the spiritual nature of the occasion, the table discussion turned to spirits and the excellent wine the friars were making there in Turkey. One old friar asked me: "Could you recognize a wonderful wine if you tasted it?" I said I could. The friar left the table and returned in five minutes with a cobwebbed bottle. A possibly irreverent friar near me remarked: "I thought he was saving that bottle for His Holiness!"

After the dinner I returned to my hotel, the Divan. I had been going in and out of there all week under the appraising eye of the tall Turkish doorman. He apparently had been trying to figure out who this man in civilian clothes was that was always accompanied by Air Force chaplains. Whether he found out who I was, I do not know for certain. But as I was leaving the next morning for Rome I felt quite sure from the farewell greeting I received that we had one thing in common—our Catholic religion.

I brought back to Rome happy memories of Turkey and the Turkish people, and the historic landmarks of Istanbul —such as the Mosque of Santa Sophia which was built by Constantine in the fourth century as a Catholic Church. Istanbul still retains the beauty it had in the days when it was called the "City of Constantine," or Constantinople.

I remember, too, the few words which someone said just before I left. They said it was the first time since the Crusades that an English-speaking mission had been given in this ancient Byzantine city which once had been the eastern capital of the Roman empire!

Chapter 10

THE SWEET LIFE

Rome brings out the worst in people.

If you have any weakness—physical, mental, or moral —the climate, the way of life, or something about the city will accentuate it. I make no claims to be a diagnostician, but I have seen it happen any number of times. People find that a physical illness, such as diabetes or arthritis, gets worse there. Normally fine women go completely berserk over some Italian *papagallo,* or Lothario, and it takes a real jolt to bring them back to their senses. Anyone would agree Rome has a strange effect on visitors if they witnessed—as I have—the antics of movie stars, the caperings of elderly men on vacation away from home, and the dear old ladies who are giving romance one last fling in Europe. I have known at least a half-dozen men and women, including members of the clergy, who have become mentally disturbed while in Rome. Obviously, the many fine Americans living in Rome and loving the Eternal City are witnesses to the fact that for many men and women the Roman atmosphere presents no problem. Saints have been made in Rome, too, and holy people today walk the ancient streets. But the ratio of saints to sinners, I have a strong suspicion, is a bit out of balance.

Rome is famous for the expression *la dolce vita*—the Sweet Life. Only a small percentage of Romans belong to the *dolce vita* set—that group of people who do nothing but spend their lives seeking pleasure. The Via Veneto, one of Rome's shortest streets (and among its most beautiful), is the heart of this *dolce vita.* At the sidewalk tables of the coffee shops on both sides of the street tourists sit for hours ogling the passers-by. Watching tourists and passers-by alike are the "hustlers"—men, women, and children—who live off the weaknesses, sensuality, or cupidity of their fellow men. If two young men are looking for trouble, let them sit at a coffee table in Via Veneto. Within ten minutes they will be accosted. Someone looks them over, "weighs them in," and quite accurately spots the Achilles heel.

Prostitutes, for example, are all over Rome. If you walk down the street between Santa Susanna's and the Piazza della Repubblica, you will be accosted by three or four of these girls. They have very definite signs by which they can be identified: the purse, the cigarette, and other means known to the initiated. Any night will find the same two girls in front of Santa Susanna's plying their "trade."

For a few years our garage was in the Via Torino. On the way back to the rectory, after putting the car away, I would pass through the Piazza San Bernardo and one or the other of the women would say: "Good evening, Father." "Good evening," I would answer. "How are you?" On several occasions I received a reply: "No good—business is rotten."

The Roman cassock is no guarantee that you will not be "approached." One morning I had gone across the street to the Grand Hotel to get Lori, a driver, to take some pilgrims to Castel Gandolfo for a Papal audience. I was a little ahead of him, as I hurried back to Santa Susanna's, when a well-dressed, very attractive girl of twenty-three or twenty-four accosted me and held out her hand. I thought for a moment she was one of the group for the Castel Gandolfo audience. I heard a snort behind me, and the girl dropped her hand fast. It was Lori, in choice Italian, telling her that if she ever did that again someone would be fishing her out of the Tiber. She was definitely a newcomer! The "regulars" of the zone were known by the policemen, cab drivers, and everyone else and would never have molested one of us from Santa Susanna's.

In the middle of all this until several years ago was a Via Veneto night-club operator, a Negro woman who was born in the poor part of West Virginia and raised on the rough side of Chicago. For half her seventy-one years she had been an international figure in Paris and Rome. Cole Porter had written songs for her; the Duke of Windsor learned how to dance under her tutelage, and Farouk used to bring her little cigars from Switzerland. Elizabeth Taylor and Richard Burton were first linked publicly in her Via Veneto club. International scoundrels and the local gentry, equally, found they were welcome, provided they used no profanity in her club. Every third drink was on the house—but you paid for it. The money was put in a locked box, and it went to charity. Thousands of dollars passed through her hands, but she kept nothing for herself except a keen sense of humor, a love of all people, and an abiding faith in God. She felt it was just as easy to be a saint in a bar room as in a cloistered convent. To everyone that would not be possible. In her case I think it would be. She had a long name that began with "Ada" and ended with "Smith." Everyone called her "Bricktop" because of her reddish hair.

Brick was a daily communicant. She would go, usually, to an afternoon Mass at one of the neighborhood churches. But if her club had remained open late, she would be at the first Mass at Santa Susanna's, sometimes with what looked like every flower in Rome, and accompanied by her dog Leo, who was slightly smaller than a full-fledged racehorse. Brick was a convert. She had begun taking instructions in 1923, not because of disappointment in love, or sickness, or any classic reason. "God just put the finger on me," she would say. "Before

I was born I was a Catholic." One influence had been a New Orleans waiter whom she had not seen in years. "You're different," she said to him. "What happened to you?" The waiter said, "Nothing"—but her questioning revealed that what was different about him was that he had become a Catholic since she had last seen him. "Well," Brick said. "If it can do that for you, what can it do for me!"

When people would ask us—as they did often enough —what kind of entertainment was available after dinner, it was not difficult to recommend Bricktop and her club. On several occasions when Brick was short on cash we helped her out. The money always came back. "You priests at Santa Susanna's are probably the only ones in the world who help support a nightclub," she said one time.

"Brick," I replied. "Yours is the only night club any of us would recommend, for it is you we recommend, and not your club. It is you we commend as first-class, honest, and a good Catholic. We don't have to know any more than that."

Necessarily, as an American pastor in Rome, I had a busy social life, and it could have been lots busier if I did not keep a brake on it. If the pastor is not to be separated from his people, he must greet them not only on Sunday as they come in and out of church, but be with them socially during the week. However, unless he is able very quickly to strike a sane balance between the needs of his parish, his visitors, and himself, he does not remain very long in the Eternal City. Many visitors who were friends of friends thought, perhaps, I was snooty when I would decline to "eat out" with them. Often I had to turn down lunch invitations from my own parishioners and Roman friends. A Roman lunch kills the day. I went to lunch one day at one-thirty with Irving R. Levine and an NBC vice-president and returned to the office at ten after five.

It is not possible to rise every morning at five-thirty, be out for lunch and dinner, work seven days a week, get home between eleven and twelve at night, and maintain any kind of a spiritual life. It is not possible to find time for reading, or to prepare for your people on Sunday the type of sermon they should have. Masses, confessions, marriages, and baptisms won't wait. Neither can the people with personal problems. Nor can you put off a convert instruction class by saying: "Excuse me, folks. I have to go out to dinner this evening. I won't be able to see you." That is why one must strike a balance. The few times I made exceptions I realized how important it was to keep this balance. I remember, especially, one Armed Forces Day which happened also to be the feast day of the Camillian Fathers. After attending a noontime dinner at the Camillian house, which lasted till 5 P.M., I returned to my office for two hours. That night each of the three branches of the military—Army, Navy, and Air Force—had its own special reception. As pastor I had been invited to each one because I had parishioners in each group—and I made all three of them. But never again! One day like that is enough.

American visitors are sometimes surprised to find a priest at a cocktail party attired in his Roman clerical garb. But we clergymen were required by the laws of the Roman Vicariate to wear our cassocks at such times.

The Rome cocktail party often was the place to make contact with the non-Catholic who was interested in the Church. This was the case with the wife of a U.S. naval attaché, himself a Catholic. She had brought up her children as Catholics, but the hurly-burly of Navy and diplomatic life never seemed to give her the time to become one herself. At a cocktail party one night I told her now was the time to do something about it—

she would never have the chance again. "Since you wanted to be a Catholic for a good number of years," I said, "we shall start instructions tomorrow morning." We did, and I know with what great happiness her husband (now a rear admiral) escorted her and two of his sons to St. Peter's, not long afterward, to make their confirmation together.

Each January we ourselves entertained the members of the English-speaking clergy—and some of our Italian clerical friends—at dinner at the Grand. The occasion was the Feast of the Conversion of St. Paul, the patron of the Paulist Fathers. The guest list ranged from sixty to eighty-five, and starting when Father Paul Maloney became our assistant, the dinner invitation would be drafted in an unusual way. One year Father Maloney couched the invitation in a Middle Eastern style reminiscent of that used in the Acts of the Apostles, and Monsignor (now Bishop) Donal Herlihy, rector of the Irish College at the time, sent his acceptance in Greek. Fortunately, we did not have to rely on our knowledge of Greek to decipher the answer because he also telephoned.

There were no speeches at our St. Paul's Day dinner. Generally I would thank everyone for their assistance during the year and ask the senior prelate present to say "a few words"—specifically, Grace. The guest of honor at our dinner in 1962 was Milwaukee-born Aloysius Joseph Cardinal Muench, who was a "neighbor" because he was Titular of San Bernardo's Church across the piazza from Santa Susanna's. He was a sick man and lived a quasi-retired life at Salvator Mundi. He had been made a member of the Roman Curia, and his death—a few weeks after dining with his fellow Americans at our St. Paul's Day dinner—once again blasted hopes of having one of our Cardinals in this supreme governing body of the Church.

At other times of the year we would have farewell

dinners when some good friend was departing. These dinners provided the one means we had for touching all the bases in the Roman way of life, since the relatively few American clergymen in Rome are scattered in a wide variety of activities, and some of us would not see one another for months at a time. We all considered such dinners as one of the highlights of our Roman life because we could get together, relax, and forget about the business of running the Church, and have a few hours of what we have often referred to as Consecrated Christian Fellowship.

One of the last of these special dinners of ours was to honor Father Malcolm Lavelle of Illinois, who was leaving after eighteen years in Rome as Superior General of the Passionist Fathers. The dinner was to be held during the period when his Community was meeting to elect a successor. To make sure that all the American Passionists in Rome would be with us, I called Father Lavelle's second Consultor, Father Theodore Foley of New Jersey. When we had finished checking over the guest list, I casually asked him: "By the way, Father Theodore, who was elected your new Superior General?"

And he, just as casually, answered: "By the way, Father Cunningham, I was."

A very interesting part of my Roman life was the contact with the ecclesiastical colleges of various nations. I was always at home at North American College and was invited there for feast days and on the occasions when distinguished ecclesiastical visitors were entertained. On December 8 each year a special banquet honoring the Blessed Mother, patroness of the United States, would be held and I would be invited. The North American College graduate school had a special dinner on St. Joseph's Day because a succession of rectors were named *Joseph*—Monsignors Lacey, Emmenegger, and Zryd—and I was on the guest list for that, too. St. Patrick's Day was the big day at the Irish College, and at my last dinner there I chatted with Eamon de Valera, who had gone to confession at Santa Susanna's during his visit to Rome. Bishop Gerard Tickle, rector of the English College, would invite me two or three times a year to dinner. Afterward, I would sit down with a dozen or so English seminarians to discuss theological problems from the point of view of the pastor.

Monsignor Peter Whitty, vice-rector of the Beda College, was a faithful golfing companion of mine for many years. On occasion Garvin Cavanagh, of the hat family (and an old friend), would be able to get away from his studies at the Beda and join the rector and myself on the golf course. I used to have fun with the Beda College students by saying there were two basic rules: 1. You may not strike the rector; 2. You may not smoke in chapel. Because these men were much older than the usual seminarian, and because Beda College has done such an outstanding job for over 100 years, it was able to stand up under my joshing.

I was frequently invited to dine at the homes of parishioners and Roman friends. Archbishop Martin O'Connor likes to tell about the time I went to dinner at the home of Ralph Fowler, the ARAMCO general manager in Rome, a good friend of mine. I was about the first to get there. Ralph's boy came to the door, looked out, and rushed back into the house. "Mother," he called, so loud I could hear him. "There's a priest at the door. Shall I let him in?" The incident got the evening off to a merry start.

From time to time I had to entertain visitors. One Easter week the three top Navy chaplains—Protestant, Jewish, and Catholic—arrived in Rome. One of them, Chaplain Joshua "Josh" Goldberg, was an old friend from Puerto Rican days. The naval attaché at the time was Captain Bill McCormick (now an admiral aboard the

Valley Forge), and the two of us arranged a cocktail party at the Grand Hotel for the chaplains. It was a nice Roman party—diplomats, nobility, Monsignori, Italian admirals and generals. But I think the chaplains, as Americans a long way from home, were impressed most of all by two American guests: Dom "Little Professor" DiMaggio, the baseball player, and Loretta Young, the movie star.

It turned out to be a long evening for me. Father John Gogarty, vice-rector of the Scots College, was celebrating his birthday that night at a dinner for a small group of us in the Augustea. I had told Loretta Young and the others at the cocktail party that I had an appointment afterward with some priests. But Loretta, knowing me of old—and possibly suspecting chicanery—asked me where I was going. I told her and her companion, Mrs. John Sharp of Los Angeles (whom I had known many years before as Mary Jane Mullen, when her father was a partner in the Mullen-Bluett department store). "Why can't we come?" the two of them asked, almost together. I warned them it might be boring. "There'll be a dozen priests, and we may talk shop."

"We'd love it," Loretta said.

With Loretta, and Mrs. Sharp and her teen-age son, I walked into the restaurant. The sight of me with these two beautiful American women caused all conversation to stop. It was a memorable evening. Several years later I visited the same restaurant with another group—this time Linda Lee Meade, Miss America of 1960 (now Mrs. John Shea of Memphis, the wife of a distinguished ear doctor), and Dr. Roland Kohen of Miami Beach, my urologist, and his lovely wife. "I waited on you the night Loretta Young entertained all the priests," a waiter said to me and described the evening.

"You are correct in every detail but one," I said. "The priests entertained Miss Young."

Loretta's name is on a plaque in Santa Susanna's, along

with the names of others from the entertainment world. The plaque is an idea of Marie Gentilcoeur, an actress. Marie was visiting Rome with her husband, Al, about the time I was thinking about restoring the Chapel of St. Lawrence, which contains the remains of St. Genesius, a fourth-century martyr who is the patron saint of actors. Marie was a friend of Mrs. Elizabeth Tine, and I was telling them and members of the guild about my restoration plans. Marie suggested making the chapel into a shrine for St. Genesius and getting people in the acting field to help finance it. Back in New York, Marie got my friend Ed Sullivan to help. Between the funds raised by the guild and those provided by the Tine-Gentilcoeur-Ed Sullivan combination I was enabled to restore this gorgeous sixteenth-century chapel.

That was in 1959. The commemorating plaque in the chapel is in the form of a working copy of a play script. It lists in alphabetical order the names of more than two dozen donors, including the American Federation of Musicians, Armando's Restaurant, Anna Brady, Danny's Hide-away, Catholic Actors' Guild of America, Irene Dunne, James A. Farley, Francis M. Folsom, Mrs. Arthur Bliss Lane, Mario del Monaco, Leo McCarey, James Petrillo, Toots Shor Restaurant, Henri R. Soulé, Ed Sullivan, Margaret and Barbara Whiting, Jane Wyman, and Loretta Young.

As far as possible, I avoided Roman restaurants which had orchestras and music. I never did like musicians spending their time at a table so that you cannot talk to people you haven't seen for a year or two. With Dolores Hope and the first Mrs. John Wayne (Josephine Saenz, whom I had met at the Los Angeles Newman Club before her marriage), I went to La Cisterna in Trastévere one night. It is a tourist "must" and in general the food is fairly good. This night their quartet of musicians in red knee breeches stood beside the table as a lusty, bosomy soprano leaned over my shoulder and sang something about going back to Sorrento. When they finished I gave the orchestra leader 500 lire—and the signal which caused them to leave us. "For that much," Mrs. Hope said, "the girl should have sung a couple of numbers." "I didn't pay her to sing," I said. "I paid her to go away."

One evening "out on the town" ended in an unexpected way. It was Thanksgiving, and since Father William Michell, my Superior General, and a few other Paulists were visiting me, I decided we would have our holiday dinner at Canepa's. A couple, with two young boys, sat at a table in the corner and the man, I noticed, kept looking over at our table of priests. He was Arthur Bliss Lane, former American Ambassador to Poland. "Didn't you arrange for Father John Burke, the Paulist, to visit the President of Mexico once," I asked, "to try to allay the persecution of the Church?" Ambassador Lane smiled reminiscently. "Not only did I do that," he said, "but I also accompanied him from the Mexican border to the President's office." The Ambassador joined us and listened to our stories, while Mrs. Lane and the boys remained at their table. When I spoke to Mrs. Lane some years later, she said the evening with us had been one of the happiest in her husband's life. He had enjoyed every moment of it. After Ambassador Lane died, she came to see me in Rome, took instructions, and entered into the Church.

I once wrote in Santa Susanna's bulletin that waiters in Rome sometimes confuse Americans by telling them they can eat meat on Friday. A few days later I had a note from the Bernini-Bristol Hotel headwaiter, saying that all their waiters were instructed to advise inquiring Americans that the law of abstinence was the same as at home. As a matter of fact, Italians from the top rank of society down to domestics are very conscious of their Catholic obligations. I am sure Jack Begon of NBC will remember the night he was entertaining Frank Folsom (chairman of the Executive Committee of the Board of RCA) with a small cocktail party. No more than fifteen persons were present. As the Begon maid was passing a tray of sandwiches, she saw me reach for one. In Italian, she half-whispered: "That is pork, Father—and today is Friday, isn't it?" Mr. Folsom, standing beside me, thoroughly enjoyed the incident.

One time, when the Fourth of July fell on a Friday and the Embassy was still having the annual get-together for all Americans, I did get the no-meat rule dropped—to a certain extent. Since hot dogs were among the things to be served at the Embassy reception, I applied to Archbishop Luigi Traglia (now Cardinal) for a dispensation. He was assistant, or Pro-Vicar at the time. Archbishop Traglia said waiving the abstinence law would "scandalize the people." I said that I would explain the reason behind it to my fellow Americans and I was sure everyone would understand. The Archbishop said he meant the *Italians* would be scandalized. Politely I remarked that not many Italians seemed to pay attention to this law anyway. The Archbishop said: "Well—write out your request, and I'll pass it on to the Cardinal-Vicar." It developed that Cardinal Micara, the Vicar, took up the matter with the Holy Father, who said that if the Cardinal-Vicar approved he himself had no objection. On the Tuesday morning before the Fourth of July the Cardinal's secretary called me and said the dispensation had been granted. I passed the word—and it went like wildfire. Then on Thursday morning he called back and said the Cardinal-Vicar had second thoughts on the matter and felt the dispensation should not apply to priests and nuns. I said it was impossible at this late date to get the word to them that they were being penalized and would not be allowed to enjoy the dispensation like other Americans. The Cardinal's secretary said: "Well—I at least have told you." I suppose the only one that Fourth of July who did not partake of the general dispensation was myself. Although the Italians love confusion, I felt words from me at that stage would only confuse things all the more.

Sunday was the one day we always ate out because it was the cook's night off. I would return from the church —a little over a block away—at one-thirty in the afternoon. The first order of the day would be to count the Sunday collection and get that out of the way, with everyone helping. Josephine, our cook-housekeeper, would keep her eye on us. When she figured we were just about ready, she would call us for dinner—and wanted no delay. After dinner, Josephine went out, leaving an empty refrigerator (in true Roman style).

Josephine had come to work for us about a year before I arrived as pastor. She was a Trieste girl, short, stocky, and in her forties. She could be difficult if she felt I was imposing on her. For instance, she did not like it when I told her without warning that there would be guests for dinner. She had the same sensitivity as a housewife suddenly finding her husband bringing home unexpected guests. But if Josephine felt I was trying to help her, I found her to be a good all-around cook and housekeeper. She learned our individual tastes—that I was allergic to oil in the cooking, for example—and very quickly had us, as it were, eating out of the palm of her hand, and liking it. She was a champion at *pasta,* but the one really good pie Josephine could make was apple.

An Italian housekeeper is a very intimate part of the family, and she is treated as such. You know all her problems and are expected to act the part of her father in helping her in every circumstance. When Josephine would receive word that one of her elderly parents was sick, she would summon her younger sister, Lilliana, who also worked in Rome, and that night the two girls would come to my room for a family council. If it was decided that Josephine should go home to Trieste, she would arrange for Lilliana or a friend to take care of her "family" while she was away. We would have Lilliana come and help out when we had specially invited guests and felt there were too many for Josephine to handle. Josephine ate and drank as we did. If there were cocktails before dinner, Josephine and her sister were always included. One of the Fathers would carry the drinks to the kitchen.

Josephine bought from one meal to the next, and there was never any surplus of food in the icebox. If there were to be four persons for dinner, she bought for four. If you suddenly told her an hour before dinner there would be another guest, she would go down to the butcher's and get an extra piece of meat. When emergencies did develop, Josephine had no qualms about buying food, already cooked, from a near-by restaurant. Such things as tomatoes filled with rice, stuffed zucchini, fruit, ice cream —even the wine—might be delivered to the door by a white-coated restaurant waiter.

During the Council, when we had more visitors at the rectory than usual, we had a basic rule that the limit for dinner was five. Often there would be as many as a dozen visiting Bishops, priests, and observers in our community room at mealtime. One of us would take our extra guests out to dinner. Before leaving the house, I would phone the restaurant and order the first course. I discovered that when you put a group of priests together they would sit down at the table and keep right on talking—completely forgetting about looking at the menu. But if you placed the first course in front of them, they would begin eating right away and then, eventually, get around to ordering the rest of the meal.

On weekends, in the two years just before the Council began, we had a special guest at the rectory. That was my teen-age grandniece, Marla. While stationed in New York as Superior General, I had become very close to my niece's two daughters—particularly Marla, the older one. When Marla was five, she was stricken with Perthes disease (the bone does not fit right in the hip socket) and was unable to walk for almost a year and a half. I frequently went to Waterbury and pushed her wheel-chair, in the company of her little friends, on long Sunday morning outings in the park. For the two summers when she could not walk, Marla swam off my back while the family was on vacation at Hitchcock Lake. Early in the morning we went fishing. I would wrap her in a blanket and carry her out to the motorboat that we used on fishing trips.

So Marla and I became good friends.

Later, when I was pastor, an uncle died, leaving some funds to my brother and myself out of which we formed an educational fund to be used in whatever manner seemed best for the youngsters coming along. When Marla was in the eighth grade, I asked her if she would like to come to Rome for two or three years, doing her high school work at Marymount. She thought this was a good idea, and we agreed to keep quiet about it till we felt it opportune to ask her parents. Her mother was really taken by surprise. The only thing she could think of to say was: "Marla—that requires an awful lot of money."

"Oh, don't worry, Mother," Marla said. "It will only be Uncle Will's money we are spending."

Her arrival coincided with a cocktail party for the new officers of the guild. I never realized the problems of teen-agers till then. "What shall I wear?" she asked me. I told her it was a formal occasion and she should wear her party dress. Her grandmother had given her a nice sequin sweater before she left, and she decided to wear that, too. Then her hair was a problem. She had to have it done, she assured me. I sent her to the *parruc-*

chière in the Grand Hotel for that. Her reaction to the Roman beauty parlor was: "Gee, Uncle James. This stuff costs a lot over here."

Marla was fifteen when she first came to Rome. She lived at Marymount, but spent a great deal of time on weekends at the rectory. She was a typical teen-ager—a brunette with a nice smile and good teeth. (Marla and I are the only ones in the family with long fingers and toes.) She and her young friends would come bouncing into the house every now and then to add a little life and color to the place. At home, young members of the family used to clap their hands loudly at the end of Grace before meals. Marla, at the time she was having her first meal at the rectory, had not forgotten this old family custom. The priests at dinner with us had been saying Grace, as usual, with bowed heads. Their heads jerked upward in surprise at the sound of Marla's hand-clapping.

"That woke them up, didn't it?" Marla said, unabashed.

On Sundays she would bring two or three of her school chums for lunch or dinner. We would go to a different restaurant each Sunday for about a month—and then start all over again. The headwaiters, and the regular customers, began to know us. One Sunday Marla brought with her Susie Smith, a charming, gracious little girl whose father was a colonel in the Air Force at Naples. Arm in arm the three of us entered Giggi Fazi's—Susie, who is colored, on one side of me; Marla on the other. The headwaiter greeted me with a warm smile and exclaimed:

"Che bellìssima famiglia—what a very beautiful family!"

Although some eight years apart in age, Marla and Josephine's sister, Lilliana, became fast friends, and for Marla's first Christmas vacation I took them to Paris. I had visited the city a number of times, but I had never received the attention I did when I had the two young ladies with me. I had a list of restaurants on the side streets where I wanted to eat, but discovered quickly that unless the place had Coca-Cola on the bill of fare the girls did not consider it a good restaurant. Their chief complaint in Paris was that the bathroom in their Left Bank hotel room leaked all night and kept them awake. The next Christmas I took them to Madrid. I was in my room only five minutes when they both rushed down the hall to where I was and escorted me back to their little suite. They stood in the reception room and ordered me to keep quiet, and LISTEN. There it was once more—the glug-glug-glug of a leaking bath.

After her first year in Rome, Marla went home for the summer, carrying with her a little Italian baby that was to be adopted in the States. Several of her school friends, traveling with her, planned to do the same thing. When their parents greeted them on arrival, with a baby in their arms, they planned to say: "Look what I brought back from home, Mother!" What a shock that would have been for all! But fortunately their plan fell through.

In her second year at Marymount Marla had a spot of homesickness due, I think, to letters from her boy friend back home, urging her return. His counsel prevailed, and she decided to do her third year at home in Waterbury, rather than Rome. By the time school started that fall, however, the boy friend could not care less. He had a different girl friend, and Marla had a new boy friend. A week after the opening of school Marla realized that not returning to Rome had been an error in judgment.

I never took Marla to the movies in Rome or to the Opera. Nor did I go myself. Priests living in Rome were forbidden to attend public spectacles. We could not attend an evening function, for instance, if there was dancing. Once, when the guild had a dance, we priests at Santa Susanna's were given permission to attend, but the music had to stop when we entered and could be resumed only when we left. When the Olympic Games came along, I did not ask for a decision as to whether it was in the spectacle category—I just went!

Swimming at Ostia, the closest beach to Rome, was also prohibited to the clergy. I always felt sort of guilty as one or two other priests and I left Rome for the beach—*beyond* Ostia. Before leaving for our swim, we would put on sports shirts and American clerical trousers underneath our habits. I emphasize "American clerical trousers" because Italian priests wear knee breeches and long stockings under their cassocks. (Usually it is very easy for an Italian to recognize an American priest because the cuffs of his trousers often reach below his cassock hem. I was told by an Italian colleague he felt this was a little indecent—like when a lady's slip shows.) Along the Passage Archaeological, about a mile from Santa Susanna's, we would pull over to the side of the road and take off our cassocks so as not to shock our Roman friends by arriving at the beach in clerical attire. On the way home we would stop at the same place and slip the cassocks on again. (One of the blessings of the cassock was that in the summer I could wear golf shorts instead of trousers—and no one was the wiser. However, when I went to the airport to meet Cardinal Spellman or Cardinal Cushing, and there was the slightest wind blowing, I wore my regular trousers underneath the cassock—just to be on the safe side. With the long trousers on a summer's day I felt as if my legs were wrapped up in blankets.)

I had been accustomed to lots of physical exercise before coming to Rome. While Superior General I swam and played handball regularly at the New York Athletic Club. (I have been a member since 1934.) In Rome I soon realized that if I was going to get any exercise it would have to be golf. My golfing companions usually were fellow priests, but once in a while golfers among our visitors played with us. One time another clergyman and myself played against Mike Stern and Perry Como. We added photographers as we went along and by the ninth hole—after many delays and many photos—we decided that we had had enough golf for that day.

Another golfing companion was Ingemar Johansson, the Swedish fighter and one-time world heavyweight champion. Ingemar knew my friend Bill Fugazy, and one time the two of them happened to be visiting Rome at the same time. Bill was with members of his family, including a sister, Mildred, who is a nun and who was accompanied by another nun. Ingemar and the Fugazy group had gotten together socially during their Rome visit. After a golf game one day, I asked Ingemar if he would like to see the Holy Father in a general audience the next morning. Apologetically he said: "I had lunch with Catholic nuns yesterday. Today I played golf with you, a Catholic priest. If I see the Holy Father tomorrow, it could be misunderstood. There are not many Catholics in my country, and they may think I am going to be one."

In those years at Rome my golf game gradually improved. Willie Goggins, after I made a particularly good drive one day, could not believe his eyes. "Father," he exclaimed. "You don't hit them that good!"

But the golf, too, had to be played discreetly at all times, and all of us golfing priests were aware of the Vicariate frown which might be directed toward us if any public mention was made of this. (I never knew a single Italian priest to play golf or—as we designated our countryside activity—"take a walk in the country.") Our timidity was such that when I won the Anglo-American Golf Tournament, I was really embarrassed. Ed Hill, editor of the Rome *Daily American*, understood my plight and headlined the story on the sports page:

JAMES FRANCIS WINS GOLF TOURNAMENT

Dick Spater, the American Club president, called up to see who this "James Francis" was. There was no such person on the club membership list, and he thought it was a ringer!

The same *nom de golf* was used when I won the tournament a second year. There was always the possibility you might be reprimanded by someone who did not understand what a great source of humility golf really is. The first lesson you learn in golf is to keep your head down!

There were winter sports, too—but not in sunny Rome. On several occasions Mr. and Mrs. Umberto Tine invited me to go skiing with them and their two children during the Christmas holidays. No matter where it was, I would say Mass each morning. At Cortina one year I said Mass in ski boots and ski clothes. The church was so cold the wine and water had to be kept on a little pot-bellied stove in the sacristy till the Gospel. Yet a large crowd of people was there day after day. As I would leave the hotel each morning to go to the church near by, I would find that a path had already been cleared for me in the newly fallen snow.

Kitzbühel was magnificent! The Austrian youngsters on the ski slopes had faces like Hummel figurines, and it was quite a thrilling experience to hear people sing "Silent Night" in the country where it was written. The *pension* where we stayed one year had a congenial mixture of many nationalities among the guests. They took turns singing their country's Christmas hymns—one day it would be the Italians; the next, another group. New Year's Day was the turn of the Americans. Since it was the first of the year, someone thought it would also be nice to have a "typical American drink." As far as I know, there is no such thing—at least one which you can whip up suddenly on an Austrian hillside. I decided on a Brandy Alexander. But since there was no brandy, I used gin. No one had told me, a neophyte in the business, that you must not mix gin drinks in aluminum pitchers. But that is what I did, and chilled the drinks by placing them for a half hour in the snow. Lunch, instead of lasting forty minutes, extended a couple of hours and none of the grown-ups were on the slopes that afternoon. When Mrs. Tine's son and I left at 6 P.M. to return to Rome, I found that many of the people I wanted to say good-bye to were still "resting."

The annual convention of the Italian department of the American Legion gave me a chance to see Italy. I was in Rome not quite a year when the rector of the American Episcopal Church, Dr. Hillis Duggins, died and I was asked to take his place as chaplain of the Legion's Rome Post No. 1. Not long afterward I became department chaplain for Italy, starting a term of office that lasted more than ten years. There were about 4000 Legionnaires in Italy at the time. They had gone to America around 1910, were taken up in the draft for World War I, and had finally returned to Italy where they were living in retirement on veterans' pensions. I found out quickly that very few spoke English. But I did discover that many of these oldtimers knew the songs of the World War I era in English and could sing them through without missing a word. At the first convention, in Taormina, I was sitting at the head table attired as an Italian priest usually is—in cassock—when one of them came up to me. He looked something like the old movie star Ben Turpin, and he said just two words: "You sing?" I told him Yes. Whereupon, he said: "Sing 'Tipperary.'" So we started off. We had not gone three bars before we were joined by a dozen others and, soon, from all over the banquet hall Legionnaires hurried over to add their voices to the group. After about twenty minutes the banquet manager, with his chef, worked his way through the crowd. "Please, Padre," he said. "Sing some other time. We want to get the dinner on the table."

No matter what the convention city was, Mass would be in the cathedral and lunch would be in the finest hotel. Everywhere we were treated with kindness and given the key to the city. On the island of Ischia, the mayor placed his beautiful yacht at our disposal, and about a dozen of us used it. On returning to the mainland, after the convention, we had to go through customs because we had arrived "from sea" on a private boat, rather than the regular ferry. With that—and because the convention meeting and the farewells had dragged on—we just missed the last evening train for Rome and had to sit on the hard benches of the Naples railroad station until the next train at three in the morning. A fellow Legionnaire from the Embassy summed up our situation neatly. "We left Ischia like millionaires," he said, "and we are arriving back in Rome like a bunch of bums."

The Legion convention was always a puzzle to the Italian pastors. "It is only Saturday," a pastor would say. "Why are all these men attending Mass? It is so difficult to get them to church on Sunday." The Legionnaires would go to confession, too. Some actually thought confession was part of the convention program. The Father Abbott at the Holy House of Loreto, after seeing the line of Legionnaires at confession, said the convention was a fine way to get the men to make their Easter duty.

On Memorial Day I would be at the service at the American military cemetery at Nettuno. Sometimes we had the three faiths represented by chaplains, but usually, as at American Club meetings, the Protestant minister from St. Paul's and I would alternate in giving the invocation and the final benediction. I said a prayer or two in English, but knowing that the Legionnaires could not respond in English I would say the *Our Father, Hail Mary* and several of the invocations in Latin. It was always a source of gratification to me—and of profound interest to the Americans present—to hear the Legionnaries and their families say with me in loud, ringing voices the Catholic prayers for their fallen comrades of all religious beliefs who were in the 8000 graves not far from the Anzio beach.

The Legion conventions were always fun for all concerned, but the spiritual welfare of the Legionnaires was always provided for. The attention the men gave to their spiritual life at these affairs was always a source of great satisfaction to me.

Chapter 11

FATHERS OF THE COUNCIL

As soon as I read the letter which arrived one morning late in the Roman summer of 1960, I knew that I was in for rough times ahead.

The letter was dated "The Vatican, 31 August 1960." In the upper left-hand corner, in a bright red, was the Papal coat of arms and the words: "Secretary of State of His Holiness." It was written on an off-white folio of outsized paper that was watermarked with the familiar crossed keys and tiara of the successors of St. Peter. With elaborate elegance the text was spread across the first page. The three other pages were blank. The message was written in Italian and signed by Domenico Cardinal Tardini. It said:

"The Holiness of Our Lord is benignly pleased to enumerate among the members of the Secretariat for the Union of Christians, for the preparation of Ecumenical Council Vatican II, the Most Reverend Padre Giacomo Cunningham of the Missionary Priests of St. Paul the Apostle."

Except for another, two-line paragraph containing formal greetings, that is all the letter said.

That was enough. I was faced with a grave decision. As pastor of Santa Susanna's, I was working on a job that occupied me seven days a week, with duties that took me to three continents—not to mention the countless special chores which devolved on me from my pastoral work. Through the years I had worked hard to build up my unique apostolate. Was I now to put aside, or assign to a very low priority, the various obligations and activities which had become part of my life as an American pastor in Rome? I knew the Papal appointment to help prepare for the Council was an honor given to no other American pastor. I also was aware that it was not merely an honorary appointment. The coming of the members of the American hierarchy for the Council would mean extra responsibilities and longer days for all of us at Santa Susanna's. Many of them would be saying their daily Mass in our church, and in one way or another we would be in contact with all of them throughout the Council. Now, in addition to getting my church ready to accommodate the leading churchmen from my own country, I was being asked by the Pope to take an active part in the preparations for the Council itself. Even then I knew I should not have accepted. But you do not refuse a Papal appointment.

I had been in Rome on the Feast of the Conversion of St. Paul the previous year when Pope John, on a visit to the Basilica of St. Paul outside-the-Walls, had dropped his "atomic blockbuster" by telling the Cardinals present of his plan to summon a General Council of the Church—the first in almost a century. The Holy Father was reported saying a few days later that these friends of his at his side—the Cardinals from the Curia—had not been at all enthusiastic when he threw out this thought about calling a Council. I could understand the point of view of such Cardinals as Tisserant, Micara, Masella, Pizzardo, and Cicognani. They were all in their seventies or eighties, and they were the men who—with the clergy of Rome—would have to prepare for this General Council.

Even before my appointment to the Christian Unity secretariat, I had been given a taste of pre-Council activity. Not long after Pope John's announcement, I was assigned to a subcommission which had to deal with motion pictures, television, and the press. I figured I had been put on it because of the association of the Paulist Fathers with the press.

Then, in an unexpected way, I was brought a step closer to the coming Council. During the time I was on this motion-picture subcommission a young Paulist priest from Milwaukee, Father Thomas Stransky, joined us at Santa Susanna's. He had been studying in Germany in the field of missiology. Now he had come to Rome to finish up his work at the Gregorian University and to write a thesis for a doctorate. A few months after he entered the Gregorian University, Father Stransky put on a mission exhibit which caught the eye of many of the Romans. When Father Stransky and I, in the preliminary stage, had discussed plans for the exhibit, it was decided that, as long as we were going to do it, we would do it as well as we could and call on the Paulist Press in New York to furnish a rather large assortment of publications. The exhibit depicted, in a graphic, interesting way, the far-ranging missionary work of the Paulist Fathers and was a great success. Shortly after this, Monsignor John Willebrands, the Secretary of the Christian Unity secretariat, said that its president, Archbishop (later Cardinal) Augustine Bea, would like to have Father Stransky on the staff. Could this be arranged? he asked me. I wrote to our Superior General in New York, Father William Michell, and told him this was not just Monsignor Willebrands who was asking, nor even Archbishop Bea. It was the Holy Father himself—and we had no choice in the matter!

With that, Father Stransky was released from studies for his doctorate, on which he had worked several years —and which he has not received—and was assigned to the secretariat. As a member of our community at Santa Susanna's, he had helped us with confessions, daily masses, and the manifold activities of the church, although his primary commitment had been his studies for the doctorate. Now his primary commitment was transferred to the secretariat, and it would have complete control over his activities, even though he would continue to be "one of us." Father Stransky indeed still gave us considerable help because he is a congenial and most cooperative young man. But his services were limited, and we recognized that we no longer had control over his comings and goings. If there was some urgent draft to be prepared at the secretariat, for instance—and he was assigned for the five-o'clock confessions—one of the others of us would have to take over the confessional.

It was after Father Stransky had been placed on the staff of the Christian Unity secretariat that Pope John appointed me to the secretariat as a member of the subcommission on motion pictures, television, and the press. I was the lowest ranking of all the members. There were Bishops and *Monsignori* among them, and professors and specialists in many fields—and men who later became Cardinals!—but none of them was a full-time pastor like myself.

The activity of the secretariat for the Union of Christians was much different, far more important, and infinitely more involved than that of the motion-picture subcommission. Instead of the few casual meetings of the past, my attendance was now required at frequent lengthy ones, with several of them lasting a week at a time. Our meetings were in Latin, French, and German. I could understand Latin and French. *Speaking* Latin was something else. My ability to speak Latin had long since disappeared. Should I take time out—two or three months, at least—to brush up on my Latin so that I could speak it again with the facility I once had? That was out of the question. There were just not enough hours in the day.

In one year I was away from Santa Susanna's on secretariat work for a total of approximately seven weeks. But it was not only meetings that took the time. Papers had to be prepared in advance of a meeting, and the subjects on the agenda had to be studied. During one week of discussions I had to prepare three papers—and in preparing papers for the finest minds in the Church you just don't "throw something together!" Furthermore, the matters examined at our meetings often were in the field of theory and planning, whereas my specialty is administration and the application of theories. My priestly experience has always been on the practical side—in the administrative or parochial life of the Church. (Cardinal Bea himself once said to me: "You are primarily a missionary, is that not so?" And he said that after I had talked at one meeting—probably too loudly, but clearly and distinctly, as one would talk to a congregation in church.)

From Cardinal Bea on down, all the members of the secretariat were, without exception, the most intelligent, learned, and, each in his own field, provocative of all the people I have ever known. I have never known a man like Cardinal Bea: humble and simple, but a giant in intellect; a strict logician, and facile in several languages. I could understand fully why Pope John chose him for the very delicate task of Christian unity. The basis of unity had to be Holy Scripture and this German Jesuit was one of our greatest Biblical scholars. He had had the confidence of Pius XII as well as John XXIII. But the clinching point, it seemed to me as I sat there and watched this program develop, was that he was a German—a man of piety, intellect, affability, and drive. Anyone who has ever lived in Europe realizes that if you have a tough job—and want it done—give it to a German!

We secretariat members were assisted by more than a dozen consultors: all men of talent and outstanding priests in the field of ecumenism. It was a multi-lingual group. Father Jerome Hamer, the French Dominican, charmed us with his beautiful Latin, French, and English. Monsignor Willebrands, who spoke several languages fluently, would interpret at meetings in case there was difficulty of communication. I suppose the one Bishop who impressed me most of all with his intellect and ability to communicate his ideas was Bishop Emile Joseph Marie De Smedt of Bruges. He speaks English fluently, but in any language it would be difficult to misunderstand him. Only once before had I been able to say that I did not know a word spoken, but completely understood everything. That had been in listening to a talk by Father Riccardo Lombardi, the Jesuit founder of the Better World Movement. Bishop De Smedt I could understand —not only his words but his ideas as well.

No more than a few Americans—and here I exclude myself—could hold their own in a Latin discussion at the beginning of the Council. Time and again it was evident to me, during the meetings of the secretariat, that priests who are taught abroad, and who learn their theology in French or German seminaries, are much better trained than those whose education has been limited to the United States. In my field of public relations in Rome, any one of these Europe-trained men would have been lost. In their field I was lost.

This goes back to seminary days. When I was a theology student, the Paulist seminary professors were outstanding examples of men of community life and were fine priests. But they were not professional teachers. I spent the last two summers of my seminary life at Johns Hopkins in Baltimore, studying history and psychology. In my last year of theology I was writing a thesis, doing my psychology studies, acting as procurator of the house, and getting ready for ordination. With Father Stransky, in this generation, it was different. He had talents and, under the direction of professional seminary teachers, was given every opportunity to develop them, with training at home and abroad. When the opportunity came to him, he was prepared to accept the responsibilities and today he is the foremost American expert in the ecumenical field.

I belong to another generation, whose basic training in philosophy and theology—possibly because of its own fault—is superficial. While this situation could have been corrected with later study, it never was. Today, therefore, I can say that my talents do not lie in that field. When the opportunity was presented to me to work as a member of the Council group, I did not have the talent, ability, knowledge of the field, or the linguistic capability either to understand the theoretical problems which the secretariat examined or to appreciate their value. A man working for his bread and butter finds that social theories leave him cold. A pastor working with everyday problems of people who are sick, sinful, and needy finds the theoretical theological discussions both boring and distasteful. I regret that I could not offer more than I did to the secretariat as a member. I do not regret that I did not fail in what I considered my primary responsibility, which was to those Americans (Catholic and non-Catholic) who looked to me for assistance—spiritual as well as temporal—as the American pastor in Rome.

My daily schedule, as the Council approached, kept getting more crowded all the time. At first the secretariat met in Rome. When it had become evident that the members were getting involved in many other things, it was decided to move the whole group to the Pious Society of St. Paul retreat house at Ariccia, a beautiful monastery in the Roman hills beyond Castel Gandolfo. In the spring and fall the scenery is magnificent there, but we had little time for scenery. Father Pierre Dumont, the Benedictine rector of the Greek-Catholic seminary, and I would leave Santa Susanna's together each morning for the fifty-minute ride to Ariccia. The day's meeting would start around nine-thirty and, except for a brief coffee break, go on until one. After lunch, subcommittees usually met (I was on the mixed-marriage subcommittee with Archbishop Lorenz Jaeger). If I had no subcommittee meeting scheduled for after lunch, I would take a forty-five minute siesta. The afternoon session would resume at four and continue until seven. After dinner I would head for Rome (unless an evening meeting was on the program) and arrive at Santa Susanna's sometime between 9 and 10 P.M. Between then and departure time the next morning, I took care of my local obligations.

The two secretaries at the church, Francesca Wagner and Anne Nealon, would have a list of messages waiting for me—a baptism, visitors in town, a marriage case, someone sick in the hospital. If any household problems had developed during my absence, my good friend Josephine would be after me: her mother was sick again—the fuses had blown out in the electric panel—the refrigerator was not working properly—she had had an argument with the *portiere!* These are the normal problems that always multiply at such times.

In addition to the day-to-day parish problems which cropped up, I was devoting a lot of my time to preparing our new rectory. We had been living in a three-bedroom apartment down the street from Santa Susanna's but, as our staff grew, it became too small. When Father Stransky arrived, there was no room for him and he had to move in at Maryknoll House. I wanted to have the community together, so I asked permission from our Superior General to get a larger place. For over a year I canvassed an area within a half mile of the church. You just cannot put five priests in a normal apartment, because the Roman apartments are built for families and not individuals. We needed something along the lines of a monastery, or a hotel, with running water, for example, in each room. It had to have sufficient bath facilities, too. You cannot have five priests trying to get into the one bathroom, at the same time in the morning, on the way to church.

Right across the street from the old place I finally
found what we wanted: two adjacent apartments in a
Condominium. I bought them, knocked out the walls, and
and rebuilt the whole thing to make a rectory of five
bedrooms, a chapel, a combined library and common
room, a maid's room, dining room, and kitchen. The one
outstanding feature of this combination was a very large
terrace. Since you can sit out in the open for seven
months a year in Rome, it was a valuable asset. Josephine
was very fond of her American-style kitchen which I had
installed, and when she was completely instructed in the
use of the new equipment she saw to it that all of it
was used. The weeks before the Council opened on October 11, 1962, were spent in getting the new rectory
ready. Just a matter of hours before the opening of the
Council we moved into our new home.

I still had the job, however, of finding a buyer for the
old apartment. In the year we had it up for sale about
300 people looked at it, and each invariably asked:
"What's going to happen to it?" The apartment was in a
building that would be torn down if the street was
widened, as proposed. But the Fine Arts Commission had
been blocking the plan because it would involve moving the *Moses* statue that was on the corner diagonally
across from Santa Susanna's. "I really don't know what's
going to happen," I would say to prospective buyers. "My
lawyer tells me nothing will be done for twenty-five
years, but I don't know. All I know is that the street-
widening project has been on the books for a good thirty
years—from the early days of Mussolini."

But it was, always, No Sale.

During the regular six-thirty Community Meditation in
church one morning, I thought of the late Mother Beatrice, a saintly woman who had been prioress of our
Cistercian convent. If I needed help at any time, I used
to say to her: "I need some prayers today, Mother." Her

prayers were always effective. This particular morning, about six months after her death, I said to myself: I have tried all angles to sell this apartment, and nothing has worked. Why not ask Mother Beatrice for help? I had done favors for her—and she had done favors for me—when she was alive. Since she was Up There now, maybe she would do another one for me.

Late that afternoon into the church office walked Andrea Marsano, an Italian shipping magnate, who had been born in New York harbor on a ship of which his father was a captain. Mr. Marsano had arrived at the Grand Hotel from Genoa the night before and in walking around the corner in the morning had seen our *For Sale* sign. He offered to buy the apartment, and we settled on a price of 16 million lire, or $25,600.

The tax structure of the Italian government starts out on the basic principle that everyone is dishonest. The tax collector assumes you made twice as much money as you declared, and Italians know they will be asked to pay half again as much tax as called for on their declaration. I saw an example of this mentality when Mr. Marsano and I appeared before a notary, with our lawyers, to close the sale. It was suggested that the sales price of 16 million lire be split into two contracts with the higher one of ten million serving as the public contract on which taxes would be paid. If we had only one contract for the actual purchase price of 16 million lire, we were told, no one would believe that—to escape taxes—there was not also another private agreement covering an additional sum. Mr. Marsano looked at the lawyers and at me and said: "We are all witnesses to this sale. We are all men of integrity. And I have a check for this amount in my hand. If necessary, we can all sign affidavits to this effect." We closed the sale and had only the one contract for the full purchase price of 16 million lire—but we may have repercussions yet!

I was happy that our new rectory was ready for the start of the Council. In the church, too, I had been busy making preparations for the arrival of the Council Fathers. For one thing, I completed our long-range restoration program by doing over the Madonna Chapel —but not without problems, naturally. A new painting of a Madonna, replacing one that had faded on the wall, pleased no one. Jefferson Caffery, former American Ambassador to France, attended Mass daily and said that he just had to turn his head away when he passed that painting. The angels surrounding the Madonna were too muscular, and one had six toes. Where people are not accustomed to fine art, it could have passed. I personally would not have done anything about it since it was a reasonably good painting. But "reasonably good" is not good enough in Rome. So, since green is a good liturgical color, I covered over the objectionable work of art by draping the wall with green damask and putting another painting in the center.

With the Council in mind, I had a new marble altar installed in the chapel and replaced the two wooden side altars with marble ones. When the Fine Arts Commission representative arrived to inspect the restoration work, he noticed the side altars. "What are these?" he asked in surprise.

"They are provisional altars for the priests and Bishops who will be saying Mass during the Council," I said.

"*Provisional*—in marble?"

By now I had been in Rome a long time. I gave him the Roman answer that is appropriate on such occasions. I shrugged my shoulders and said: "Buh!"

To make sure we could take care of the Council Fathers, I had extra portable-type altars made and set them up around the church. (We had twelve altars at the start and added six more during the second session of the Council.) Three of these extra altars I placed in the corridor between the sacristy and convent. This created a problem because of the cloister. No one is permitted to enter the cloister, even the clergy, without special permission. The request for permission traveled from the Mother Abbess to the Father Abbott of the Cistercian Order and then to the Vicariate of Rome. Because of the Council, the Cardinal-Vicar granted permission.

For these extra altars we needed an equal number of sets of vestments, chalices, missals, candlesticks, crucifixes, and altar cards. Hosts, candles, and wine had to be provided. Far ahead of time I discussed all our church needs for the Council with the Mother Abbess. Purificators, amices, and finger towels were made by the nuns during the six months before the Council began. Arrangements were worked out to change the personal altar linens of our visitors weekly. (In the first month of the Council our Sisters laundered almost 400 purificators!) We realized that at each altar special attention would be required to make sure that the alb worn by someone the size of Bishop John F. Hackett of Hartford, who is five-foot-eight and 150 pounds (maybe less), would not be the same one prepared for a person of the stature of Bishop Ernest L. Unterkoefler, now of Charleston, who at 250 or 260 pounds is one of the largest members of the American hierarchy. The ordinary church does not have sufficient vestments to outfit as many altars as we had. But Santa Susanna's is not an ordinary church! Even the matter of providing a sufficient number of altar boys presented quite a problem. Men from the Embassy, such as Major General N. A. Costello, the head of the U. S. Military Assistance Advisory Group—tall, slim, and who looked like a general!—volunteered to supplement our few altar boys. When the Council got underway, we were prepared in every respect.

On the night before the Council opened, the midnight Mass of the Holy Spirit was celebrated at the main altar by our Titular, Cardinal Cushing, while eleven other Bishops were saying Mass at the same time at other altars. The church was jammed. NBC-TV was filming the Cardinal's Mass on video tape, which was to be shown later in the United States. Because of the lateness of the hour, and the fact that not only the Bishops but many of the people present had a heavy day ahead of them, I asked His Eminence not to speak. He had finished the Mass without giving a sermon and was almost out of the sanctuary when he looked up and saw the large number of people in the church. With that he went back to the center of the altar. "I promised Father Cunningham," he said, "that I would not speak. But I feel I should say a few words." By actual count these "few words" extended to fifty-four minutes. All this time Bishop Charles Mulrooney of Brooklyn, with his vestments on, patiently waited in the sacristy for his turn to say Mass after the Cardinal!

One week later nine Cardinals and 300 Bishops were present in Santa Susanna's for the funeral of Bishop Joseph A. Burke of Buffalo, the first of the Council Fathers to die.

The arrival of the Council Fathers worked a complete change in our house schedule and in my way of living. My day began about an hour earlier in the morning and ended an hour later at night. Before the Council I used to open the church and say the six o'clock Mass each morning. That was now changed. At least two of the Council Fathers would arrive to celebrate Mass at ten minutes to six. This meant that I would say Mass after opening the church at five forty-five. I could set my watch by Bishop Ralph Hayes of Davenport (known as the "noblest Roman of them all," because he had been rector of North American College for almost a decade, starting in 1935). Each morning at six-thirty Bishop Hayes was at the altar for Mass. Archbishop (later Cardinal) Lawrence J. Shehan, with whom I in the past had had special dealings on Newman Club work in Baltimore, was a great help by saying the seven o'clock Mass at the main altar each morning. This made it possible for the other Paulists and myself to be available for confessions and for directing traffic during the early-morning hours. Mrs. Elizabeth Tine, after watching a very busy morning when more than sixty-five priests and Bishops said Mass, remarked that I had missed my vocation—I should have been a traffic cop. "At least," I replied, "I'd have a day off once a week."

The time I went to breakfast each day would depend on how busy we were at the church. (In pre-Council days it was usually around seven-fifteen.) I would stop on the way from church to pick up the rolls and hot pastry for breakfast so that Josephine would not have to make a trip downstairs to get them. We ate the continental-type breakfast at the rectory, rather than the American kind. For me this generally meant some fruit and a cup of coffee. A few ulcers which had developed *before* the Council prevented me from having my favorite Italian breakfast: the doughnut-like *ciambelle*.

American and other English-speaking Bishops came to confession at Santa Susanna's because we were there and available. If I was busy talking to someone in the office when a Bishop arrived, he would stand in the doorway and point to the back office. That was the signal he wanted to go to confession. After the first session of the Council, Archbishop Paul J. Hallinan of Atlanta made a different kind of confession. He came into the office to say he was returning a hat of mine which he had picked up by mistake after coming to confession some weeks earlier.

Many of the Council Fathers were old friends. Bishop Christopher J. Weldon of Springfield (Massachusetts) and I had been Navy chaplains together. Bishop Unterkoefler, as a student at Catholic University, had worked in our Paulist seminary in Washington. Bishop John J. Russell of Richmond, whom I knew from Catholic University, had given a most gracious review of the book which I had written on the life of Christ some years before. High among my memories of very happy Council evenings in Rome are two or three I spent with my seminary class-mate, Bishop Mulrooney of Brooklyn, and with Bishop John J. Boardman, another Brooklynite. Bishop Board-man, in celebrating his birthday at a dinner in the Berar Dino restaurant one night, reviewed some of his early days as a priest and his subsequent experiences as head of the Propagation of the Faith in the diocese of Brooklyn. He was like the father of a family, teaching the younger members of his household those qualities—such as the love of one's flock—which are characteristic of an apostolic priest.

I have always felt a little embarrassed with regard to Bishop Andrew Grutka of Gary, for I took advantage of his kindness and prevailed upon him to speak to the American Club at the time of the steel strike. Bishop Grutka gave a magnificent talk. He was a Bishop who had begun as a steelworker. In his twenties he had to decide whether he should try to become a foreman in the steel mills or a "spiritual" foreman. At our American Club lunch Bishop Grutka said ninety per cent of the people of his diocese did not want a strike. The statement was picked up by the Associated Press and caused consider-able unpleasantness for the Bishop when he got back to his home in the steel town of Gary. Union officials snubbed him, I understand, and he was not invited to the banquet celebrating the settlement of the strike. But David Mc-Donald, president of the steelworkers' union, insisted on his presence. At the banquet Bishop Grutka read the prayer which the diocese had been saying—and which he himself had prepared—petitioning God for the successful conclusion of the strike. As the Bishop sat down after the prayer, the steelworkers' president turned to him and said it was not ninety—but ninety-nine—per cent of the people who had been against a strike.

Our parishioners had a ringside seat at the Council. We were able to obtain tickets for them—and for visitors as well—to attend the public functions. They had the feeling of not only living in a Golden Age of Church reform but also being a very vital part of it. Many parishioners came day after day for the early-morning Masses of the Bishops. Two parishioners one busy morning called to my attention that Bishop John J. Carberry of Lafayette, Indiana (now of Columbus, Ohio), was serving the Mass of Bishop Weldon. It was a wonderful example, they said, to see a Bishop kneeling on the cold marble floor to serve another. Special preachers, closely associated with the Council, occupied our pulpit on Sundays. Cardinal Cushing himself spoke several times.

The Cardinal did not remain in Rome throughout the Council. He asked permission from Pope John to go home and gave as a reason that he did not understand what was going on and was needed back in Boston to raise funds for charity. His Holiness saw in Cardinal Cushing a kindred spirit. Both men were truly pastors. Both loved people and had a deep-seated and abiding affection for the Church and the *people of God*. They could communicate without words. Cardinal Cushing was not a well man; yet there is no evidence of any kind that he has ever complained. Pope John said to him: "Certainly you may go home. We recognize you as a modern St. Charles Borromeo." John saw deeply—and he saw more profoundly than those who stood about and heard the remark. I have often thought what a wonderful reunion there will be when Angelo Roncalli and Richard Cushing, stalwart heroes of the Church and zealous apostles, meet in the Kingdom of God.

Since I was not a Bishop—or a *peritus*, a designated expert—I, of course, could not attend actual meetings of the Council itself. (Cardinal Bea called me a "private" *peritus*.) Nor did I wish to accept Council attendance as a daily burden. One American Bishop offered to appoint me as his *peritus*, but I regretfully declined. For one thing, I did not wish to embarrass the organization of which I was a member. Also, in all honesty, I had to say I just could not absent myself from Santa Susanna's for the several months which each session lasted.

There were other sides to my Council activity.

A month or so before the Council started, my old friend Irving R. Levine of NBC said he would need a regular source of advice and technical aid for reporting on it. I told Irving I myself could not be of much help because of the complicated life I was leading, but I said I had a brilliant young doctor of philosophy coming within a few days after a half-dozen years of teaching in Washington. I was referring to Father Robert O'Donnell, who had studied at Louvain University in Belgium. Father O'Donnell relates that he had scarcely put his suitcase on the floor than he was told: "Tomorrow you will have lunch with Vice-President Johnson (whom he had never seen in all his years in Washington), and this afternoon Irving Levine will call you. You are to work with him and help wherever you can in NBC's coverage of the Council."

Irving Levine and Father O'Donnell made a great team. I had a special telephone installed in the back office so that even when Father O'Donnell was on duty at the church it would be possible for him to keep in contact with NBC. It is hard to get new phones installed in Rome. To simplify things I asked that the old rectory number be used for the new phone. I thought this would speed things up. Our old number was 48-45-97. The telephone company mistook my way of writing "7" for "1" because I did not put a bar through it in the European manner. The new phone was installed within twenty-four hours, as I hoped, but my effort at being helpful was a waste of time. It had the old rectory number—except for the last numeral. It was 1 instead of 7.

Rarely did a day pass at the Council but some reporter was calling me up to check on a story or to ask for specific information. Sometimes they had important doctrinal questions. Other times it was something which, for a priest, was simple but to a non-Catholic journalist could be confusing. The late Milton Bracker of the New York *Times* telephoned one afternoon. "Father," he said, "I am embarrassed to ask you this question, but since I must file my story accurately I hope you don't mind." I assured him I would be glad to answer any question I could. Earlier that afternoon Mr. Bracker had heard two English-speaking Bishops speak. One had begun his talk by invoking the Father, the Son, and the Holy Ghost; the other—the Father, the Son, and the *Holy Spirit*. Mr. Bracker wished to know the distinction between the two terms used for the third person of the Trinity. I answered him that both meant the same thing. The apparent difference, possibly, was between a conservative Bishop and a progressive one. The conservative Bishop, like all of us, had learned his prayers with the words *Holy Ghost* and was not changing to the term *Holy Spirit*, which had found its way into our prayer life a few years ago.

One of my favorite reporters was Ben Bolton of the Associated Press. He had no hesitation in calling up to verify points in the story he was writing. Jack Casserly, a very good friend, was busy covering for ABC. At other times I had considered Paul Blanshard as violently anti-Catholic in his writings, but when he was in Rome for the Council I found him gracious and personable. I made him at home in our library and arranged for him to see some of the individuals in whom he was especially interested.

Among the authors with whom I had more than a passing acquaintance was Alden Hatch. I met him first at one of our Embassy receptions and was amazed at the courage of this man who was so seriously crippled that he was never removed from his crutches. Yet, in addition to being an indefatigable worker, he has a sparkling wit and a sharp mind. It was a pleasure to be associated with him and to realize how men are not overcome by serious physical handicaps but, because of their indomitable courage and innate ability, can hold their own with the best in the field. His biography of Pope John, *A Man Named John,* has been the most popular book so far written about that beloved pontiff.

Another author, Morris West, came to Rome from New South Wales to get the feeling of the Eternal City once again and to overcome what he said were roadblocks in a new book. We talked at length about these, and his penetrating questions so held one to the point that there was no wandering. I was able, in several ways, to help him, but when he started to question me on speculative theology I had to admit my knowledge was practically non-existent. However, an education does not mean you have to know everything. It means, rather, that you know where to look for information you do not have yourself— and I knew two very intelligent young priests with whom he could profitably engage in conversation. One was our own Father Stransky, and the other was Father Francis X. Murphy. We had lunch at the Flora Hotel—the four of us. It began around one. I left at two-thirty. But the others did not finish until about five. Mr. West wrote me later that after the luncheon he went to his typewriter and typed for several hours. The get-together had cleared away most of his "roadblocks." The book resulting from this visit was *The Shoes of the Fisherman,* a national best-seller.

One question—asked *confidentially*—was: "Is Father Murphy really Xavier Rynne?" That was a question discussed in most clerical circles as soon as this mysterious

"Xavier Rynne" appeared on the best-seller list. The thesis was: If it looks like a duck, walks like a duck, quacks like a duck—it *is* a duck. Our Roman literary detectives said it is his style, he has used the same phrases in other writings, it is his method of presentation, and it shows the same scholarly research you will find if you listen to his lectures in the *Alfonsianum*. My reply could only be: "I agree with all you say. But, when I point-blank asked Father Murphy if he was the author of *Letters from Vatican City*, he told me No."

The fifth room in our new rectory during the Council was used by Father John Sheerin, editor of the Paulist Fathers' *Catholic World* Magazine. He came over for the first session, as I recall, to spend only a couple of weeks so that he could see how the Council went. After he had been in Rome a few days I spoke to Monsignor Tucek, the head of the NCWC news bureau, who was helping Council officials. I asked if Father Sheerin could be of any assistance—particularly during these difficult days for journalists. In no time at all, Monsignor Tucek had Father Sheerin on the press panel which briefed journalists.

At mealtime in the rectory, when only the five of us Paulists were present, our unique family relationship was emphasized. This was best represented by a casual comment made by Father Stransky at the dinner table one evening. Father Sheerin mentioned conversationally that in acting as procurator that day for an American Bishop who could not be present at the Council meeting he had signed Conciliar documents. "I helped write them," Father Stransky remarked. Thus, when a Council matter was being discussed among ourselves, we reacted in five different ways: Father Stransky—making sure nothing would slip by his lips that would involve his oath of secrecy; Father Sheerin—looking at it from a standpoint of information to the world at large; Father O'Donnell—

wondering if there was something here which would give Irving Levine a special *scoop;* Father Paul Maloney—storing up material to be released in Santa Susanna's *Sunday Bulletin;* and myself—considering how our parishioners would be affected.

From the start there was a rapport between a number of the non-Catholic observers and the Paulist Fathers through Father Stransky. It was not at all unusual to find one or two observers at the rectory with Father Stransky when I returned from Santa Susanna's in the evening around seven-thirty. They would sit in the community room, talking over together the events of the day or coming projects. The observers became good friends, not only of the Paulist Fathers but of the other priests and Bishops who would drop in during the evening for a visit. But toward the end of the first session it became apparent that some of our Bishops would be returning home without having met the American non-Catholic churchmen who had been invited by Pope John to attend the Council as observers. The observers sat in a place of honor in St. Peter's, occupying a major tribune close to the Holy Father. But apart from the constant contact they had with Father Stransky, Father John Long, S.J., and the late Father Gus Weigel, S.J., the Americans in the group of several dozen observers were, as one of my non-Catholic friends put it, "really separated brethren."

One night at supper I discussed this matter with Father Stransky and asked whether it would not be possible for us to put on a reception at the Grand Hotel for the American Bishops and observers. Within a day the Christian Unity secretariat decided that this could be done, and I made arrangements for the first meeting. I went to Cardinal Shehan—at the time an Archbishop—and asked him if he would give the lead-off talk. He protested, but I said: "You are in ecumenical work, you are gentle and gracious, you are familiar with the problems of our separated brethren—and I do not know how this meeting is going to turn out." I owe him a great debt that the gathering was so successful, because, with his opening words—rendered with such tact and grace—there was no longer concern about the outcome of this important meeting.

It was to be two hours. The first hour, I decided, would be for formal speechmaking and a question-and-answer period. In the second hour the ladies of our guild and their husbands would act as hosts at an informal reception. Except for Jim O'Neill, representing the American Catholic press, I excluded all other correspondents—almost. I had not as yet met Sanche de Gramont, who had replaced Barrett McGurn as the New York *Herald-Tribune* correspondent in Rome. When Sanche appeared at the doorway, I asked: "Are you an observer?" Before Sanche could reply, a Bishop passing behind me said: "He certainly is an *observer*"—and I invited him in. I thought nothing more about it until the next day when I was surprised to see Sanche's article about the meeting in the *Herald-Tribune*. Only then did I realize that the good Bishop had the laugh on me.

I opened the meeting by introducing Father Stransky on behalf of the Paulist Fathers and Santa Susanna's (the Bishops called this "the commercial"). He in turn presented Archbishop Shehan. After the Archbishop's talk, Father Stransky called upon Dr. Douglas Horton, the former dean of Harvard University's Divinity School, who acted as leader of the observers and introduced them. The Bishops then proceeded to ask questions of Dr. Horton, and he would pass them on to the observer who had a special interest in the particular field. As we were concluding the formal part of the meeting, Bishop Frank Reh (now rector of North American College) asked if we could not end with prayer—and Dean Horton led the whole group in the *Lord's Prayer*.

I had every hope that the meeting would work out well, but it surpassed my hopes. As one Bishop said, it was the first time in history that over 100 American Catholic Bishops and experts in Church matters had been lectured to by Protestants—and liked it! At the reception which followed, many Bishops got acquainted with observers from their own cities or states whom they had never met before. The reception, instead of ending at seven as I had anticipated, was not over till nine o'clock. I found that this opportunity for the Bishops and observers to engage in friendly chitchat was probably the most valuable part of the meeting. Robert McAfee Brown, professor of religion at Stanford University, met many of our Bishops at this reception (and at the second one I arranged in 1963). When he subsequently wrote a series of articles in *Look* on "Protestant Expectations of the Council," the Bishops and *periti* reading them were impressed not only by the views he expressed but because they knew him. To them, Dr. Brown was not an impersonal observer, but a personable and knowledgeable minister of the Gospel whom they had met, and with whom they had had friendly conversation, at the Bishops-and-observers meetings.

These public meetings also led to private ones. Thus, men of good will and sincerity on both sides were able to sit down and talk, not only as members of the Council but as American clergymen who had a profound interest in the future and the hopes of their country and its fundamental religious beliefs.

Some Bishops, too, discovered for the first time—and were able to evaluate—the sincerity of the observers and the absolute certainty these non-Catholics had of the truth of their religious convictions.

Chapter 12

THE YEAR IT SNOWED

The year 1963 started out exactly like any other.

Early on the morning of January 6, with several bottles of wine in my arms, I walked out into the middle of Piazza San Bernardo, where the *vigile* was directing traffic in front of Santa Susanna's. As the policeman gave me an extra special smile, I placed the bottles among the gifts which grateful Romans were already piling up around his traffic stand in return for favors received in the past year. Gift-giving traditionally takes place also at Easter and the August holidays, but the Feast of the Epiphany is the main time. In the Mass for that day the words of the epistle beseech: "Lift up your eyes roundabout, and see; all these are gathered together—they are come to you." If a scriptural text was needed to describe Epiphany in Rome, that would be it. The postman, the street-cleaner, the telegram deliveryman, the *portiere* at the building where we have our rectory, the garage attendant who keeps our car clean and available for instant use—these and others were on our gift list, as usual. There were about fifty people altogether. You don't have to look for them. They find you.

In bringing my gift out to the *vigile*, I reflected, as I always did on such occasions, how typical this custom was of the characteristics of the Italian people and their sensibility to obligations—if you do a person a favor, it must be returned. It is done with a graciousness all its own; there is none of the crass commercialism that is evident with tips and gifts in other areas of the world.

We owed a lot to the policemen on the corner. They were always unfailingly courteous. Once, on the way back to Santa Susanna's from the Quirinale, my car broke down. A *vigile* took off his white gloves, lifted the hood, and in three minutes had the car running again. The *portiere* from the apartment house across the street from the Belgian College came rushing over with a towel in his hand for the policeman. In the doorway, meanwhile, was the wife of the *portiere*, making signs to say she had a basin of water. It is said that in Italy everyone gets in the act—and sometimes you are overwhelmed by the kindness of the actors.

Nor did I forget Epiphany gifts for the doormen and messengers at the Vatican congregations. I saw to it also that the Swiss Guard received a case of wine as a gesture of good will from Santa Susanna's to the defenders of the Pontiff. Four or five men in the "audience office" at the Vatican were always helpful. Since they were providing invitations for our American people—and since our American people in turn were generous to us—I had something for them.

On my regular visiting day before Epiphany I distributed my Christmas gifts at the Vatican bank. If I had to deal with the people these fine young tellers face, hour after hour, all year long, I should have been an out-and-out anti-cleric by now. Yet they never showed impatience, nor were they ever resentful, despite much provocation. By 1963, Vatican bank tellers had already begun to advise the nuns among their clients to make out their deposit slips ahead of time. It had not always been that way. I recalled how, in my early years as pastor, I would have finally worked my way up toward the front of the line on more than one occasion when a nun, holding a single check in her hand, would suddenly appear. She first would look over those in the line to decide which one was the softest touch. Then, addressing me, she would say:

"May I present this check, Padre?" Not wishing to bring the wrath of the good nun down on me I'd say: "Why certainly, Madre." Then, when she would get to the teller's window, she would—without any warning—reach into the cavernous folds of her habit and retrieve all kinds of checks, coins, and bills. The teller would then have to list the various items, doing the work she should have done at home—as I had done the night before. The teller would know—the nun would know—and I would know that she had "conned" me into giving up my place!

The beggars—"our customers," as we called them—came by for their regular Epiphany gifts that year, too. On such festive days they always expected twice as much as their normal weekly allocation because, as one once solemnly told me, of the "greater graces" we would receive.

Various friends I knew from past experience would send us funds throughout the coming year, enabling us to continue to share our own blessings with the people who "made the machinery go." Regular benefactors had been such people as Barney Wiegard, a New York broker, and Charlie Gallagher, a retired oil man and an old friend from Westwood Village days—in fact, my book about the life of Christ is dedicated to him and to his wife, "Buster." I could always count on running into kind people. One time, after a Roman doctor removed a small growth from my eyelid, I asked him what the fee was. He assured me he would send a bill. But he didn't. So at Christmastime I sent around to him a case of nice wine. He wrote me a friendly thank-you note in which he said: "It's much better not to send a bill—see?"

In the week or two before Epiphany a large number of Mass offerings had arrived from people in the States. Such requests to say Mass for a person's intention were particularly numerous during the Christmas season, but they arrived the year round and we at Santa Susanna's could not possibly take care of all of them. Some I would turn over to the Roman Vicariate for distribution to old and retired priests; others would go to Don Giovanni Brazzani, the chaplain at the Rome railroad station, who would pass them along by an engineer or train conductor to priest friends in Yugoslavia, who were desperately in need; others would be for the rural, rugged Abruzzi area, where priests find living difficult—and a Mass offering when it comes (which is rare) is forty cents.

It would seem strange, but even in places like St. Peter's Basilica, these Mass offerings were welcomed. For instance, Don Angelo Del Savio, the vice-rector of the parochial office (and a person who did a dozen favors a day for people), was frequently in need of assistance for himself, and for others working with him, through these intentions. In this manner the wishes of our American people, who wanted to have Masses said, were complied with. Their offerings helped priests in real need. They also enabled the Vicariate priests and those working in the Roman offices to assist us in carrying out our obligations, while at the same time providing for them a source of personal support and assistance in their priestly activities.

It had been a particularly merry Christmas. At the conclusion of the first session of the Council, three weeks before Christmas, not a single American Bishop left Rome without leaving a considerable donation to Santa Susanna's. The average was well over $100. The initial expense of providing all the extra equipment at Santa Susanna's for the Council had been a bit heavy on our budget, as no particular fund had been set up for it. But the investment was repaid a hundred times over. There was an unexpected Christmas bonus, too, in the form of drugs, toilet articles, cigarettes, and clothing which the Bishops left behind rather than take back to the States with them. Bishop Jeremiah Minihan of Boston left his *greca*—a long shoulder-to-ankles double-breasted coat worn by Roman clergymen (I used it until my departure from Rome and then passed it on to one of the other Fathers). The Bishop also donated several unused sets of underwear sent by his sister. Three priests who lived in colder apartments—or were less robust and vigorous than Bishop Minihan—found this gift a great charity.

They were probably very glad to have that warm underwear on January 31. That night Rome had its first real snowfall in seven years. Several inches of snow blanketed St. Peter's piazza, the Roman Forum, and the Seven Hills of the Eternal City in a strange, spectacular way. As if to demonstrate that it was not all some kind of a mirage, snow fell again the following day. The Rome *Daily American*—our consistent and ever-faithful ally during my years in Rome—reported that the two-day fall amounted to more snow than in any entire Roman winter since the war.

Right after that unusual snowfall, I, as Procurator General of the Paulist Fathers, joined the representatives of the other male religious communities in Rome for an official call upon the Holy Father. Candlemas Day, or the Feast of the Purification, as February 2 is known, is the one time in the year when such a call is mandatory. Like the others who gathered with me in the Apostolic Palace, I carried a profusely decorated candle about four feet long for presentation to His Holiness as a token of fealty and devotion. These candles were usually given to the poor churches of Rome, but under Pope John they became *Unity* candles and were sent to non-Catholic churches around the world. (Ours one year turned up in an Orthodox church in Beirut, and since Santa Susanna's name was on it, as customary, the recipient dropped us a note of thanks.) On three different occasions, when I was presenting the Candlemas Day candle to Pope John, he asked me why I did not invite him to Santa Susanna's.

The first two times I went back to the office and prepared a grandiose invitation, written in special Italian style. Nothing happened. I felt that I had done enough and that in his own good time Pope John would come. But he did not. On the third occasion—which turned out to be my last visit with him—he talked about Cardinal Cushing and again said: "Why don't you ever invite me to Santa Susanna's?"

"Your Holiness," I replied, "I have invited you twice, and you have never come."

He reached over and, tapping me on the hand, said: "My boy—invite me again."

He never did visit Santa Susanna's, but he did show his affection for Santa Susanna's in many ways. After one audience, in which he had given me some medals and a rosary, Pope John discovered that Felici, the Vatican photographer, had not taken a picture. Picking up another medal from Monsignor Mario Nasalli Rocca, the *maestro di camera*, His Holiness came over to me, and I knelt down again. Smiling, as he handed me the new medal—this time in front of the photographer—Pope John said: "I think you need another medal."

Just before the start of spring, one of the most impressive and memorable events during my years in Rome took place. The previous January Cardinal Spellman had been in Rome on Council business at the time of our annual St. Paul's Day dinner. It was being held at the Grand Hotel, where he was staying, and I had invited him to join us. Shortly before the dinner, the Cardinal called me from his room to say he had just gotten back from a meeting and would I come up to see him. Regretfully he said he could not be with us at dinner because he had to leave almost immediately for another meeting. His Eminence then told me he would be coming to Rome with a large group of pilgrims for the beatification of Mother Seton in March. In passing, His Eminence asked about the capacity of Santa Susanna's. But, limited as it is to some 400 people, Santa Susanna's obviously could not hope to contain the large numbers expected. So without further discussion the Cardinal said the triduum services would be held in his Titular Church of Sts. John and Paul, and he wished that I would explain this to Father Malcolm Lavelle, who was one of our guests in the ballroom downstairs. (Father Lavelle was Superior General of the Passionist Fathers who administer the Cardinal's church.) His Eminence then went on to say that he hoped I would give one of the sermons in the solemn triduum.

The beatification ceremony for this native New Yorker who had founded America's first religious community—and who herself was a convert and a widow!—was set for St. Patrick's Day, a Sunday. Cardinal Spellman led a flight of chartered planes carrying hundreds of Sisters of Charity to Rome for the beatification of their founder —the first native-born American to be beatified. In addition, 1200 civilians flew from the States. These were thrilling days. His Eminence said Mass at Santa Susanna's as soon as the pilgrimage arrived in Rome, and from then on our church was filled with the visitors. Some of the nuns were old friends of the Paulists. (One was a sister of our Superior General, Father John Fitzgerald.) The Sunday afternoon beatification ceremony in St. Peter's was wonderful. When Pope John addressed the thronged Basilica to speak about Mother Seton, Cardinal Spellman sat on the dais, one step below His Holiness, and translated his Latin words into English. Joseph Cardinal Ritter, Archbishop of St. Louis, said the Pontifical Mass at the triduum service on Tuesday night, and it was then that I gave the sermon.

On entering the sacristy that evening, after I had paid my respects to Cardinal Ritter, I was asked by him how long I intended to talk, and whether I planned to preach my sermon or read it. I said it would run about fifteen minutes, and I would "preach it."

"I would prefer you to read it," the Cardinal replied. "Once you fellows start talking, one never knows how long you'll go."

I did not want to tell him that I had been a teacher of homiletics at North American College almost all the time I had been in Rome, and had always looked with considerable disfavor upon the *read* sermon. I felt the *read* speech had a place at certain times—an address at a university, for instance, or on a political occasion. But the idea of reading a sermon from the altar distressed me. However, I said: "As Your Eminence wishes." When I went to the pulpit later, I placed the four typed pages of the sermon on the lectern. I did not know how I would explain this to my students at the College. As I had said I would, I finished in fifteen minutes. In the sacristy afterward Cardinal Ritter said: "That was a well-read sermon."

Laughingly, I said: "Your Eminence, I could have given it blindfolded, word for word." I was not exaggerating. A sermon on an occasion like that is a rare opportunity, and I had prepared it as well as I could. In it I said that Mother Seton, who was born just seven days prior to the opening of the first Continental Congress, had "blazed a trail of holiness in the wilderness that was America, and proved to the world at large that sanctity of life can be an American product."

Cardinal Spellman had invited me to the banquet at the Grand that night after the services. As he passed by the table at which I was to sit, he said: "That was a very good sermon." I thanked him for the opportunity he had given me.

Then we sat down to one of the most unusual banquets the Grand Hotel has ever seen. Never had Rome itself seen such an outpouring of American nuns. They were there, 550 strong. Some were past seventy, and others even much older. The banquet had in it all the elements of pure joy and happiness. The prayers of Mother Seton's nuns for over fifty years had been answered with her beatification. Ninety per cent of the nuns at the banquet had never been abroad before. Now they were in Rome—the hope of all their desires and dreams. They had seen the Holy Father not once but several times, and the heart of all these activities was their founder. Here at the Grand, in the presence of their benefactor, Cardinal Spellman, they were relaxed and enjoying themselves like members of one big, happy family. A quartet of priests led them in singing "East Side, West Side" and a number of other songs we all knew from childhood. It was a warm, enthusiastic American gathering.

Easter was beautiful in Rome, and scores of thousands of people knelt in St. Peter's Square for the blessing of Pope John. Early in May, accompanied by Monsignor Andrew Landi, I left on a month's trip to the Far East. The trip developed unexpectedly one night at dinner with the James Murray family in Rome. Both Mr. and Mrs. Murray are championship-caliber golfers. As we ate, the conversation turned to golf in Japan where Mr. Murray has commercial activities and commitments, and he said to the Monsignor and myself: "Why don't you two come out and play golf in Japan as my guests?" It took me about three seconds to catch my breath. Then I gasped: "Why, of course. I'd be delighted to go." And the Monsignor and I went! The last few days in Japan, however, were a bit on the uneasy side due to the unhappy reports emanating from Rome about Pope John's declining health. Monsignor Landi and I made tentative arrangements to cut our trip short, if necessary, but we were able to stick to our schedule.

Pope John's death made Rome sad and quiet. As I wrote to my New York friends Walter and "Bunny" O'Connor (after I had knelt at his catafalque): "He was a great and good man, and we will miss him."

On June 10, eleven days before Cardinal Montini was elected as the successor to Good Pope John, I celebrated my thirty-third anniversary as a priest. Then, on July 1, the morning after Paul VI was crowned in St. Peter's Square, President Kennedy arrived in Rome.

Cardinal Cushing, who had come to Rome for the funeral of Pope John and the election of his successor, remained until President Kennedy concluded his visit. I accompanied His Eminence to the airport and in the waiting room asked if there was anything special he wanted done. "Yes," he said, "send a cable to Joe Kennedy at Hyannisport to say that the President was terrific, the reception was wonderful, and the impression on the Italian people tremendous." I gave this, and one or two other messages of the Cardinal, to Larry Lotito, a TWA official, who was standing by. His Eminence then spoke to me about sending him some relics for new churches in Boston and paintings of the new Pope for his seminary and home. When Larry Lotito reported back to me that the messages had been sent, I told the Cardinal: "Everything is taken care of." He smiled and said: "You should be in the movies."

Our new Pope had been trained by Pius and had been made a Cardinal by John. Yet those of us who followed his career knew that he had a mind and a will of his own and would lead the Church into new fields of endeavor. Shortly after his election I had a private audience with him, and he asked: "Shall we speak in English or Italian?"

"Whatever Your Holiness wishes," I said.

We began in Italian. But after two minutes I found that we were speaking English—and Pope Paul's English is better than my Italian!

It was a busy summer for Pope Paul, as he sought to

familiarize himself with his many Papal duties and functions. His supreme decision of these days was to continue the Council, and at the end of September it began its second session.

Two weeks later Pope Paul conferred the title of *Blessed* on Bohemia-born John Neumann, the fourth Bishop of Philadelphia—the second American to be beatified in little more than six months. When the date for Bishop Neumann's beatification had been fixed late that summer, Archbishop John J. Krol of Philadelphia asked me to work out details for the triduum of Masses with the Postulator of the Cause, a Redemptorist Father from San Alfonso's. (The triduum was to follow the Sunday morning and afternoon ceremonies in St. Peter's.) Bishop Neumann had been a Redemptorist, but San Alfonso's would be too small for the large pilgrimage expected to come from Philadelphia with Archbishop Krol. So would Santa Susanna's.

The Postulator and I discussed the possibility of the Basilica of St. Mary of the Angels, which was designed by Michelangelo when he was eighty-eight. It is a large church, and it is where Italy buries her national heroes. But when we inspected it, they were digging a big ditch down the center aisle. So I said to the Father Postulator: "What is the matter with St. Mary Major's? It is sufficently large, it is close to the Redemptorist house, it is beautifully located transportation-wise in the heart of the city, and, furthermore, you Redemptorists are in charge of the sacristy there."

He agreed that St. Mary Major's would be ideal. At that point I remarked that Archbishop Krol had told me to make the arrangements, and I was sure St. Mary's would be satisfactory to him. "So let's consider it agreed upon," I said to the Father Postulator. That morning I had a cable off to Auxiliary Bishop Gerald V. McDevitt of Philadelphia, telling him of the arrangements made and asking for final approval. I had it in twenty-four hours.

Unlike Mother Seton's beatification, I did not speak at the triduum. Archbishop Krol, however, asked me to arrange the reception which was to conclude the religious ceremonies. The Grand Hotel put all of its ballroom facilities at our disposal. The problem was to get more than 1000 people through a reception line between seven and nine in the evening. We managed. It turned out we had eighteen Cardinals and over 300 Bishops at the reception. In keeping with the Roman custom, each Cardinal was received on arrival by the *maggiordomo* of the hotel and two members of his staff bearing candles. With the candlebearers in the lead, the Cardinal would then proceed into the ballroom to where Archbishop Krol was standing, flanked on the right by the Father General of the Redemptorists and on his left by Bishop McDevitt.

I saw to it that no one was allowed to linger in the reception line. If Archbishop Krol wished to delay a guest, he could, of course. But otherwise, after fifteen seconds, one of our guild ladies (dressed in their evening gowns) would reach out and touch the guest, saying: "Would you come this way, please?" She would lead the way to one of the many groups in the two large ballrooms. Each guest received from the Archbishop a specially blessed Bishop Neumann medal, beautifully enclosed in an open-faced box.

Nothing was lacking to make the reception a complete success, because there is probably no hotel in the world as well equipped as the Grand to care for a group of this kind as completely and as perfectly, with exquisite services. The Grand Hotel outdid itself in food and beverages. Tables for both were set up around the ballrooms, and several of our ladies poured tea and coffee with an air of *la dolce vita, tipo americano*.

Our church bulletin of October 13—the Sunday Bishop

Neumann was beatified—carried details of the ceremonies. It also called to the attention of our parishioners that bazaar time was approaching. Our annual bazaar was scheduled for Saturday, November 23, at the Palazzo Barberini, and it promised to be the best one yet. In reminding parishioners that the top prize was a six-day Mediterranean voyage for two, we said in the bulletin: "Don't forget the opportunity you may have of a cruise through the Greek Isles in the wake of Jackie Kennedy and Onassis' yacht, *Christina.*"

On Friday evening, November 8, American Bishops and non-Catholic observers met for the second time at the Grand, at the invitation of myself and the other Paulist Fathers of Santa Susanna's, and I felt very happy that I had thought of this unique get-together during the Council's first session.

Two weeks later, on November 22, I had another "night out." Mike Stern was putting on a private film showing. Mike had access to new American films being "dubbed" in Italian, and when a good picture came along, he would set up a screening for some of his friends in the Warner Brothers projection room. This particular night the film was *The Great Escape.* About fifty American clergymen and laymen were there, including all of us from Santa Susanna's except Father Thomas Stransky, who had decided to remain at home. While we were watching Mike's movie, *The Great Escape,* Father Stransky heard over the radio in the rectory that President Kennedy had been assassinated. Without losing a moment he rushed by taxicab to bring the news. Before he opened his mouth I knew the gravity of what he had to say because I noticed he had forgotten to put on his cincture on leaving the rectory. When Mike Stern announced the news that Father Stransky had brought, our people were stunned. It was by far the most tragic American event to occur in my years as pastor. Obviously our American people would look to us for leadership in this hour of calamity. The three other Paulist Fathers and I left the projection room together. As we had not eaten as yet, we stopped at the little Italian resaurant we usually went to for a late dinner. There was no hunger, but we had to eat something while we made plans for the morrow.

Six months of planning had gone into the bazaar that was scheduled to take place the next day. But the bazaar had to be canceled. That was Father O'Donnell's job. It was my job to reach Cardinal Spellman and ask him to say Mass at Santa Susanna's the following afternoon at five o'clock. Father Maloney and Father Stransky were to get the church ready and handle all details. North American College had to be asked to send servers for His Eminence—preferably young men from his own archdiocese of New York.

By the time I arrived at the Grand Hotel where the Cardinal was staying it was 11 P.M. I called Cardinal Spellman on the house phone and apologized for disturbing him at that late hour. He was most gracious and at once agreed to say the Mass.

Celebrities, Bishops, and ordinary citizens "stormed" Santa Susanna's for the Mass for our late President. The walls of the sanctuary were completely draped in black, and superimposed behind the main altar was a huge cross of gold. The symbolic catafalque, built up for this special occasion, was covered with black drapes embossed with gold cloth in the form of a cross, and a large black and gold pillow was at the head. The friars of the Third Order Regular choir sang. Senior American officials from the Vatican—Monsignor Paul Marcinkus of Chicago; Monsignor (now Bishop) Pius Benincasa of Buffalo; Monsignor Henry Cosgrove of Brooklyn—helped in taking care of the crowd.

The following Monday, at the same time as the funeral ceremonies in Washington, Cardinal Spellman celebrated a Pontifical Requiem Mass in the Basilica of St. John Lateran, the traditional church of the Bishop of Rome, and at the invitation of His Eminence I assisted him as the archpriest. No American priest had ever been given such a honor before. The Cardinal had also named Monsignor James F. Chambers, vice-rector of North American College, and Monsignor Andrew Landi as deacons. At the rehearsal on Sunday afternoon, Monsignor (now Cardinal) Enrico Dante, the Papal master of ceremonies, advised Cardinal Spellman that the use of deacons would not be appropriate. I immediately offered to withdraw as archpriest, leaving place for one of the Monsignors. Raising his hand slightly, Cardinal Spellman said: "There shall be no withdrawals."

Cardinal Spellman invited me to ride with him and Count Enrico Galeazzi to St. John Lateran's. Fifteen thousand persons were in the Basilica, including the whole American hierarchy. Ambassador Frederick Reinhardt headed a large group from our Embassy. Every Embassy in Rome was represented. This was the official Italian government Mass for the President, and it was celebrated on the altar normally reserved for the Pope. A formal rescript, posted in the sanctuary, announced that Paul VI had given exceptional permission for use of his altar.

I had with me the English-language ritual which Cardinal Spellman had asked me to bring. The Papal master of ceremonies did not especially care to have English prayers recited, but Cardinal Spellman wanted to say the prayers in English as a special honor for the President. As the eyes of everyone turned to the catafalque, which was draped in the American flag and flanked by U.S. marines and Italian *carabiniere*, Cardinal Spellman solemnly intoned the final prayers of absolution in English. After the Mass, the Cardinal, in his vestments, greeted Italian President Antonio Segni, who had come from his sickbed to attend the service, and Ambassador Reinhardt.

Signor Segni stood there weeping as he recalled the vigorous young American President who had visited him less than five months before.

On Sunday, December 22, one month after the President's assassination, a Month's Mind Mass was offered at Santa Susanna's at the request of Ambassador Reinhardt, and Father Francis X. Murphy spoke at it. This terminated the official mourning period prescribed by the State Department.

It had been a full month. Early in December the second session of the Council ended, and I had then turned my attention to our postponed bazaar. We rescheduled it for December 21. It was our ninth annual bazaar, and it was a great success.

As Christmas got closer, visitors thronged the church to see the Christmas crib of our nuns. This Christmas the crib looked especially beautiful. When I had first come to Rome, the nuns had a crib which suffered in comparison with those in other churches. I had it replaced by one with some sixty or seventy antique, Neapolitan-style figures and distinctive miniatures of fruit baskets, jewels, and animals. (The *Bambino* was a delicate wood-carving.) With the annual packing and unpacking, there had been some breakage, so this Christmas Margaret Cassidy Manship, an American sculptress, restored the broken fingers and arms. The nuns were very grateful. (The nuns were always appreciative of anything done for them. A couple of years earlier delegates from other Italian convents meeting at Santa Susanna's elected our Mother Abbess as the head of the Cistercian Confederation of Italy. *"Per merito suo—thanks* to what you have done," she said to me. She meant that the Cistercian visitors had been impressed by the restored convent at Santa Susanna's, with its modern facilities, the new floor in the choir hall, electricity, and—an unheard-of thing in the average Italian convent—hot and cold showers. "Cardinal Cushing gave the money for all this," I said. "All I did was ask for it.")

A few days before Christmas, Jack Herfurt of the Embassy called and asked if I would deliver a talk on Monday, December 23, at a joint luncheon of the American Club and the American Women's Association. Laughingly I asked Jack: "What have we run out of? Money, speakers, or gift wallets [which each guest speaker received]?" "We've run out of nothing, Father," he said. "We'd just like you to give a little Christmas message. After all, this is our family Christmas dinner."

I was happy to oblige. The American Club was ten years old this year. In those years no member had ever felt the slightest hesitation to call on me, or one of the other Paulists at Santa Susanna's, if there was need of assistance for any American, or for advice and counsel. "We are a closely knit group of many faiths and of a dozen different racial backgrounds," I told my fellow Americans at the Christmas dinner. "We have learned to have a high regard for each other, and to recognize the good we see in each other." Then I offered the toast which I have used many times across the world: "Here's to us—better people are hard to find!"

But I was terribly tired.

During the previous month or so I had had a number of bad nights. I am sure this was not the fault of the Council, as the younger men took it in stride. But there had been no letup. Right after the Council there was the customary arrival of several hundred parents and friends of the latest class of North American College seminarians to be ordained the week before Christmas. There was, too, the pre-Christmas activity of confessions, visits to the church, etc. All of this activity together becomes more fatiguing as one gets older. I felt that nothing less than a twenty-one-day round trip to Miami would set me straight again. But the twenty-one days became three months. I did not return to Rome until just before Easter in 1964—after major surgery and a long rest which I had not anticipated.

Father Paul Maloney had to present the candle of the Paulist Fathers to Paul VI on Candlemas Day in 1964 because I was hospitalized in Miami Beach. I had missed another audience with His Holiness but, on that occasion, my absence considerably embarrassed me. I had asked for an audience for our guild, as I regularly did each year. It was made part of a general audience in St. Peter's, but the four officers were to be presented personally to Pope Paul. After getting the group settled in a special tribune, I took the officers up front to a place beside the Papal throne. "Gerry" Ryan, the president, and the other officers knew what to do—how to kneel before His Holiness and what to say—because I had rehearsed them.

But on being presented to Pope Paul they were completely taken off balance when the master of ceremonies asked: "Where is Father Cunningham?" All that the four ladies knew—fortunately!—was that I had gone back to the main group. But the question confused them and His Holiness and took a little of the glamour from the meeting. I had anticipated the audience would be over by noon and had made a golf date for one-fifteen. When I saw the audience was running late, I surreptitiously made my escape from the Basilica, not expecting anyone would be asking for me except the three friends with whom I was going to play in the annual Anglo-American Club golf tournament. From the game I played that day, it would have been better if I had remained in St. Peter's!

One Sunday, during these last months, Cardinal Cushing was to speak at our ten-o'clock parish Mass. Since we had another Mass at eleven o'clock, I asked His

Eminence please to be brief, and he said he would. The topic he had chosen was "Good Pope John and Good Pope Paul." Bishop Coleman Carroll of Miami was to say Mass at a side altar as soon as the Cardinal finished talking. Five minutes after the time set for the end of the sermon, His Eminence was still speaking about Good Pope John. I persuaded Bishop Carroll to go out and begin his own Mass anyway. He was reluctant to do this until I assured him the Cardinal would not mind. Cardinal Cushing, on seeing the Bishop, ended his sermon in a minute or two, without ever getting to the *Good Pope Paul* part.

In June I went to New York for the Chapter of the Paulist Fathers. I had completed two six-year terms as pastor of Santa Susanna's. As my new assignment, effective in September, the Chapter appointed me as pastor of Old St. Mary's, an American landmark, because it was the first parish established in Chicago.

The summer of my departure was very hot, and we were overwhelmed by tourists. I was standing at the door of Santa Susanna's one day when a passing woman asked me, in a pronounced British accent, "Do you speak English?"

"No," I replied. "I speak only American."

After checking my accent, she said: "How right you are!"

Among the things that had to be packed were a *Pro Ecclesia et Pontifice* award from Pius XII; a decoration as a Knight (and a subsequent one as a Knight Commander) of the Legion of Merit of the Republic of Italy, and certificates of my appointment as a Chaplain of the Knights of Malta and of the Knights of the Holy Sepulchre. I had originally declined the Malta chaplaincy, thereby embarrassing the kind friends who had proposed me. I was so busy at the time with so many things I couldn't handle another activity and, mistakenly, I envisioned hospital visitations and involvements beyond my ability to cope with.

With the Knights of the Holy Sepulchre it was somewhat different. The award came through the instrumentalities of clerical friends who felt some recognition of my years of work in Rome was in order. The request for my appointment was presented through Count Enrico Galeazzi. It was turned down on the ground that I was a priest, and therefore not eligible. The Grand Master of the Knights of the Holy Sepulchre was Federico Cardinal Tedeschini. The Cardinal was a sick man and was said to be unconscious about ninety per cent of the time. My friends apparently did not take No for an answer, because it was announced one day that I had been given the award. A clerical friend called to say he was glad that I had "made it" and described the approving signature as "one of Cardinal Tedeschini's last *unconscious* acts." And I don't know to this day whether it was or not, because Cardinal Tedeschini died a day or two after I was made a Knight of the Holy Sepulchre!

I also had received a scroll—which I framed and now have hanging in my room—attesting that I am a member of the Hole-in-One-Club!

The caddies at the Acqua Santa golf club sent me a nice farewell note thanking me for everything. I have always been a firm believer in helping those who try to help themselves, and the caddies were trying to do this. Three or four times a year the caddy master would select five or six of the poorer boys, and our faithful Palermo, after picking them up, would pass by Santa Susanna's, where Francesca Wagner would join them. Off they would go to a public market in Trastévere, a poorer section of town. I would give Francesca $100 to clothe the boys "from the skin out!" So she would inquire at the first stand or pushcart what the underwear cost and would be told, for instance, 500 lire. Invariably the pushcart woman would ask: "Are all these your boys, *Signora?*" Francesca would explain they were poor youngsters from the country for whom she was buying clothes. "For you, then, *Signora,*" the woman would say, "the price is 200 lire." And that is the way it would go. If Italians find out you are trying to help someone, they make special concessions and show approval in many ways. Francesca always managed to have a little change left over to give to the boys on their way home.

My last golf game in Rome, in the latter part of August 1964, coincided with the funeral of Palmiro Togliatti, the head of the Italian Communist Party. Coming back through St. John Lateran's Gate, I was stopped by one of the hundreds of policemen in the area. "Padre," he said, "I don't think you'd better drive through the piazza. The funeral procession is already starting to move." He suggested that if I wished to see it I could go along the periphery of the line of march.

I stopped at a church on the corner of Via Taranto and Via Monza to watch. The church—the Immacolata— is famous for its mosaics. I had visited it once with Monsignor William Doheny, C.S.C., of the Sacred Rota. (I was interested in putting mosaics in the Madonna Chapel of Santa Susanna's and the Monsignor, knowing about the Immacolata mosaics, suggested that we look them over.)

There were literally thousands of massed flags for the Togliatti funeral procession. All along the way buses were parked. People coming in from the country had eaten their lunches in the shade of the buses and were now parading toward the cemetery in the hot Roman sun of summer. Some 500,000 persons were in the line, carrying the red banner with the hammer and sickle. The men wore red shirts. The women had flimsy red scarves around their shoulders and clutched rosaries in their hands. As they passed the church, on whose steps I was standing, row after row of these people—the men, too—blessed themselves in the peculiarly Italian fashion. The women threw a kiss in the direction of the church and bowed to the Madonna looking out at them, silently, from the golden mosaic panel above the doorway.

I thought of Clare Boothe Luce's words: "Italy is a nation of lovable but frustrating people."

In my last sermon at Santa Susanna's, on Sunday, August 30, 1964, I made a kind of summing-up. I told my Roman parishioners that many years before, while working in the mountains of Tennessee, I had been engaged in the building of a church. The laborers were from the countryside, and one of the workers was an old man named Sam who made the best moonshine in the country —and drank most of it. He had been a lawyer by profession, but gave up after his first case because the court accused him of drinking the evidence. After some persuasion on my part—and my agreement to certain conditions, such as that his lunch would have to come out of a jug—he went to work on my church as a stonecutter. He worked reasonably well, and at the end of our contract this old non-Catholic mountaineer would not take his final check. After much prodding, he told me why. He gave me the answer in a series of statements.

"One day you will come into the country to find Old Sam dead—(That is right)—By the time you find me I will have had to stand in front of that man Up There— (Correct)—He is going to say to me: "Sam, you have been a bad man"—Reckon you're right, Lord—"Sam, did you ever do anything good?"—He is going to push me a little there and I'll scratch my head and say: "Well, I once worked for a whole week for nothing on a Catholic church"—And he is going to say: "Come right in, Sam. Lots of room for fellows like you."

By this time in my life, I had learned that no one is 100 per cent perfect. Seventy-five is *very good*. Even seventy. Sometimes you have to settle for thirty! I had done my best.

The parish's farewell party for me was in the home of Mr. and Mrs. Umberto Tine on the Aventine. My first meal as pastor in Rome had been there. The parishioners had a surprise for Pennsylvania-born Mrs. Tine. Loretta Young, many years earlier, had given me a beautiful gold medal of St. Genesius, the patron of actors who is remembered with a chapel in our church. The medal was encrusted with pearls and hung from a gold chain. We made it the prize at our annual bazaar that year, and the winner was Mrs. Vincent Barnett, wife of the Counsellor for Economic Affairs at the Embassy. She wore it once or twice, but then returned it, feeling it should be given to a Catholic woman for whom it would have more meaning. I kept it in the church safe for several years, but decided that it did St. Genesius no good there, nor was it in the interest of the donor. When a St. Genesius Award was decided upon by the guild in the year of my departure, the Loretta Young medal was it. Officers of the guild voted that the one who most deserved it was Mrs. Elizabeth Tine, and it was presented to her at my farewell reception in her home.

Lou Fugazy's thirteen-year-old daughter, Melina, was at the reception. Lou had been my yeoman in San Juan during the war. Since I had officiated at the wedding of Lou and Doris (a Hunter College graduate)—and had baptized five of the six children (and am godfather of the sixth)—I could be called a "friend of the family." Melina had been visiting relatives of her mother in northern Italy. When parishioners saw her with me at the reception, they asked what she was doing in Rome. "I thought Father might feel badly about leaving Rome,"

Melina said, "so my aunt and uncle brought me down from the Piedmont to cheer him up."

Someone at the reception suggested a toast: "To Father's promotion!"

Everyone raised their glasses and repeated the words joyfully. But, being "old Romans," they knew that after Rome there is no promotion—there is only change.

I knew it, too.